# Human Perception

# Basic Topics in Psychology series
## *R. A. Champion, Editor*

P. E. H. Barratt
*Bases of Psychological Methods*

R. A. Champion
*Learning and Activation*

R. H. Day
*Human Perception*

J. A. Keats
*An Introduction to Quantitative Psychology*

L. Mann
*Social Psychology*

J. Ross
*Mathematics as Applied to Psychology*

P. van Sommers
*The Biology of Behaviour*

I. K. Waterhouse
*Personality*

# Human Perception

**R. H. DAY**

Monash University

JOHN WILEY & SONS AUSTRALASIA PTY LTD

Sydney   New York   London   Toronto

Library of Congress catalog number: 74-75659
National Library of Australia registry number: AUS 69-13

Composition by Craftsmen Type-Setters Pty Ltd, Sydney, Australia
Printed in Hong Kong by Toppan Printing Co., (H.K.) Ltd

# Foreword

FROM time to time teachers of psychology in Australia have regretted the relative lack of text and reference books written by Australians primarily for use in Australia. The series of which this book is part has been organized with a view to making good the deficiency. The regret has arisen not so much from criticism of books written overseas as from recognition of the fact that Australian students have somewhat different backgrounds and needs from their contemporaries elsewhere; Australian authors might be able to communicate information and ideas to them just a little more effectively. This is not to deny the possibility that, while Australian students have profited immensely from the use of overseas books, students elsewhere might enjoy a slight Australian flavour in their reading diet.

The topics chosen for the series are chiefly those found in introductory texts, but we have been bold enough to depart from convention, especially in quantification and the applications of mathematics. The material has mainly been written at a level deemed appropriate to the typical first-year course in Australia, either for text or reference purposes. Account has been taken of the increasing time being allowed students in their secondary school studies and of the inclusion there of an increasing amount of material on psychology, albeit in disguise. Some topics in the series, such as the biology of behaviour, and learning and activation, may be useful at the advanced secondary level. At the other extreme, the overriding determination to encourage authors to give rein to their own ideas at the expense of complete, detailed coverage, and not to pander to students, may mean that the series will also find some use in second or third year courses, depending upon the level at which the various topics are introduced in different institutions.

*R. A. Champion*

*TO GRECIAN*

# Preface

PERCEPTION is defined here as the organism's maintenance of contact with its environment, its internal state, and its postures and movements. The problems and issues of perception can be usefully studied from a variety of viewpoints including those of development, ethology, information theory and personality. While the approach adopted in this treatment owes a little to each of these and other viewpoints, it centres on a general principle of perception developed in the course of teaching and researching in perception and clarified in many discussions with colleagues and graduate students.

The general principle, perceptual resolution of stimulus equivocality, has proved useful in bringing together and explaining in common terms perceptual phenomena hitherto treated more or less separately. Among the most important of these effects are perceptual constancy, illusion and instability, the last including perceptual reversals or fluctuations. Because this central notion is involved in the description and explanation of a variety of perceptual phenomena, the contents and treatment may appear on first sight to depart radically from those of other introductory texts. Most of the above material in perception is covered, however, although the order and grouping may be different.

Chapter 1 is introductory and deals with background material, definitions, general issues and methods. Chapter 2 is mainly devoted to acuity and sensitivity in human perception. In Chapters 3, 4, 5, and 6 the principle of perceptual resolution of stimulus ambiguity is introduced in the treatment of constancy, illusion and instability. In order to bring out common features associated with adaptation to light, colour, sound, pressure, and to spatial features such as size, shape and direction perceptual adaptation and after-effect are treated in Chapter 7. An attempt has been made to avoid the highly artificial distinction between adaptation to spatial and non-spatial features of stimulation. A common basis for adaptive effects and aftereffects is suggested in Chapter 7. Finally, in Chapter 8, three aspects of the complex relationships between perception and learning are discussed.

It is not possible to acknowledge in full the debt I owe to many colleagues and students of the last ten years who have been directly or indirectly involved in the preparation of this book. My greatest debt is acknowledged as a dedication on an earlier page. I wish especially to record my appreciation of the critical comments made by Dr F. M. Coltheart of a first draft. I am very grateful also to Professor R.A. Champion, the editor of this series, for his criticisms and careful editing. Mrs Lola Pasieczny, Miss Pamela Ward and Mrs Margaret Bourton undertook with considerable patience the tedious task of typing various drafts. Mr Vladimir Kohout showed much imagination and care in the preparation of figures and illustrations. I acknowledge with gratitude the contributions to this book made by these and many others.

*Melbourne 1968*                                                    *R. H. Day*

# Contents

# 1. Nature and Measurement of Perception

IN BROAD terms perception can be defined as the organism's maintenance of contact with its environment, its internal state, and its own posture and motion. Two points need to be clear from the outset. First, perception involves not only keeping in touch with objects and events physically removed from the animal, but also its internal states and self-induced activity. Second, perception is not a peculiarly human activity; animals from simple unicellular organisms to highly developed vertebrates must maintain contact with events in the interests of environmental adaptation and survival. Much research and most textbook material, however, stresses perception in man. While this book is mainly concerned with human perception it is as well to approach the main issues through a consideration of animal perception in general terms.

From a biological viewpoint the animal's preservation is dependent not only on its structure and processes but in large part on its capacity to achieve and maintain contact with internal and external events. As structural and physiological processes have evolved so have the means whereby contact is maintained. Natural selection of the means of contact maintenance is as much a central principle in perception as it is in animal form and structure. The detection and capture of prey, avoidance of harmful situations, care of the young, defecation and urination, and discrimination of posture and movement all involve keeping in touch with events occurring within or outside the organism.

Information about events is conveyed by the impingement of electro-magnetic, mechanical, and chemical changes on the sensory cells or receptors. These impingements are essentially changes in energy; changes which occur over space or time and to which the receptors are specially adapted or "tuned".

The *process* of perception includes the reception of changes in impinging energy, its transduction into electrical impulses, and the encoding of the impulses to preserve the information which the impingements convey about events. The study of perception must begin, therefore, with a consideration of the electromagnetic, mechanical, and chemical stimuli, the information which they carry, the sensory cells and systems which receive and transmit

1

the information, and the manner in which information is encoded. The further study of perception involves consideration of the way in which highly complex situations are perceived as relatively stable despite enormous variations in the patterns of change which occur at the receptors.

The study of perception is not clearly distinguishable from the study of learning, motivation, or individual differences in behaviour. Maintaining contact with events may change with practice (*i.e.,* may be learned), exhibits individual differences, and depends upon the organism's motivational state. Much of the study of perception is closely tied to the study of the learning process, the range and determinants of individual differences in behaviour, and motivational states.

# Stimulus Energy, Receptors and the Encoding of Information

Electromagnetic, mechanical, and chemical changes impinging on the receptors carry information about the external environment, the internal state of the organism, and the organism's activity. The energy changes constitute stimuli. Electromagnetic stimuli include impinging light and radiant heat. Mechanical stimuli involve sustained and intermittent activity, the latter including acoustic and other vibrations. Chemical stimuli are constituted of numerous solid, liquid, and gaseous substances. The essential feature of stimulation is energy. Whether the stimulus is a pattern of light on the eye, pressures on the skin, or chemical solutions on the tongue, energy is transduced into electrical events in the nervous system. Since through natural selection different organisms have evolved in different environments, the type of information essential to the organism's adaptation and survival varies. Accordingly, the classes and ranges of energy to which different animals are sensitive, and the form, structure, and arrangement of their sensory equipment vary widely.

## STIMULUS PROPERTIES

### Classes and Ranges of Stimulus Energy

The total electromagnetic spectrum ranges from cosmic rays with wavelengths in the vicinity of $10^{-3}$ millimicrons (m$\mu$) to electromagnetic waves of wavelengths around $10^{12}$ m$\mu$ (a millimicron is a millionth of a millimetre).* For the human observer the *visible* spectrum composed of light waves consists of only about $\frac{1}{70}$th of the total and includes light with wavelengths extending over 390–700 m$\mu$ (Fig. 1.1). A few examples will serve to show, however, that

*Recently the term nanometre ($10^{-9}$) metre, has been adopted in place of millimicron.

some animals maintain contact with environmental events through sensitivity to light with wavelengths above and below those to which man's photoreceptors are sensitive.

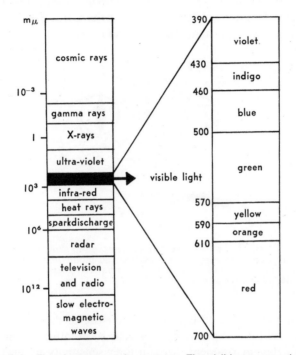

**Figure 1.1**   The electromagnetic spectrum. The visible spectrum is about $\frac{1}{70}$th of the total and extends from about 390 to 700 millimicrons (m$\mu$). (Adapted from J.R. Brett, The eye. In *The Physiology of Fishes*, Vol. 2, New York, Academic Press Inc., 1957. Copyright Academic Press Inc.)

Various experiments with honeybees show clearly that bees are capable of discriminating light in the ultraviolet region of the spectrum. If feeding dishes containing sugar syrup are illuminated by light of different wavelengths and the bee trained to fly to the dishes and collect the syrup, it will respond readily to dishes illuminated with ultraviolet light. In point of fact, the honeybee is capable of discriminating wavelengths in the range 300–360 m$\mu$ in addition to longer wavelengths.

Some snakes, including the rattle-snake and certain species of viper, can locate and accurately strike at a rodent which remains quite still in absolute darkness and at some distance. Snakes are not particularly sensitive to airborne sounds and there is no evidence that the eyes of the snake differ markedly from those of other vertebrates. The basis of the rattle-snake's extraordinary accuracy in detecting and striking prey in the dark consists of receptors sensitive to infrared light. It can be seen in Fig. 1.2 that in front of the eyes there is a pair of openings pointing slightly forward. These organs contain receptors which, while they do not respond to light waves in the visual range, do so when infrared rays fall on them. Infrared rays ("warmth") emitted by a rat or mouse are detected through the receptors of the pit-organs, thus permitting the rattle-snake to strike and capture.

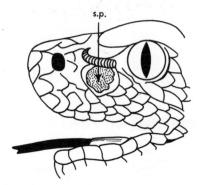

**Figure 1.2**   Head of pit viper with tissue removed to show the sensory pit (s.p.) which contains receptors for infrared radiation. (Adapted from J.H. Bullock and F.P.J. Diecke, Properties of an infra-red receptor. In *J. Physiol.*, 1956, 134, 47–87. By courtesy of *J. Physiol.*)

Ultraviolet and infrared light waves lie close to those of man's visible spectrum. By virtue of special sensory cells some other animals maintain contact with the environment through their sensitivity to electromagnetic energy with wavelengths much removed from those to which man is sensitive. An African river fish *Gymnarchus* swims with equal facility backwards or forwards. When obstacles are encountered fore or aft they are avoided and crevices are entered tail first. *Gymnarchus* possesses a unique tail organ which generates weak electrical impulses of about 3–7 volts at a frequency of about 300 per second. When objects which are either more or less conductive than the surrounding water come within range of these emitted pulses the lines of current flow in the electrical field are distorted, as shown in Fig. 1.3. It is believed that pores in the head region which lead into tubes filled with a jelly-like substance contain receptors sensitive to these changes in the direction of current flow.

Wide variations occur also in sensitivity to mechanical stimulation, of which sound is one form. As shown in Fig. 1.4, sound waves are successive compressions of air molecules giving rise to waves of pressure on the ear. Sound is normally specified in terms of the frequency of recurrent cycles of compression and decompression per unit time. In specifying an auditory stimulus both the amplitude and frequency of sound waves are given, the

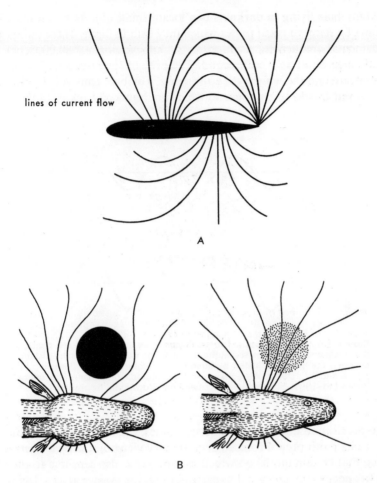

lines of current flow

A

B

**Figure 1.3** *A* Electric field of *Gymnarchus*. *B* Distortion of lines of current flow by objects. (*A* from H.W. Lissman and K.E. Machin, The mechanism of object location in *Gymnarchus niloticus* and similar fish. In *J. exp. Biol.*, 1958, 35, 451–486. *B* from H.W. Lissman, Electric location in fishes. In *Sci. Amer.*, 1963, 208, 50–59. Both by courtesy of H.W. Lissman.)

first specifying the amount of energy and the second the frequency of compressions. The human ear is sensitive to sounds with frequencies between about 20 and 20,000 cycles per second (cps*). For the most part, only young observers with acute hearing can respond to sounds of 20,000 cps, the upper limit for a normal adult being about 12,000–15,000 cps.

*Recently the term Herz, designated by H, has been adopted in place of cycles per second. Thus 500 H is used instead of 500 cps.

Many bats flying in darkness can locate small objects by means of the echoes of a series of vocal pulses which they emit in flight. These pulses have fundamental frequencies as high as 80 kilocycles (*i.e.*, 80,000 cps) and durations as short as 1 millisecond. The prey of insectivorous bats appear to be located on the wing by echo-ranging. The bats emit vocal pulses at a rate between 5 and 100 per second which are bounced back from the insect.

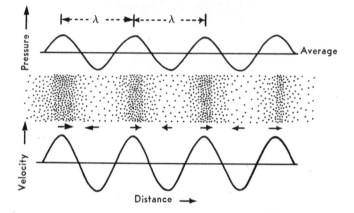

**Figure 1.4**  A sound wave. The molecules of air are crowded and dense at the crests and more dispersed at the troughs. The wave length is the distance between the crests indicated by lambda ($\lambda$). From W.A. van Bergeijk, J.R. Pierce and E.E. David, *Waves and the Ear,* London, Heinemann Educational Books Ltd, 1961. By courtesy of Heinemann Educational Books Ltd.)

By responding to these high frequency echoes, the bat is able to locate and capture its moth prey. From an evolutionary viewpoint it is not surprising to find that certain moths on which bats prey are also sensitive to the bat's high frequency cries and are thus capable of taking evasive action. In Fig. 1.5 are shown recordings of bat cries and the response from the simple ear of a moth, together with tracings of the moth flight when a bat emitting its cries cruises nearby.

Different species also exhibit widely different sensitivities to chemical stimulation. Such sensitivity can be ascertained by observing whether different chemicals trigger impulses in the nerve fibres connecting the receptors with the central nervous system. For the human observer water is regarded as a relatively tasteless substance. By splitting up the nerve from the tongue into fine strands it can be shown that certain receptors are sensitive to the application of water to the tongue but not to a weak salt solution, and that others respond to the application of salt solution but not water. The tongues of the cat, dog, and pig contain sensory cells which respond to water. The rat's tongue, however, does not reveal this sensitivity.

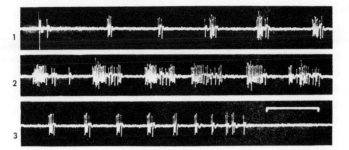

**Figure 1.5** *A* (1) The recorded sounds of a cruising bat emitted at about 10 per second. (2) Electrical recordings of the response from the ear of a nearby moth (*Noctua*). (3) Time line, 100 milliseconds. *B* Pursuit of moth by a bat using echolocation. (*A* from K.D. Roeder and A.E. Treat, The detection and evasion of bats by moths. In *American Scientist*, 1961, 49, 135–148. By courtesy of *American Scientist*. *B* from F.A. Webster, Active energy radiating systems. In *Proc. Internat. Cong. Technology and Blindness*, Vol. I, 1963, 49–135.)

This brief review makes clear that maintenance of contact with external events is achieved by different animals in a variety of ways. The range of sensitivity of the human receptors to electromagnetic, mechanical, and chemical changes in the external environment is but one example. Depending on the animal's habitat, behaviour, and requirements, sensory cells have evolved which are tuned to ranges of energy far outside those to which man is sensitive. Contact with events is maintained through sensitivity to energy of different classes and ranges in different species.

### Stimulus as Change

The environment with which the organism must cope, and to which it must continually adjust to ensure survival, is seldom static. The organism itself moves about within its surroundings, and other objects and features move in relation to it. Light, sound, heat, and pressures on the sensory receptor cells vary over a wide range. These changes occur over both space and time to give patterns and gradients of stimulus energy. It is not surprising then that the sensory systems respond primarily to changes in stimulation. In fact they are often rendered non-functional by perfectly static

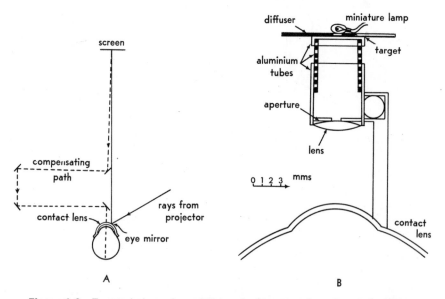

**Figure 1.6** Two techniques for stabilizing the image on the retina. *A* Rays from the object are reflected from a small mirror mounted on a contact lens. *B* The miniature optical system and target are mounted on a contact lens. (*A* adapted from L.A. Riggs, F. Ratliff, J.C. Cornsweet and T.N. Cornsweet, The disappearance of steadily fixated visual test objects. In *J. Optical Soc. Amer.*, 1953, 43, 495–501. By courtesy of *J. Optical Soc. Amer. B* adapted from R.M. Pritchard, W. Heron and D.O. Hebb, Visual perception as approached by the method of stabilized images. In *Canad. J. Psychol.*, 1960, 14, 67–77.)

or uniform patterns of energy. The importance of stimulus change in the maintenance of contact with external events is demonstrated when the projection of light energy on the retina is held perfectly constant. The eye is suspended between three pairs of muscles (see Fig. 1.7C) and is continually in a state of oscillation or tremor. No matter how hard we try to hold our gaze steadily or fixedly on an external object, the image on the retina oscillates so that no single group of receptors is subjected to unvarying stimulation for more than a brief moment. By attaching the object to a short stem mounted on a contact lens which, because of suction, moves with the eye, the pattern of light reflected from object to receptors remains fixed relative to the receptors. The same stabilization of the visual stimulus can be achieved by means of another optical system. The two methods of rendering the pattern of light on the eye stable are shown in Fig. 1.6. Under these conditions of uniform or unchanging stimulation the object disappears rapidly or fades out after a few seconds. The human eye is primarily sensitive to *changes* in light energy.

Common observation provides further evidence for the role of change in stimulation of sensory receptors. If spectacles or a hat are worn for a period of time during which their pressure on the skin of nose and head is unchanging, their presence can no longer be easily detected. Likewise the pressure of the band of a wrist-watch soon disappears.

### Sensory Adaptation

Decline in sensitivity to stimulation of constant intensity is referred to as sensory adaptation. The examples just given are examples of a wide range of adaptive changes which will be considered in more detail in Chapter 7. If the receptors of the eye are subjected to continuous stimulation by a light of constant intensity, sensitivity progressively diminishes. This change can be demonstrated by establishing the minimum intensity of light necessary to elicit a response from the organism at regular intervals after the onset of continuous, constant stimulation. Sensitivity varies as a function of the stimulus intensity, and the time taken for recovery from adaptation is a function of stimulus duration (see Fig. 7.1 and 7.2). Adaptation which is characteristic of all sensory systems during continuous stimulation is correlated with decline in the frequency of neural impulses generated in the receptors and their associated cells (see "*Encoding of Information*", p. 18).

## STRUCTURE AND ARRANGEMENT OF SENSORY SYSTEMS

Just as organisms differ in the classes and ranges of energy on which they depend to maintain contact with events, so the sensory cells or receptors adapted to receive this energy vary widely in their detailed structure and distribution.

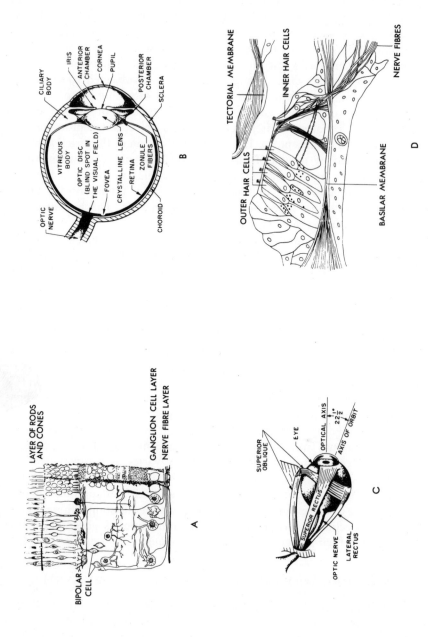

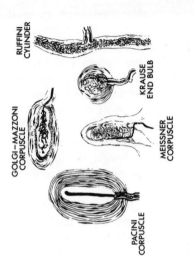

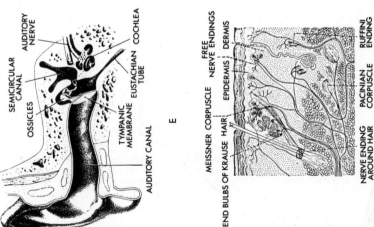

**Figure 1.7** Structure and arrangement of sensory cells and sense organs for vision, hearing and touch. *A* Detailed structure of the retina showing rods and cones, bipolar cells and ganglion cells. *B* The right eye seen from above. *C* The eye showing the three muscles which control eye movement. *D* The organ of Corti in the human ear showing arrangement of inner and outer hair cells on the basilar membrane. *E* Schematic drawing of the ear. *F* The principal receptors of the skin. *G* Cross-section of skin showing arrangement of the three main layers and distribution of receptors. (*A* and *E* from T.A. Rogers, *Elementary Human Psychology*, N.Y., John Wiley & Sons Inc., 1961; by courtesy of John Wiley & Sons Inc. *B* and *C* from J. W. Wulfeck, *Vision in Military Aviation*, Air Research and Development Command, Ohio, 1958; by courtesy Air Research and Development Command. *D* from J.D. Lickley, *The Nervous System*, London, Longmans, Green & Co. Ltd, 1919; by courtesy of Longmans, Green & Co. Ltd. *F* and *G* from F.A. Geldard, *The Human Senses*, N.Y., John Wiley & Sons Inc., 1953; by courtesy of John Wiley & Sons Inc.)

**Receptors and Sense Organs**

Receptors, sensory cells which are adapted for the reception of energy, may be widely distributed throughout the superficial or deep tissue, grouped in restricted regions such as muscles, joints and tendons, or concentrated together in a sense organ. A sense organ usually includes some means whereby the energy is conducted to and focused on the receptors. In Fig. 1.7 are shown examples of the individual receptors of the human skin, eye, and ear, the manner in which they are distributed and grouped, and the structure of the sense organs. While the contact pressure receptors of the skin are widely distributed with varying concentration, the pressure receptors of the ear and the photoreceptors of the eye are concentrated in the organ of Corti and the retina respectively. In the latter cases the sense organ has a complex series of conducting mechanisms which convey the impinging energy to the site of the receptors.

Differences between sense organs which are adapted for different types of stimulation were exemplified in the fish *Gymnarchus*, which responds to changes in a self-emitted electrical field by means of receptors contained in pores situated in the head (see Fig. 1.3). Two further examples will serve to stress the extraordinary range of specialized receptors and sense organs.

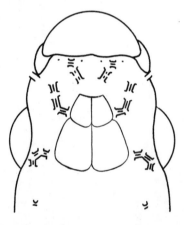

**Figure 1.8** The surface-dwelling fish *Aplocheilus lineatus* showing modified lateral line receptors which detect surface ripples. (From E. Schwartz, Bau und Funktion der Seitenlinie des Streifenhechts. In *Z. vergl. Physiol.*, 1965, 50, 55–87. By courtesy of *Z. vergl. Physiol.*)

The surface dwelling fish *Aplocheilus lineatus* depends on surface ripples on the water to detect the direction and distance of prey. Receptors sensitive to surface ripples are located in shallow troughs on top of the animal's head. The troughs are oriented in different directions, the animal receiving information for the direction of prey according to which trough receives the mechanical stimulation. These organs are sensitive to the distance as well as the source of the ripples. The receptors and sense organs of *Aplocheilus* are shown in Fig. 1.8. The diagram of the human eye in Fig. 1.7 shows the lens by means of which impinging light is brought to sharp focus on the mosaic of receptors in the retina. The primary functions of the lens is that of achieving a sharp clear image of the external scene on the retina. While this focusing function is served by the lens in many species, its role in other animals is that of concentrating as much light as possible on the receptors.

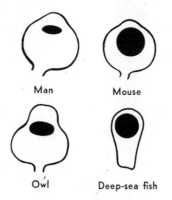

Man      Mouse

Owl      Deep-sea fish

**Figure 1.9**   Relative proportion of lens to eye, in eye of man, mouse, owl and deep-sea fish. The larger lenses collect more light at the expense of a clear image and are characteristic of nocturnal animals and those whose habitat is dimly lighted. (Adapted from E. Lowenstein, *The Senses*, Harmondsworth, Penguin Books, 1966. By courtesy of Penguin Books.)

Fig. 1.9 depicts the lens system of man, mouse, owl, and deep-sea fish. In the mouse and deep-sea fish the lens occupies a relatively greater volume of the optic chamber. Such lenses are capable of collecting very much more light at the expense of a clear image, but for the mouse whose habits are mainly nocturnal and the deep-sea fish dwelling in a light-reduced environment, the sheer amount of light rather than a sharp image is of critical significance in the detection of predators and of obstacles and in hunting.

**Arrangement of Sense Organs**

Sense organs, especially those containing receptors sensitive to light, sound, gravitational pull, and movement, tend to be bilaterally paired, *i.e.,* located symmetrically on either side of the body. This bilateral pairing is itself highly functional in maintaining contact with the spatial location (distance and direction) of external objects and events. The functional significance of bilateral pairing of sensory structures in perception is well illustrated in human vision and hearing and is depicted in Fig. 1.10. Because the eyes are set about 6–7 cm apart, the patterns of stimulation given by light projected on them from an external object are slightly different. The closer the object to the eyes the greater the disparity between the two retinal images. This difference between the two retinal images thus serves as a basis for distance discrimination. In other words, the different patterns of light stimulation at the two eyes provides information about the distance of objects from the observer. Retinal disparity, as this difference is called, is an important factor in three-dimensional or stereoscopic vision. In somewhat similar fashion the bilateral arrangement of the ears gives rise to

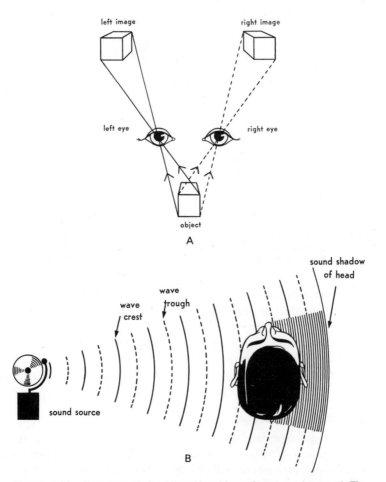

**Figure 1.10** Function of the bilateral pairing of eyes and ears. *A* The separation (about 60–70 mm) of the two eyes results in a small disparity of the two retinal images which serves as a basis for depth discrimination. *B* The separation of the ears serves as a basis for the localization of sounds; the sound at the far ear is less intense because of the sound shadow of the head, reaches the far ear later, and is often out of phase with the sound at the near ear.

differences in the patterns of auditory stimulation at the two groups of auditory receptors. When the sound source is located to the right or left of the observer's median plane (*i.e.,* a hypothetical plane bisecting at right angles the plane through the two ears, see Fig. 8.5), the time of arrival, phase, and intensity of the sound wave differ for the two ears. The observer's ability to detect the direction of a sound source is dependent on these binaural differences in stimulation. The significance of bilateral pairing of the ears for auditory localization is depicted in Fig. 1.10.

Bilateral pairing of sense organs is not confined to man, for numerous animal species exhibit this characteristic arrangement. But whereas in man and some other animals such an arrangement of the eyes results in stereoscopic or depth vision, in other species still the spacing of the eyes simply allows an almost complete field of view. In the rabbit, for example, the eyes give panoramic vision through nearly 360 degrees.

### Relationships between Sensory Systems

In discussing perception in general terms it would be misleading to regard each of the sensory systems in isolation, without considering the manner in which they interact in the overall function of maintaining contact with internal and external events. The sensory systems can be roughly but conveniently classified into three groups. The exteroceptive systems, with receptors sensitive to energy from the external environment, are represented by vision, hearing, touch, taste, smell, and the system responding to changes in environmental heat. The interoceptive systems have internal receptors in the deep tissues, digestive tract, and other organs, which are tuned to changes in the internal activities of the body. Finally, the proprioceptive systems mediate changes originating in the organism's movements and postures. The kinesthetic receptors of the joints and tendons of the limbs respond to movements of the body parts, and the muscle-spindle cells are sensitive to changes in muscle stretch and contraction. Receptors in the non-auditory structures of the inner ear are stimulated by changes in the posture and movement of the head and body. The arrangement of these labyrinthine receptors is shown in Fig. 1.11.

The interaction between the exteroceptive and proprioceptive systems can be illustrated by an activity such as tying a shoe-lace. We look down and observe that the lace is untied, the visual stimulus from the lace initiating the action of bending down to re-tie it. As we bend and reach out the hands and arms the kinesthetic receptors of the body joints are stimulated, thus providing information for limb position. Movement of the head and body downward stimulates the receptors of the semicircular canals and permits us to monitor body movement and posture. The visual stimulus initiates the initial response (tying the lace) and the response pattern itself (bending, reaching out, and tying) stimulates the receptors of the proprioceptive systems, thus providing information by means of which the response is monitored. The extent and direction of the response is thus controlled and directed by information which derives from the very act of responding. The proprioceptive systems function as feed-back mechanisms permitting corrective movements during the course of responding.

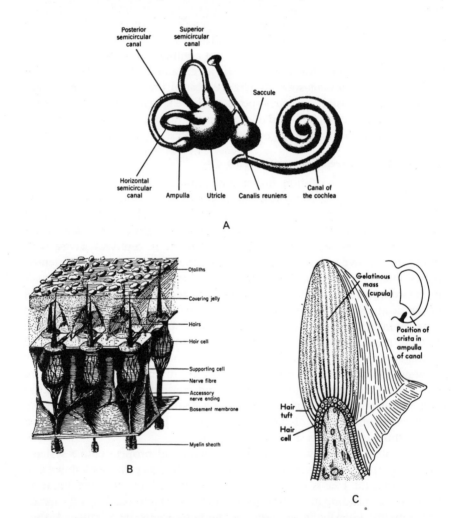

**Figure 1.11** *A* Diagram showing the labyrinthine system including the semicircular canals, utricle and saccule, and the cochlea. *B* Detail of the otolith organ of the utricle. *C* Crista located in the ampulla of the semicircular canals. (*A* from T.A. Rogers, *Elementary Human Physiology*, N.Y., John Wiley & Sons Inc., 1961; by courtesy of John Wiley & Sons Inc. *B* from W.J.S. Krieg, *Functional Neuroanatomy*, Illinois, Brain Books, 1953; by courtesy of Brain Books, *C* from E.G. Boring, *Introduction to Psychology*, N.Y., John Wiley & Sons Inc., 1932; by courtesy of John Wiley & Sons Inc.)

## TRANSDUCTION AND ENCODING OF STIMULUS ENERGY

The energy impinging on the receptors carries information about external and internal events. This information must be preserved in the chains of electrical impulses which pass along the nerve fibres between receptors and central nervous system. The process whereby energy is converted into neural impulses is called energy transduction, and the preservation of stimulus information in the patterns of impulses is stimulus encoding.

### Transduction

A great deal remains to be found out about the process in which one form of energy is converted to another in the sensory structures. In some sensory systems transduction is achieved mainly through a series of mechanical steps, as in hearing, touch, and the kinesthetic and muscular systems. In vision, however, photochemical processes intervene between the impingement of light and the generation of impulses. The receptors of the retina of the eye contain substances which undergo chemical change when light strikes them. In the rod receptors of the retina, receptors which are sensitive to reduced intensities of illumination, a substance called visual purple or rhodopsin decomposes in light to two further substances, retinene and Vitamin A. In darkness these products recombine in a reversible reaction to rhodopsin. The detailed cycle of events involved in the breakdown and re-generation is actually much more complex and involves numerous intervening sub-steps. The final steps between the decomposition of rhodopsin and the initiation of neural impulses are not fully known. The complete transduction process in vision runs from the absorption of light energy by photochemical substances contained in the receptors to the triggering of electrical impulses.

The transduction processes in those receptors of the skin, joints, muscles, and ears sensitive to mechanical energy involve the conversion of the distortion or movement of the receptors into electrical energy. Sound waves result in a disturbance of the endolymph fluid of the inner ear. The wave travelling through the endolymph causes the hair cells to bend or shear and so evoke electrical charges in the fibres leading from the cell itself to the auditory nerve.

The conversion of chemical stimulation of the tongue and nasal cavity into electrical energy in the nervous system is by no means clear and has been an issue of considerable enquiry and speculation. It has been suggested recently that in the case of the sense of smell the size, shape, and electrical charge of the gas molecules entering the nasal cavity are critical in the transduction of energy. It is argued that different sizes and shapes of molecule are accommodated in appropriate sizes and shapes of minute pockets or pits in the sensory hairs of the nasal mucosa (see page 43). Beyond this

point there is little information on the transformation of chemical characteristics into electrical impulses. The possible relationship between molecular
size, shape, and charge and the first stages of the transduction process for
smell is shown in Fig. 1.12.

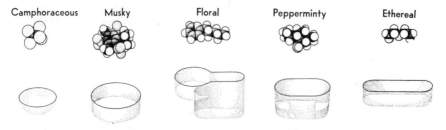

**Figure 1.12**   The stereochemical theory of odour; molecular size and shape are
believed to be the basis of sensory coding. (From J.E. Amoore, W. Johnston and
M. Rubin, The stereochemical theory of odour. In *Scientific American*, 1964, 211.
Copyright 1964 by *Scientific American* Inc. All rights reserved.)

## Encoding of Information

The stimulus at the receptors is essentially energy which carries information about internal and external events of significance to the organism.
For example, the visual stimulus is a pattern of light brought to focus on the
retinal receptor mosaic by the lens system of the eye. The external object
or event from which light is emitted or reflected has certain properties; objects
vary in their shape, size, direction, distance, and the amount and composition
of light which is reflected from their surfaces. An observer can respond to and
discriminate among all these properties. We observe bees discriminating
between different coloured flowers and animals withdrawing from hot
surfaces. Insects avoid predators and approach food. Clearly the sensory
systems which receive stimulation are capable of preserving the information
about events in the patterns of impulses in the nervous system. This preservation of relevant information in the nervous system is called stimulus coding
and the manner of achieving it is encoding. It should be noted, however,
that while the manner in which certain properties of stimulation are encoded
is fairly clear, the way in which other stimulus properties are preserved in
the patterns of neural activity is by no means fully understood.

If the total electric potential of a nerve trunk consisting of a bundle of
fibres is recorded while the intensity of the stimulus is increased, the evoked
potential also increases. The size of the evoked potential in the main nerve
trunk from the taste receptors of the tongue as a function of the concentration
of a salt solution is shown in Fig. 1.13. As the concentration increases so does
the total output from the trunk. The first point to note about the encoding
of stimulus intensity is that it is represented grossly by the size of the evoked

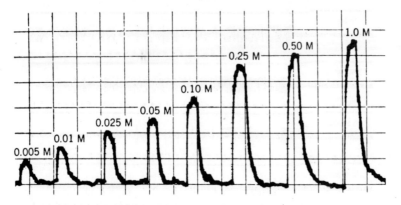

**Figure 1.13** Summated electrical activity of the nerve serving the taste receptors of the tongue in response to salt solutions of concentrations between 0·005 and I·OM. (From L.M. Beidler, Mechanisms of gustatory and olfactory receptor stimulation. In W.A. Rosenblith (Ed.), *Sensory Communication*, Cambridge, Mass., The M.I.T. Press, 1961. By courtesy of The M.I.T. Press, Copyright ©, 1961, by the Massachusetts Institute of Technology.)

potential. If, however, recordings are made from single nerve fibres instead of the nerve trunk as a whole, the magnitude of each recorded impulse remains constant despite variations in stimulus intensity, a well-established principle of neural action referred to as the all-or-none law. The *frequency* of impulses per unit time, however, does change with intensity; the greater the intensity of stimulation the greater the frequency of impulses, as shown in Fig. 1.14 for single fibres of the gustatory (taste) and visual systems.

The evoked potential (Fig. 1.13) represents the summated impulses from a number of fibres, so that its magnitude is a function of both the number of individual nerve fibres involved and the frequency of impulses in each fibre. Thus intensity of stimulation is encoded by both impulse frequency and the number of fibres which are activated by the stimulus. In most sensory systems the frequency of impulses in a single fibre characteristically rises as the intensity of stimulation increases.

No single mechanism is involved in the encoding of stimulus qualities such as wavelength of light, frequency of acoustic stimulus, or chemical composition of olfactory or gustatory stimulation. At the level of the receptors themselves, however, it is becoming increasingly clear that different receptors exhibit a considerable degree of specificity for certain qualities or ranges of quality. In other words, the first stage in encoding is the particular receptors which respond to a certain stimulus quality.

Although it has long been suspected that there are three types of cone receptors in the retina, each responsive to a limited range of wavelengths, only recently has this suspicion been confirmed neurophysiologically. All

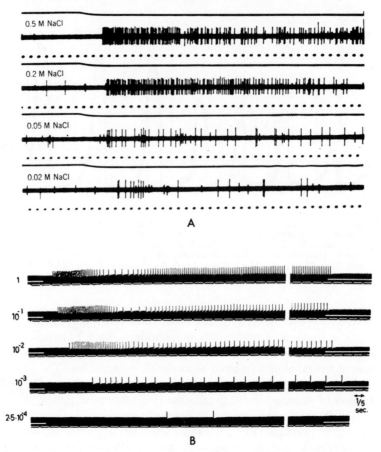

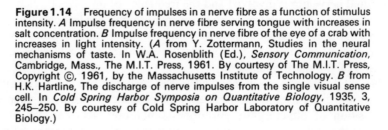

**Figure 1.14** Frequency of impulses in a nerve fibre as a function of stimulus intensity. *A* Impulse frequency in nerve fibre serving tongue with increases in salt concentration. *B* Impulse frequency in nerve fibre of the eye of a crab with increases in light intensity. (*A* from Y. Zottermann, Studies in the neural mechanisms of taste. In W.A. Rosenblith (Ed.), *Sensory Communication*, Cambridge, Mass., The M.I.T. Press, 1961. By courtesy of The M.I.T. Press, Copyright ©, 1961, by the Massachusetts Institute of Technology. *B* from H.K. Hartline, The discharge of nerve impulses from the single visual sense cell. In *Cold Spring Harbor Symposia on Quantitative Biology*, 1935, 3, 245–250. By courtesy of Cold Spring Harbor Laboratory of Quantitative Biology.)

discriminable colours in the visible spectrum can be produced by mixing appropriate proportions of light from the red, green, and blue regions of the spectrum. This fact, known to Isaac Newton, lead Thomas Young and later Hermann von Helmholtz to argue that there are three types of cone receptor, each sensitive to a limited band of wavelengths. More recently it has been shown that there are indeed three classes of receptor, as shown in Fig. 1.15. In analogous fashion, the thermo-receptors of the skin are clearly distinguishable into "warm" and "cold" receptors both in terms of their excitation by warm and cold stimuli and their depth in the skin. The encoding of stimulus qualities is not, however, entirely a matter of receptor specificity. At higher levels of the nervous pathways, interactions between nerve cells occur such that one type of cell inhibits another. For example, in the ganglion cell layer of the retina one cell may be excited primarily by a group of red-sensitive receptors and inhibited (*i.e.*, prevented from responding) mainly by green-sensitive receptors. Other cells are affected conversely, being excited by green and inhibited by red receptors.

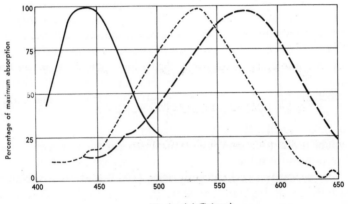

**Figure 1.15** Spectral sensitivity curves of three cone pigments in the retina; the peak sensitivities are 447, 540 and 577 millimicrons. (From E.F. MacNichol, Three-pigment color vision. In *Scientific American*, 1964, 211, 48–56. Copyright 1964 by *Scientific American* Inc. All rights reserved.)

It seems then that in at least some of the sensory systems, receptors specifically sensitive to particular ranges of stimulus quality effect an initial sorting out. At higher levels of the nervous pathway, however, the fibres from these receptors converge on cells which are excited or inhibited by specifically sensitive receptors. There is a great deal more to be found about the preservation in the transmitted chains of impulses of information carried by the stimulus. The problem of the encoding of spatial information, of size, shape, and direction of vision, has not been dealt with here mainly because its manner is less clear. It is enough to note at this stage that information is preserved in neural activity as a first step in the perceptual process which enables the organism to maintain contact with internal and external events.

# Methods of Investigation and Measurement

Perception was defined broadly in the last section as the organism's maintenance of contact with its environment, its internal state, and its posture and movement. This contact is initiated through energy changes or stimuli which impinge on and excite receptors which in turn transduce and transmit the information in coded form to the central nervous system. Irrespective of whether the investigator's interest centres on subjective experiences or observed responses (an issue which will be discussed later), perception is indexed by the organism's behaviour. The detection, discrimination, and recognition behaviour of the animal indicates that it is in contact with internal or external states of affairs. These behavioural responses may be muscle twitches, skilled movements, or verbalizations. If a source of infrared emission is struck at by a pit-viper whose ears, eyes, and olfactory receptors are masked from stimulation, then it can be said that the snake is in contact with the external source (see pp. 3-4). In short, it can be said (providing the response is made consistently) that the animal perceives. If, on the other hand, no such response is made to the stimulus when the pit-organ (a small pit in which are located sensory cells sensitive to infrared radiation) is sealed off then one can say that the animal is not in contact with the external event or, more briefly, that it fails to perceive.

It will be useful to begin with a typical experiment in perception in which verbal responses from human subjects index perception of external objects. A problem recently investigated by Rice (1967) and his associates at the Stanford Research Institute concerns the perception of objects by blind subjects using information provided by echoes from self-emitted sounds. More specifically, the question was: what is the minimum size of an object which a blind person can detect when it is placed at different distances? There were five subjects and they were seated as shown in Fig. 1.16 with a metal disk suspended in front. Subjects were allowed to choose their preferred sound, words, clicks, hisses and "F" sounds. After a series of practice periods, the experimenters chose five sizes of disk, the largest being selected on the basis of results from the practice trials and the smaller ones each being 60 percent of the size of the next larger one. At each distance (24, 30, 36, 42, 48, 67, 87 and 108 inches) there was a separate set of five disks, the average size being greater for the longer distances. For each of the distances the five disks were presented 100 times each in random order and there were 100 occasions when the disk was not presented at all. The subjects emitted their preferred sound and indicated whether or not a disk was present in front. For the small targets they were frequently wrong whereas for the larger disks they were more frequently correct in their detection. In Fig. 1.17 the average percentage frequency of correct response is plotted as a function of disk diameter for each of the eight distances. The disk diameter which resulted in subjects giving correct responses on 50 percent of the occasions is a traditional and convenient index referred to as the threshold (see p. 32), in this case the detection threshold for disks. It can be seen that the threshold increased with distance. In physical terms the angle subtended at the observer by the disk giving 50 percent correct detection responses remained relatively stable at about 4.63°. That is, at a distance of 24 inches the threshold diameter was 1.9 centimetres and at 108 inches about 8 centimetres.

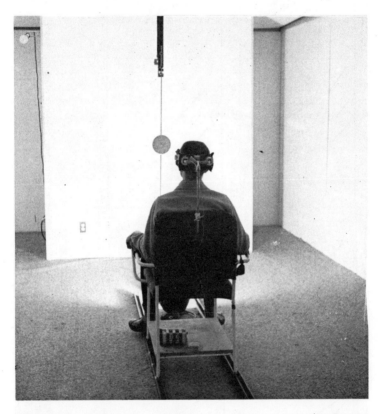

**Figure 1.16** Experimental arrangement for studying size discrimination by a blind subject. (From C.E. Rice, Human echo perception. In *Science*, 1967, 155, 656–664. By courtesy of *Science*, Copyright 1967 by the American Association for the Advancement of Science.)

The point to be made by describing this experiment is that the perception of objects at a distance by a blind person is indicated by his responses, in this case "yes" and "no". Irrespective of what is inferred from these responses about subjective experiences, the blind subject's contact with external objects through echo-sounding is indicated by what he does. With this point

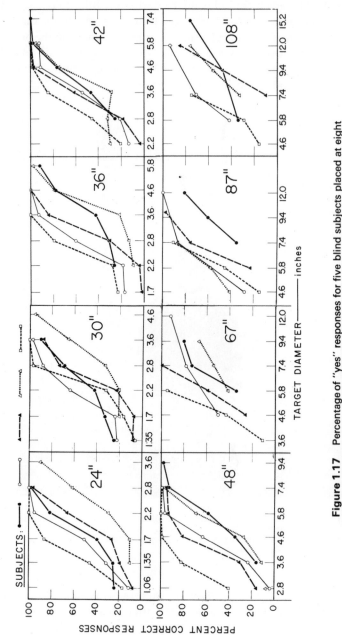

**Figure 1.17** Percentage of "yes" responses for five blind subjects placed at eight distances from targets of different sizes. (From C.E. Rice, Human echo perception. In *Science*, 1967, 155, 656–664. By courtesy of *Science*, Copyright 1967 by the American Association for the Advancement of Science.)

established the principal methods for investigating perception can be out-lined, *viz.,* analytical introspection and psychophysical methods, the latter having numerous variants.

## ANALYTICAL INTROSPECTION

Consciousness, perception, and introspection are bound up with the origins of scientific enquiry in psychology. Introspection provides a convenient opportunity to discuss briefly the background to the study of perception. Scientific psychology formally began with the establishment by Wilhelm Wundt of the first experimental laboratory in 1879. Wundt held that psychology is the science of experience or consciousness. The main problems of psychology for Wundt were the analysis of conscious processes into their elements, the manner in which these elements are connected, and the laws which govern their connection. In an attempt to solve these problems Wundt developed and applied introspection, later described by William James in 1890 as "... looking into our own minds and reporting what we discover". It was later argued that the elements of consciousness were sensations and that these were connected by association.

If immediate experience is regarded as the subject matter of psychology, then introspection (looking into and describing one's own sensations) is an obvious means of examining it. The method was, however, called into ques-tion and later dropped for three reasons; its unreliability, changing con-ceptions of the subject matter of psychology, and the rise of animal psycho-logy. First, it is expected that an experimental method will give reliable data, *i.e.,* results that are consistent from one study to another providing the same procedures and conditions are employed. This, introspection failed to do. Different trained observers reported different sensations under identical conditions of stimulation, a disagreement which derived in large part from the different meanings given to descriptive terms. Second, the emphasis in psychology swung slowly from the study of consciousness to the study of behaviour, leaving less of a place for subjective description of sensory phenomena. Third, interest increased progressively in animal behaviour, especially in regard to learning processes, an area of psychology in which introspection is obviously impossible. Overriding all these considerations, however, was an increasing demand for and emphasis on precision and quantification in experiment which was not obtainable using introspection. It was for this last reason that psychophysics eventually triumphed as the basic procedure for the study of perception.

## PSYCHOPHYSICAL METHODS

The history of psychophysics is even longer than that of formal, analytical introspection. Its founder, Gustav Fechner, in 1860 was concerned mainly with the relationships between mind and body, between the psychical and physical. To this end he developed psychophysical techniques and appropriate methods for the treatment of data. The metaphysical issues in the context of which psychophysics developed are no longer central, although its ingenious methods remain in numerous forms as the mainstay for the investigation of perception. Psychophysical methods offer a means of precisely investigating and quantifying four classes of behaviour which indicate perception: detecting, discriminating, recognizing and estimating. These classes are by no means discrete and are simply a descriptive convenience. An example will clarify the four aspects.

A common task is that of watch-keeping, monitoring, or invigilating. A naval watch-keeper is required to scan the surroundings for objects such as ships, periscopes, and lighthouses. He may report a blur on the surface (detection) and later report that the blur is in fact two smaller blurs (discrimination). Later he may report that the two blurs are fishing craft (recognition) at a range of about three miles (estimation). Detection, of course, is discriminating between background and object, and estimating is discriminating distance. Nevertheless, it is convenient to group perceptual indicators into these four classes.

In general, detection, discrimination, recognition, and estimation can be quantified using one or more groups of psychophysical methods: conventional or classical psychophysics, scaling, and signal detection methods.

## Classical Psychophysics

The classical psychophysical methods are those of average error or adjustment, limits or minimal changes, and constant stimuli. These three methods can best be described in the context of a particular problem. Let it be assumed that the problem concerns the "straight-aheadness" of a point of light. We wish to establish in which position a point of light must be in order to be judged straight ahead in an otherwise dark room.

The method of average error simply requires the observer to adjust the point of light with a suitable control mechanism to the straight-ahead position on a number of occasions. To overcome biases the starting position of the point is normally varied from occasion to occasion. The judged straight-ahead would be the average of a suitable number of trials, say ten with starting position to the left and ten to the right.

The method of limits involves the experimenter positioning the light successively in a series of equally-spaced positions, beginning on the right and left equally often. On each occasion on which the light is presented the subject is merely required to indicate at each position whether it is to the right or left of the straight-ahead. If the procedure is begun from the right the observer might respond by saying "right, right, right, right, right, left, left". The position halfway between the last "right" and the first "left" would then be accepted as the straight-ahead for that trial. On the next trial the procedure might begin from the left and the point of light presented step-wise at equally-spaced intervals towards the right, with the subject saying "left, left, left", etc., until a "right" response is given. The average straight-ahead based on a number of trials would then be found, the straight-ahead for each trial being the halfway point between one type of response ("right") and the other ("left").

The method of constant stimuli involves the presentation of the point of light at, say, five positions equally spaced on either side of a pre-established rough estimate of the straight-ahead. These five positions are used on an equal number of occasions (say, 50) but are presented in a random sequence. Each time the point is presented in one of the five positions the subject indicates whether it is to the right or left. Positions further to the right and left are normally judged correctly most of the time. Those near the position of the subject's physical straight-ahead would be sometimes judged "right" and sometimes "left". The subject's straight-ahead is that position of the light (computed or read from a graph' which is judged left on half the occasions and right on the other half.

Generally, the method of constant stimuli is preferred to the others in that it eliminates more sources of error. Since the subject cannot predict what the next stimulus will be, there is less "expectancy" effect and less error due to starting positions.

### Scaling Methods

While psychophysical methods are concerned mainly with establishing acuities and sensitivities in judgments of sizes, shapes, positions, intensities, and other properties of objects, scaling methods deal with the relationship between judgmental and physical continua. For example, if a light increases in intensity by equal increments, how does its judged or perceived intensity (*i.e.,* brightness) increase? We can put this problem another way. As light intensity increases in physical terms the observer through his photoreceptors maintains contact with the change. To what extent does his response to intensity accord with physical intensity?

Fechner in his *Elemente der Psychophysik* first considered this problem using two assumptions. First he assumed Weber's Law, which states that the size of a just noticeable difference (jnd) in stimulation is a constant proportion of the total stimulus intensity. Thus if one candle added to ten candles results in a jnd then ten candles must be added to a hundred. Second, he assumed that a sensation is the sum of all the jnds coming before it in the scale. Fechner proposed that where $S$ is sensation, $K$ a constant, and $R$ the stimulus, $S = K \log R$. That is, the experienced intensity is a logarithmic function of the stimulus. Since Fechner's investigations, both the basic assumptions have been questioned and different methods developed for establishing the relationship between physical and perceptual scales.

Category and magnitude scaling methods are among those in current use. In category scaling the individual is instructed to order the relative magnitudes of an object property such as length, intensity, or weight. He is told to place the least into category 1 and the greatest into category 7. Then he is told to distribute the other stimuli in such a manner that the intervals between them are equal. In the magnitude estimation method the individual is required merely to estimate an object property by assigning values in units of length, intensity, or weight. Unfortunately these two methods do not give rise to the same scales, as can be seen from Fig. 1.18 for estimations of length. Because the magnitude estimation scale is more closely associated with the stimulus itself, the view is often expressed that this method better depicts the perceptual effects of stimuli to which the observer must adapt. The basis of the difference between the outcomes of category and estimation procedures is, however, unsettled.

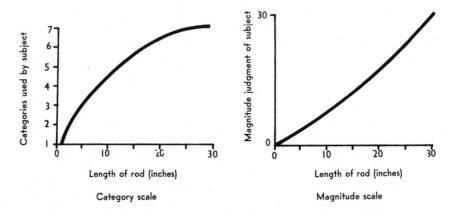

**Figure 1.18** The effect on judgments of length of requiring subject to assign the lengths of objects to different categories (category scale) and to estimate lengths (magnitude scale). Both procedures are reliable but result in different scales. (Adapted from E. Galanter, Contemporary psychophysics. From *New Directions in Psychology* by Roger Brown, E. Galanter, E.H. Hess, and G. Mandler. Copyright © 1962 by Holt, Rinehart and Winston, Inc. Adapted and reprinted by permission of Holt, Rinehart and Winston, Inc., Publishers, New York.

## Signal Detection Methods

If faced with a task involving the reporting of signals, as in radar-watching, the observer's responses may take one of four forms; he may respond when the signal occurs (a hit) or not respond when there is no signal. Alternatively he may fail to respond when there is a signal (a miss) or he may respond when there is no signal (a false alarm). The frequency of these four classes is a function of factors other than stimulus (signal) strength. The attentiveness of the observer and, more significantly, the rewards and punishments given for these various responses profoundly affect the pattern of responding. In signal detection studies the emphasis is shifted from sheer sensory detection to the decision-making characteristics of the observer or operator, reflecting the fact that perception is intimately bound up with motivation.

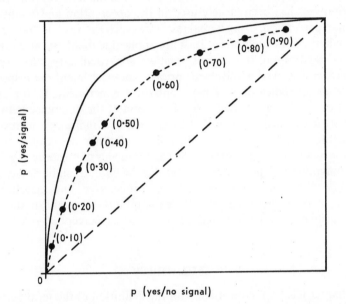

**Figure 1.19**  An iso-sensitivity curve or response operating characteristic obtained by plotting the probability of "yes" responses when there is no signal, against the probability of "yes" responses when there is a signal. When the signal is rare the subject does not say "yes" very frequently even when the signal is presented. (Adapted from E. Galanter, Contemporary psychophysics. From *New Directions in Psychology* by Roger Brown, E. Galanter, E.H. Hess, and G. Mandler. Copyright © 1962 by Holt, Rinehart and Winston, Inc. Adapted and reprinted by permission of Holt, Rinehart and Winston, Inc., Publishers, New York.)

By systematically varying the rewards and punishments for various types of responses in a so-called pay-off matrix, the patterns of responding may be altered. The probability that a signal will occur, the pay-off matrix, and the strength of the stimulus interact to determine the individual's perception, his contact with the external state of affairs. In Fig. 1.19 is shown a typical curve, referred to as a "response operating characteristic", for a signal of intermediate intensity with its probability of occurrence systematically varied. The probability of the observer responding positively to a signal is plotted against the probability that he will respond positively to no signal. The individual clearly responds in accord with signal probability.

### Special Psychophysical Methods

The discussion of classical psychophysics, scaling, and signal detection methods may well convey the impression that in this chapter the emphasis has shifted from perception in general terms to human perception. But while psychophysics has been largely used in the observation and quantification of human perception, using verbal responses such as "yes" or "no", "larger" or "smaller", some methods at least are applicable to infants and subhuman subjects. By training the animal to make a particular response (pecking, head movement, paw withdrawal) prior to an experiment the response can be used as an indicator in a psychophysical experiment. If, for example, interest centres on an animal's discrimination of the difference between the diameter of two disks, it can first be trained or conditioned to respond to such a difference. Thereafter five or more small differences can be presented using the method of constant stimuli. The frequency of response as a function of the magnitude of the differences can then be used to establish the animal's difference threshold. Similar training procedures and psychophysical methods may be used successfully with infants to establish their visual acuity, taste discrimination, and numerous other perceptual sensitivities.

# Summary

This chapter has been concerned with the definition of the term perception, the basic structures and processes involved in perception, and with methods of investigation and measurement in studying perception.

Perception can be defined as the organism's maintenance of contact with its environment, its internal state, and its own postures and motions. In this sense, animals simpler than man can be said to perceive, a capacity which is essential for their survival. The perceptual process consists of the reception of changes in energy impinging at the receptor cells, the transduction of this energy into electrical impulses in the nerve cells, and the encoding of the impulses to preserve the information about external and internal events conveyed by the patterns of energy stimulation.

The forms of energy to which the sensory cells are tuned and which convey information about events are electromagnetic, mechanical and chemical. The ranges of these energy forms to which some animals are sensitive are vastly different from those to which man is sensitive. Certain species of snake, fish and bat (to mention only a few) respond to energy ranges to which man is quite insensitive. Accordingly the structure and processes of the receptor cells and sense organs vary widely among animal species.

While the intensity of stimulus energy is encoded in the form of impulse frequency in single fibres of the nervous system, the encoding of stimulus qualities such as wavelength in vision is dependent on the specific properties of certain receptors and nerve fibres. Visual receptors exhibit considerable specificity for certain wavelengths of energy, a basis of information coding observable in senses other than vision.

While analytical introspection was once the principal technique for the study of human perception, it has been replaced by psychophysics. Classical psychophysics, including the methods of adjustment, limits, and constant stimuli, with their many variants, continue to be widely used in the study of human and non-human perception. In addition, scaling methods are frequently employed in establishing relationships between physical and judged properties of the stimulus. Recent developments in methods for studying perception include signal detection techniques and special psychophysical methods for studying non-human perception using operant conditioning procedures. In signal detection methods the emphasis in perception is shifted from the stimulus and its properties to the decision-making behaviour of the observer.

# 2.   Basic Perceptual Capacities

LIMITS are imposed on perception by the sensitivity and the spatial and temporal resolving power of the various sensory systems which mediate contact with internal and external events. Certain minimal conditions of stimulus intensity, and spatial and temporal properties, are necessary for responses to occur. The index of these basic perceptual capacities is the threshold found by means of psychophysical procedures described in the last chapter. The purpose of this chapter is to review the minimal amounts and changes of stimulus energy necessary for perception and, in some cases, the sensory structures involved. Since the perceptual threshold is the standard measure of capacity, it is necessary to examine this concept before discussing the minimal conditions of intensity, space and time for perception to occur.

## Perception of Intensity and Quality

### THE THRESHOLD AS A MEASURE OF PERCEPTUAL CAPACITY

The threshold can be found using any of the standard psychophysical procedures outlined in the last chapter. It is not, however, a fixed value but varies from time to time. Its variation can best be shown using the method of constant stimuli. If the frequency of positive responses is plotted as a function of stimulus values, the graph assumes a typical form as shown in Fig. 2.1. The shape of the graph is that of a typical probability function. Usually the threshold is taken to be that value of the stimulus at which perception (*i.e.,* positive responses) occurs on fifty percent of the occasions on which the stimulus is presented.

The fifty percent point may vary according to a variety of factors including the motivational state determined by the pay-offs for "hits", "misses" and "false-alarms", the number of "blanks" (*i.e.,* trials on which no stimulus is presented), the state of the sensory system, and the sequence in which the stimulus values are presented. Fluctuation of the threshold with variation in these factors has led to a view that the measure is unstable and to procedures for rendering it more stable or reliable. The threshold as a measure of perceptual capacity is not, however, necessarily any more unstable than other measures. The volume of a gas varies according to its temperature and pressure and in stating volume it is usual to specify the temperature and pressure. So far there is no standard specification for pay-off structure, number of "blanks" per hundred presentations, or sequential

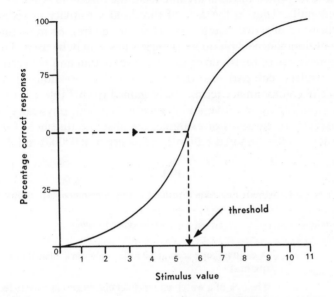

**Figure 2.1** Percentage of correct or positive responses as a function of stimulus value. The threshold is that value at which 50 percent of the responses are correct.

pattern of presentation. There is no reason, however, why careful specification of the conditions of measurement should not apply in statements of threshold values. For most general purposes measurements are made rather loosely. In measuring the length of a table we seldom bother to state the temperature. In like fashion most measurements of threshold are made psychophysically without employing standard conditions.

## PERCEPTION OF INTENSITY

As is the case with most stimulus properties, two aspects of perceptual sensitivity arise in connection with stimulus intensity; the minimum perceptible intensity and the minimum perceptible difference in intensity. The first refers to what is traditionally called the absolute threshold or limen and the second to the difference threshold, limen, or just noticeable difference (jnd).

**Minimum Perceptible Intensity**

The absolute threshold is normally established using one of the psycho-physical measures after a period of "rest" during which the sensory system recovers from prior stimulation. Depending on the particular problem, and the purpose for which the data are intended, the threshold is stated in terms of various units. Thus in the case of threshold sensitivity in vision either ergs, a measure of work (1 erg = 1 dyne/centimetre), or millilamberts (a measure of luminance or photometric brightness), may be used. The use of different measures of threshold sensitivity both within and between sensory systems renders comparisons difficult. Some impression of absolute thresholds in commonplace terms can be gained from Table 2.1. Generally, the senses are highly sensitive and compare well with physical systems in their sensitivity to energy. For example, the absolute threshold for light is of the order of a few hundred billionths of an erg or 0·000001 millilamberts.

TABLE 2.1

**Some approximate detection threshold values in commonplace terms**

| Sense modality | Detection threshold |
| --- | --- |
| Light | A candle flame seen at 30 miles on a dark clear night (ca. 10 quanta). |
| Sound | The tick of a watch under quiet conditions at twenty feet (ca. 0.0002 dynes/cm$^2$). |
| Taste | One teaspoon of sugar in 2 gallons of water. |
| Smell | One drop of perfume diffused into the entire volume of a 3 room apartment. |
| Touch | The wing of a bee falling on your cheek from a distance of 1 cm. |

(From *New Directions in Psychology* by Roger Brown, E. Galanter, E. H. Hess, and G. Mandler. Copyright © 1962 by Holt, Rinehart and Winston, Inc. Adapted and reprinted by permission of Holt, Rinehart and Winston, Inc., Publishers, New York.)

For hearing the absolute threshold is −73·8 decibels with reference to a pressure of 1 dyne/cm$^2$. In the case of the pressure sensitive system of the skin, threshold pressure is a force of about 85 milligrams acting on a surface of 0·1 millimetre radius. Thresholds for taste vary widely according to the chemical composition of the substance in solution. Whereas the threshold of sugar is about 0·7 percent solution, that for quinine sulphate is a 0·00003 percent solution. The amounts of chemical substances in air for the sense of smell at threshold are often so minute as to make accurate measurement difficult. For vanillin, a very powerful odorant, only about two ten millionths of a milligram per cubic metre of air is necessary for a threshold response.

**Minimum Perceptible Difference**

Discussion of the minimum or threshold differences in stimulus, of the just noticeable difference, must begin with consideration of the Weber ratio which was mentioned briefly in the last chapter. E. H. Weber in 1834 maintained that the stimulus must be increased by a constant fraction to be just noticeably different. In other words, if one gram added to fifty grams gives a just noticeable difference in weight on fifty percent of the trials (*i.e.*, a threshold difference) then two grams would need to be added to a hundred and four grams to two hundred. The Weber fraction is often written

$$\Delta I/I = K$$

*i.e.*, the threshold difference in stimulation stated as a fraction of the stimulus is a constant. Generally this law holds over a broad range of stimulus values for the various senses but does not apply for extreme conditions of stimulation such as very bright or dim light, very heavy weights, or light and very loud or soft sounds.

## PERCEPTION OF QUALITY

In addition to intensity of stimulation the sensory systems mediate contact with numerous other properties which can be conveniently referred to as qualities. The wavelengths of light from objects, the frequency of sounds, and the chemical composition of solutions and gases can all be treated as qualities of stimulation. It will be convenient to treat perception of quality in terms of the individual sensory systems. It is not intended to deal with all aspects of quality discrimination but to treat vision, hearing, taste, and smell as examples.

**Colour Vision**

The human observer is capable of discriminating between about 7,500,000 different colours when intensity, wavelength and purity of light reaching the eye are varied conjointly. If, however, wavelength alone is varied the average observer exhibits about 128 jnds in the visible spectrum some of which are as large as 22 m$\mu$ and others as small as 1 m$\mu$.

If red light from the long-wave part of the spectrum is combined with a green in different proportions the resulting mixtures are matched by an observer to orange, yellow and yellow-green. A particular red (671 m$\mu$) and green (536 m$\mu$) yield a yellow which is matched to a yellow of 589 m$\mu$. Some pairs when mixed are matched to white, *e.g.*, red (671 m$\mu$) and blue-green (493 m$\mu$), and are known as complementary colours.

Since Newton's experiments with light it has been known that all the discriminable colours can be obtained through mixing "primary" wave-lengths from the long-wave, medium-wave, and short-wave regions of the spectrum. These primaries, which must not be confused with "artist's primaries", are red, green and violet. A general equation can be written in the form

$$C = xR + yG + zV$$

where $C$ is the discriminated colour, $R$, $G$ and $V$ wavelengths from the red, green and violet regions, and $x$, $y$ and $z$ coefficients signifying the proportions of primaries in the mixture.

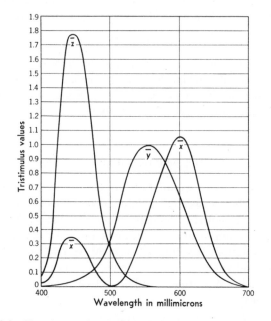

**Figure 2.2** The International Commission on Illumination "standard observer". The values $\bar{x}$, $\bar{y}$ and $\bar{z}$ indicate the amount of the three primary colours required to match a unit amount of radiant energy. (From A.C. Hardy, *Handbook of Colorimetry*, Cambridge, Mass., The M.I.T. Press, 1936. By courtesy of The M.I.T. Press, Copyright © 1936, by the Massachusetts Institute of Technology.)

Wavelengths may be mixed in a variety of ways including that of over-lapping on a white screen three circular patches of light from three projectors. By placing filters transmitting different wavelengths in each projector different wavelengths can be mixed on the screen. A simpler but cruder method is to use three sectors of different colours (*i.e.,* reflecting different wavelengths) arranged on a disk. When the disk is rotated at high speed the three are mixed or "fused". If the sectors are adjustable in area different proportions of the different wavelengths may be added to the mixture.

If three wavelengths, each selected so that none can be produced by a mixture of the other two, are mixable to produce any colour, then it should be possible to specify any colour in terms of three selected primaries. This is in fact the case. A "tristimulus specification" can be arrived at for a given visible wavelength. In 1931 the International Commission on Illumination (I.C.I.) (now *C.I.E., Commission Internationale de l'Eclairage*) drew up a standard system for specifying tristimulus values based on the colour matching responses of subjects whose settings were in good agreement. These are shown in Fig. 2.2. The values $\bar{x}$, $\bar{y}$ and $\bar{z}$ indicate the amount of each of the I.C.I. primaries required to match a unit amount of radiant energy at each wavelength.

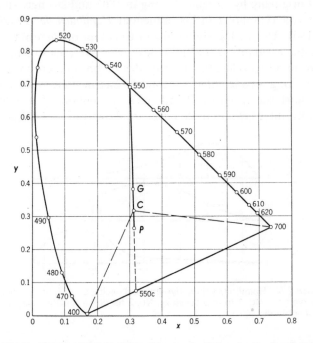

**Figure 2.3** Chromaticity diagram; the sample *G* lies on the line between illuminant *C* ("daylight") and 550 millimicrons identifying it as yellowish green. (From A.C. Hardy, *Handbook of Colorimetry*, Cambridge, Mass., The M.I.T. Press, 1936. By courtesy of The M.I.T. Press, Copyright ©, 1936, by the Massachusetts Institute of Technology.)

An outcome of the tristimulus specification of a colour is the "chromaticity diagram" which permits identification of any colour and its relationship to others. Such a diagram is shown in Fig. 2.3. The axes *x* and *y* are called chromaticity coordinates; the curved line represents the location of all spectral colours in the visible spectrum, and all colours are represented by points within this curve and a straight line joining their termini. The point *C* near the centre is the location of white "daylight". A particular colour *G* can be specified in terms of its dominant wavelength by drawing a line from *C* through *G* to its spectral locus. For *G* this is about 550 m$\mu$, a yellowish-green. Since *G* lies only about 20 percent of the distance from *C* to spectral green it is said to have a purity of 20 percent.

The fact that a maximum of only three wavelengths is required to reproduce or match every colour in the visible spectrum suggests a basis for an explanation of visual wavelength discrimination. Rather than having to assume that there are as many different classes of receptor units as there are discriminable wavelengths, it is sufficient to assume three. Such a view was expressed originally by Thomas Young in 1807 and strongly supported by Hermann von Helmholtz in his influential *Handbuch der Physiologischen Optik* in 1861. The Young-Helmholtz three-colour or trichromatic theory is based on the assumption that all colour sensitive cones of the retina are responsive to all wavelengths in some degree but one group is maximally sensitive to long wavelengths, a second to intermediate wavelengths and a third to short wavelengths. Helmholtz's conception of the "excitation" curves for the three types of mechanism are shown in Fig. 2.4. Later enquiries

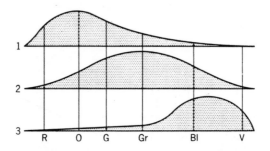

**Figure 2.4**  Helmholtz's three hypothetical excitation curves for three kinds of nerve fibre; No. 1 for red sensitive, No. 2 for green sensitive and No. 3 for violet sensitive.

suggested that the basis of differential sensitivity at the level of the retinal receptors lies in the photosensitive materials contained by the three groups of cones. In a series of elegantly precise experiments investigators have recently passed a beam of light of known wavelength through cones from monkeys and humans. The composition of the emerging beam when compared with that of an uninterrupted beam from the same source indicates the particular wavelengths absorbed by the cone. By taking a large number of such measurements it has been possible to show that cones fall into three groups in terms of the absorption characteristics of their photosensitive materials (see Fig. 1.15). Thus the initial "sorting" of the multitude of wavelengths falling on the eye occurs in the retina; three different classes of receptor mechanism are respectively tuned to long, intermediate and short wavelengths. In psychophysical terms three wavelengths when mixed are sufficient for the reproduction of all visible colours.

Although it is possible to discuss the perception of stimulus intensity independently of spectral composition of light when the latter is held constant and *vice versa* these two stimulus variables interact when they are jointly varied. Except for certain invariable points in the spectrum judgments of wavelengths shift slightly towards yellow or blue with increases in intensity, a phenomenon called the Bézold-Brucke effect. Three spectral points, 572 m$\mu$, 503 m$\mu$ and 478 m$\mu$ are, however, invariant with changes in intensity. These invariant points and the shifts in hue judgments for other points with variations in intensity are shown in Fig. 2.5.

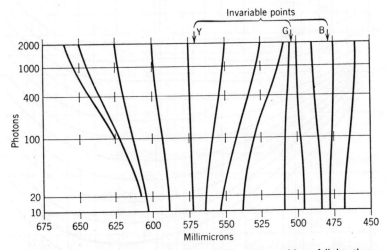

**Figure 2.5** Constant hue contours for different intensities of light; three spectral points yield constant hue regardless of intensity. (From D.M. Purdy, The Bézold-Brucke phenomenon and contours for constant hue. In *Amer. J. Psychol.*, 1937, 49, 313–315. By courtesy of *Amer. J. Psychol.*)

## Hearing and Frequency Discrimination

In addition to intensity of sound an observer can also discriminate between frequencies. Tones are described as "high" or "low", a subjective quality referred to as pitch. It has already been noted that the approximate range of frequency discrimination for a young human observer is between about 20 and 20,000 cps. In the case of some species of moth, bat and dolphin the range of frequency discrimination is extended upward by some thousands of cps.

Although the normal human observer can discriminate frequencies between about 20 and 20,000 cps, by no means all of these are separately discriminable. Depending on the psychophysical procedures used, the method of presenting the pure tones to be compared, and their intensity, there are about 1500 jnds in the audible range of frequencies. As in the case of visual wavelength discrimination the jnds vary in magnitude; at 1000 cps a change as small as 3 cps can be detected whereas at 5000 cps at least 15 are required for discriminable change.

Sound intensity and frequency jointly determine discrimination. In the range 1000–2000 cps significantly lower intensities are necessary to equal judged intensity at the lower and higher frequencies. In Fig. 2.6 are shown

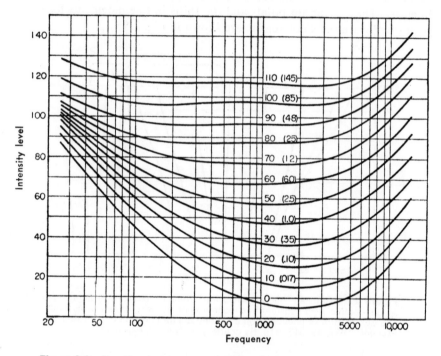

**Figure 2.6**   Equal loudness contours for frequencies between 20 and 10,000 cycles per second and the relation between intensity level and frequency. (Adapted from S.S. Stevens and H. Davis, *Hearing: Its Physiology and Psychology*, N.Y., John Wiley & Sons Inc., 1938. By courtesy of John Wiley & Sons Inc.)

contours of "equal loudness' for different frequencies. It can be seen that not only judged loudness varies with frequency but the relationship between the two is affected by the overall intensity level.

Discrimination of acoustic frequencies is achieved through the cochlea acting as a sound analyser in a way originally demonstrated by Georg von Békésy. If the cochlea (Figs 1.7 and 1.11) were uncoiled, it would have the general form shown in Fig. 2.7. The sound vibrations are transmitted to the cochlea by the three small ossicles of the middle ear and enter through the oval window. The stirrup footplate (Fig. 1.7E) acts like a piston and displaces the incompressible fluid, the perilymph, towards the apical end.

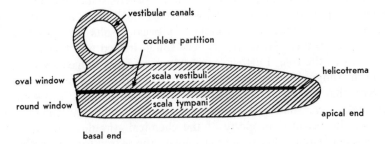

**Figure 2.7** Diagram of the uncoiled cochlea. The cochlear partition is bounded by Reissner's membrane and the basilar membrane which contain between them the sensory receptors for hearing. (From W.A. van Bergeijk, J.R. Pierce and E.E. David, *Waves and the Ear*, London, Heinemann Educational Books Ltd, 1961. By courtesy of Heinemann Educational Books Ltd.)

When a pressure wave impinges on the oval window the perilymph displaces the cochlear partition which bends or bulges downward into the scala tympani. The bulge occurs first at the basal end and travels toward the apex, the time taken for the bulge to travel the length of the cochlea being about 3 milliseconds. In the case of pure tones, as each peak of a sine wave pushes in the oval window the bulge or wave starts down the partition and reaches its maximum amplitude at a place determined by its frequency. In the case of high frequency tones this maximum is at the basal end and for low tones closer to the apical end. Thus, the sound wave at the oval window creates a travelling bulge whose maximum amplitude is a function of the frequency characteristics of the sound. This maximum stimulates the hair cells (Fig. 1.7D) which generate impulses in the fibres of the auditory (VIIIth) nerve. A particular region of the cochlear partition, the basilar membrane and organ of Corti, is, therefore, associated with a particular range of frequencies. The cochlea thus serves as a sound frequency analyser by virtue of the travelling wave induced in the stiff partition by the impinging vibrations at the cochlear partition.

### Gustatory Quality

Certain qualities of substances stimulating the tongue can be discriminated in addition to their concentrations. These qualities are related to chemical composition although, unlike wavelength and frequency in vision and hearing, the actual property of composition which determines such judgments is not yet fully known. Human observers respond to chemical substances on the tongue by describing them as sour, salty, sweet and bitter. Generally, sour tasting chemicals are associated with the hydrogen ion and the degree of sourness is roughly related to the degree of hydrogen ion dissociation. Saltiness is associated with soluble salts composed of positive and negative ions in their crystalline state. Sweetness occurs mainly with organic compounds such as alcohols, glycols and sugars, and bitterness is associated with the molecular weight of inorganic salts. This classification in terms of chemical properties is very rough indeed and there are many exceptions to the rule. Further, a substance which is judged sweet on one part of the tongue may be classed as bitter on another. It is generally agreed, however, that the subjective descriptions of taste qualities into sour, salt, sweet and bitter exhausts the range of classes into which judgments fall.

Since the essential property of the chemical stimulus correlated with variations in taste quality is not yet known, the search for the mechanisms and processes involved is rendered much more difficult than in the cases of vision and hearing. Having established wavelength of light and frequency of vibration as the main determinants of colour vision and pitch discrimination respectively, the analysis of the mechanisms in terms of sense organ structure, mechanics and processes could proceed. In the case of taste and smell the search is held back because the basic stimulus property underlying judgments of sweetness, sourness, saltiness and bitterness remains obscure.

It is known that different parts of the tongue exhibit different sensitivities to chemical solutions, an observation which has been subjected to considerable enquiry. While there is little variation in sensitivity to salty solutions and not very much to acids, different regions of the tongue vary in their sensitivity to sweet and bitter substances. In general, the tip of the tongue is more sensitive to sweet and the base to bitter. This difference between tip and base is obvious with a substance such as magnesium sulphate (Epsom salts) which tastes salty when placed at the tip and bitter when placed at the base. Since the tongue has four types of taste bud, fungiform, foliate, circumvallate and filiform, there has naturally been speculation as to whether these are associated with the four taste sensations. Such is not the case. Among the most interesting observations so far are those involving electrical stimulation of the tongue. When the tongue is stimulated with alternating currents the taste reported by the subject is dependent on frequency of alternation. With low frequency alternations of the order of 50 cycles, a sour taste is reported while in the neighbourhood of 1000 cycles, the taste reported is mainly bitter. Direct current applied to the tongue also gives rise to taste reports, the particular quality reported being dependent upon the direction of current flow. When the anode is placed on the tongue the sensation is similar to that for low frequency alternating current; a sour taste is reported. The significance of "electrical taste" is not as yet fully understood. The observations are of interest in suggesting that the chemical solutions on the tongue are transduced at the taste buds into electrical activity with varying frequencies. These frequencies can be reproduced by direct electrical stimulation. The problem concerning the chemical properties of solutions responsible for variations in taste qualities still remains unclear and further research will be necessary to isolate the essential features of stimulation.

## Olfactory Quality

Like quality discrimination in taste the stimulus basis for smell discrimination is not clearly understood. To complicate matters, there are different views as to how many phenomenal qualities there are. An early view is that of Zwaademaker who suggested a nine-fold classification of ethereal (fruits, wines), aromatic (spices, camphor), fragrant (flowers, vanilla), ambrosiac (musk, sandalwood), alliaceous (garlic, chlorine), empyreumatic (coffee, creosote), hircine (rancid), foul (bed bugs) and nauseous (carrion). The classification proposed by Henning, however, was generally accepted for a long period. Henning's "smell prism" locates flowery, foul, fruity, resinous, spicy and burnt at the six corners of a wedge-prism. This classification is based partly on observations and partly on rational considerations but, in general terms, has not been confirmed by experiment. It is not possible to locate intermediate odours between the six primaries.

More recently Amoore and his associates have argued that odours can be classified into seven categories which they call primary odours. These are camphoraceous, musky, floral, pepperminty, ethereal, pungent and putrid. There is a point to these attempts to classify odours into primaries. In somewhat similar spirit to the facts of colour mixture, the basis of odours (and indeed tastes) in a small number of primary odours could facilitate the search for the sensory mechanisms involved. If there are seven basic classes of odour the question can well be raised as to whether the members of each class share some common feature and, if so, whether the sensory cells are adapted for receiving and transducing the particular stimulus feature. Amoore suggests that substances which give rise to a camphoraceous odour have a similar molecular size and shape and that these substances are accommodated by minute receptor pits or sites in the olfactory cells. When such a site is occupied by its molecule, excitation of the cell is initiated. In brief, Amoore argues that there are seven primary odours and that substances giving rise to these odours are characterized by certain stereochemical properties, by certain sizes and shapes of molecule (see Fig. 1.12). Further, the sensory cells of the olfactory system contain sites which accommodate particular shapes and sizes of molecule. The sensory basis of olfactory quality is thus said to lie in molecular properties. This view is yet to be amplified and confirmed and should not at this stage be taken as fact. It is, however, a plausible hypothesis and, among other things, suggests a basis for taste quality as well as smell quality. It is not inconceivable that sour, bitter, salty and sweet tasting substances may each have characteristic stereochemical features.

# Perception of Spatial and Temporal Properties

## PERCEPTION OF SPATIAL PROPERTIES

The sensory systems vary in their spatial acuities. It is convenient to discuss basic capacities in spatial discriminations in terms of the individual sensory systems.

### Visual Spatial Discrimination

A fundamental question in visual space perception concerns the smallest detail which can be detected. Visual acuity or "visual resolving power" is expressed either in terms of the angle subtended at the eye by a detail or as a ratio between the distances at which the detail can be detected by a particular and a "standard observer". The smaller a detail the smaller the angle it subtends at the eye (Fig. 2.8). The reciprocal of this angle is often used as

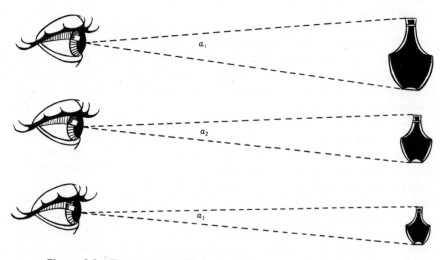

**Figure 2.8** The concept of visual angle. The angle $\alpha$ subtended at the eye varies as a function of object size. See also Fig. 3.1A and 3.2A.

an index of acuity. For clinical purposes acuity is stated as the ratio between the distance at which a detail can be discriminated and that at which a "normal" observer can discriminate it. Thus 20/20 or normal vision means that an individual can distinguish a detail at 20 feet, the same distance that it is discriminable by a normal eye. In clinical terms 20/10 is better and 20/40 worse than normal. The term mean normal vision refers to the discrimination of a detail subtending an angle of 1 minute at the eye. Expressed as the reciprocal of the angle, therefore, 20/20 vision is 1·00, and 20/40 is 0·50. The reciprocal of the visual angle is used, rather than the angle itself, so that good acuity (*e.g.*, 20/20) will have a higher value than poor acuity (*e.g.*, 20/40).

Numerous tasks are used in the assessment of visual acuity. Each gives a different result when expressed in visual angle terms. Minimum *visible* acuity refers to the perceptual capacity to detect a point, a task in which the intensity of the stimulus is the main determinant of acuity. Minimum *perceptible* acuity is the capacity to discriminate small objects or lines against a plain background, and minimum *separable* acuity to the capacity to discriminate between details (lines, points) when they are close together. Minimum *distinguishable* acuity, sometimes called vernier acuity or "form sense" refers to the capacity to distinguish irregularities or discontinuities. Typical test patterns for minimum perceptible, minimum separable and minimum distinguishable are shown in Fig. 2.9. While the minimum perceptible task with a fine line averages around 1 second of arc, the minimum separable requires an angle of about 1 minute of arc. Under ideal conditions with a bright uniform background the minimum perceptible acuity may be as low as 0·5 second of arc, a value which would be found if a line $\frac{1}{16}$ inch wide were discriminated at 1 mile. This finding is of considerable theoretical interest in that the individual receptors of the central retina are greater in angular size than half a second of arc. It must be concluded, therefore, that visual resolving power is not finally limited by the size of the receptors, *i.e.*, by the coarseness of the retinal grain. In photography it is necessary to have a film grain finer than the grain or texture to be resolved. Visual resolving power is affected by a variety of determinants besides that of sheer detail size. The wavelength and intensity of the light reflected from the detail, the contrast between detail and background, and the duration of exposure are all critical determinants.

The resolving tasks just described are not those commonly employed in the clinical or optometric assessment of visual acuity. For the most part tasks involving visual recognition of letters or, in the case of children, pictures, are used clinically and acuity is expressed relative to a normal observer as described earlier, *i.e.*, as 20/24, 20/18, etc. Using figures similar to those shown in Fig. 2.9D, acuity testing by recognition requires the observer to name the object (letter or symbol) or to specify some critical aspect of it.

As well as the capacity to discriminate between details which are laterally separated, *i.e.*, minimum separable acuity, details which are separated in depth relative to the observer can also be discriminated. This is called depth acuity or, where binocular vision is used, stereoscopic acuity. A common

A                                                          B

Minimum distinguishable
or Vernier acuity

C

Recognition acuity

D

**Figure 2.9**  Typical test patterns for the measurement of visual acuity. For *A*, the task is that of detecting a small dot, for *B*, that of discriminating separate white and black lines, for *C*, that of detecting the "break" in the line, and for *D*, that of recognizing the (Snellen) letters.

apparatus for measuring visual acuity for separation of objects in depth consists of two vertical rods, one stationary and the other movable, which the observer views through a rectangular aperture (about 20 × 12 cm). At a viewing distance of about 6 metres the threshold for discrimination in depth is established by means of one of the standard psychophysical methods.

The threshold difference for binocular vision is about 14·4 mm and for monocular vision about 285 mm. That is, binocular depth acuity is about 20 times better than monocular. Such factors as viewing distance, lengths, widths and separation of the rods, and brightness of background influence the threshold for discrimination of differences in depth.

The basis of markedly superior visual acuity for separation of objects in depth with binocular vision is to be found in the differences between the images falling on the retina of each eye, a difference called retinal disparity. Since for two vertical rods separated in depth the separation between their images on one retina is greater than on the other, the relative depths of the two rods can be discriminated. Retinal disparity is among the primary determinants of visual depth perception. This basis for stereoscopic acuity is shown in Fig. 2.10. Since the discrimination is based essentially on the different angles subtended at the two eyes by the distance between the two rods, stereoscopic acuity is usually expressed in terms of the difference between these angles.

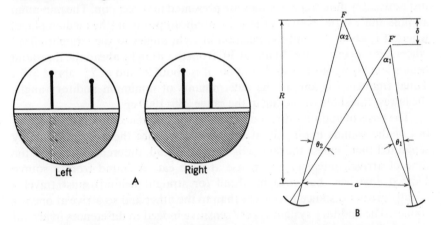

**Figure 2.10** *A* Left eye and right eye views of two flagpoles behind a stone wall; the lateral separation of the flagpoles is seen as smaller in the right eye view. *B* Geometry of the situation depicted in *A*; flagpole F is farther than the F' and the angle ($\theta_1$) subtended at the right eye by the separation is less than that ($\theta_2$) at the left eye.(Adapted from C.H. Graham *et al.*, *Vision and Visual Perception*, N.Y., John Wiley & Sons Inc., 1965. By courtesy of John Wiley & Sons Inc.)

## Tactile Spatial Acuity

The skin, like the retina of the eye, contains a mosaic of receptors which vary in density from one skin area to another. Depending on their distance apart, two points pressed on the skin can be separately discriminated and using psychophysical techniques the minimum separable acuity or the "two-point" threshold of the skin can be found. The two-point threshold varies from one part of the skin surface to another. In the region of the ankle two points need to be separated by about 40 mm to achieve the threshold, while on the lips and finger tips only a few mm of separation are necessary. The most sensitive area for tactile acuity is the tip of the tongue where the separation threshold is about 1 mm.

### Auditory Spatial Localization

The human observer is not only capable of discriminating the direction of a sound source but also its distance. Distance discrimination is based on echoes of footsteps, taps and clicks which are made by the observer himself.

Auditory direction discrimination, sometimes referred to as sound localization, is a basic auditory capacity analogous to acuity in vision and touch. Two separate sources of sound subtend an angle at the centre of the head so that the threshold for auditory direction is usually expressed as the minimum audible angle. This is defined as the angle formed at the centre of the head by lines projecting to two sources of sound whose positions are just noticeably different when they are presented in succession. The minimum audible angle varies between the straight-ahead position (the median plane) where it is about 1°, and the position at right angles to the straight-ahead where it is indeterminate. At about 30° from the straight-ahead the threshold begins increasing steeply so that at 60° it is about 2° and at 75° about 5–6°. Tonal frequency is among the determinants of minimum auditory angle, the lowest threshold occurring in the range 250–1000 cps.

The basis of auditory direction acuity is the differences in the characteristics of the sounds impinging at the two ears. Since the ears are spatially separated then, unless the source is straight ahead, differences occur in the time of arrival, intensity and phase at each ear. A sound from a source located anywhere but straight ahead (or straight behind) must travel a slightly greater distance to one ear than to the other and so arrive at one ear sooner. The auditory system is very sensitive indeed to differences in arrival time at the two ears and is capable of responding to differences as small as 0·00003 sec. Since a sound travels further to one ear than to the other more energy is absorbed en route and, when the sound is angularly displaced from the straight-ahead, one ear lies in the "sound shadow" of the head. In consequence the intensity of sound at one ear is less than at the other. In addition, since one sound travels further to the ear it may be out of phase with the sound at the other at the point of arrival. That is, one part of the wave-form, *e.g.*, the peak, may arrive at one ear while the trough reaches the other (see Fig. 1.10). Differences in intensity and phase also serve as a basis for the auditory resolution of direction, the phase difference being effective mainly at frequencies below about 1500 cps. Further, intensity differences are most effective at high frequencies and arrival time differences chiefly at frequencies in the range 2000–4000 cps. Intensity and arrival time differences are about equally effective in the discrimination of auditory direction. The basis of auditory direction acuity is shown in Fig. 1.10B

## PERCEPTION OF FORM AND PATTERN

Traditional methods for the measurement of acuity or spatial resolving power are concerned mainly with the size of detail which an observer can resolve. Although capacity to discriminate shapes and patterns includes the resolution of fine detail, other factors are also involved. In general terms, the study of form and pattern perception has two aspects. The first is a practical consideration involving which particular shapes of letters, dial patterns, symbols

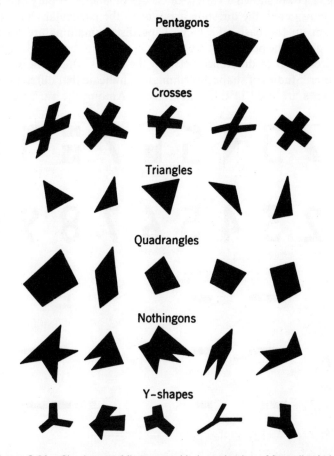

**Figure 2.11**   Six classes of figures used in investigation of form discrimination. (From R.M. Boynton, Recognition of critical targets among irrelevant forms. In J.W. Wulfeck and J.H. Taylors (Eds), *Form Discrimination as Related to Military Problems*, Committee on Vision, National Academy of Sciences—National Research Council, Washington, D.C., 1957.)

and signs are most readily discriminable, especially in the presence of "noise" or distracting background. The second is a more theoretical issue concerned with those features of forms and patterns which permit discrimination of one from the other. Although by far the greatest volume of enquiry has been directed to visual form discrimination, the overloading of the visual sense by complex arrays has resulted in a search for alternative sensory modes capable of similar discriminations. Thus recent studies have been concerned with shape discriminations by the tactile-kinesthetic or "haptic" sense.

### Visual Form Discrimination

In Fig. 2.11 are shown a variety of classes of shapes. If only one of these classes is considered, the question arises as to the particular characteristics of the form on the basis of which shape discriminations are made. For example, each of the pentagons are similar in their number of sides and there is not a great deal of difference between the angles which one side makes with another. Studies of shape discrimination indicate that different features of the shapes are used in different degrees. Among the variables are the

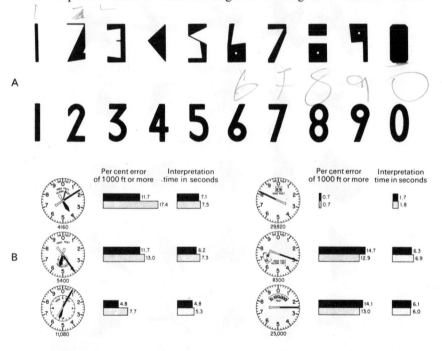

**Figure 2.12** *A* The Landsell numerals (upper) and Mackworth numerals (lower); the Landsell numerals are more legible under various illuminations. *B* Errors and time in reading different dials. (*A* by courtesy of *Canad. J. Psychol. B* from W.F. Grether, Instrument reading: I. In *J. Appl. Psychol.*, 1949, 33, 363–372. By courtesy of W.F. Grether.)

number of sides of the form, symmetry, angular variability, and $p^2/A$ (the ratio of the square of the perimeter to the area).

From a practical point of view interest centres on which letter-shape, dial arrangement or pattern can be most readily discriminated especially when the conditions of illumination or exposure-time are poor. These issues are important considerations in the design of instrument panels, road signs, and in other situations where perception must be quick and accurate. Letter shapes and dial arrangements which result in greater ease of discrimination are shown in Fig. 2.12.

### Haptic Form Discrimination

Form discrimination is by no means the exclusive domain of visual perception. Both the tactile and kinesthetic senses are singly and jointly capable of mediating a wide range of spatial judgments. A blind person, for example, can discriminate Braille patterns. Many other tasks involve the

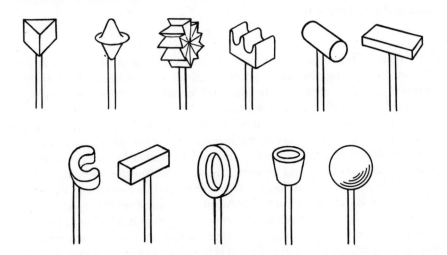

**Figure 2.13** Eleven shapes which are least confusing in the design of controls. (From W.O. Jenkins, The tactual discrimination of shapes for coding aircraft-type controls. In P.M. Fitts (Ed.), *Psychological Research on Equipment Design*, U.S. Army Airforce Research Report, 1947. By courtesy of W.O. Jenkins.)

perception of shape exclusively by means of sensory systems associated with the skin, joints, and tendons. Handles, turning knobs, keys, and switches are examples of control devices which an observer must frequently discriminate largely in terms of tactile-kinesthetic or haptic information. Examples of three-dimensional forms which are more readily recognized than others are shown in Fig. 2.13.

## PERCEPTION OF TEMPORAL PROPERTIES

Stimuli vary in duration, the sharpness or gradualness of their onset and offset, and in their temporal patterns. In discussing spatial acuities in the previous section questions were raised concerning the minimum perceptible and the minimum separable. In similar spirit, questions can be asked regarding the minimum time a stimulus must last to be perceived and the minimum time difference between successive stimuli necessary for their separate discrimination.

For very brief stimuli, duration, along with area (in the case of vision and cutaneous sensitivity) and intensity, determine the amount of energy impinging at the receptors. The problem of the minimum duration is therefore intimately related to a minimum area and intensity of stimulation at threshold. Within certain limits a constant amount of energy must be delivered by a stimulus for detection to occur. In vision the product of stimulus intensity and duration is constant at threshold so that where $L$ is the luminance of the flash and $t$ its duration,

$$Lt = C$$

This relationship between time and intensity in visual perception is the Bunsen-Roscoe law, sometimes known as Bloch's law. A similar relationship called Ricco's law applies to the area and intensity of stimulation in vision provided the stimuli are small in area.

Temporal acuity or "temporal resolving power" is the capacity to discriminate two stimuli occurring in close succession as separate, *i.e.,* to perceive two stimuli as successive in time. In measuring temporal acuity it is necessary to distinguish between "flicker" and true discontinuity. When repeated stimuli are close in time they are judged as continuous or fused. With greater durations of interval between successive stimuli they are judged as flickering, an effect which in phenomenal terms is marked by a rise and fall of intensity rather than by a clear break or interruption between successively presented stimuli. Thus it is possible to speak of a threshold for flicker (referred to as flutter for hearing and vibration for touch) and discontinuity. The threshold for discontinuity varies as a function of stimulus intensity and of qualitative properties. It is roughly about 10 milliseconds for hearing and touch, and about 100 milliseconds for vision. In the case of flicker discrimination the threshold time between stimuli is about 1 millisecond for touch (vibration) and hearing (flutter) and about 16 for vision. It must be emphasized that these threshold values are markedly affected by numerous stimulus properties and at the most are very rough approximations which permit a crude comparison of temporal acuity between the sensory systems. Touch and hearing are better adapted for the resolution of stimuli over time than vision.

Visual flicker is among the most extensively investigated aspects of visual perception. The most commonly employed threshold is that of critical flicker frequency or CFF, the rate of stimulus intermittence at the point of transition from flicker to a steady appearance. Apart from the light which studies of visual flicker throw on the temporal resolving power of the visual system, it can also be used as a method of investigating numerous problems in colour vision, spatial vision and the manner in which information is encoded and preserved in the visual system. Visual flicker has also been used in photometry for comparing the effectiveness of different spectral compositions of light. If two different wavelengths are alternated and the intensity of one varied until the CFF is achieved, the relative stimulus effectiveness of the two chromatic compositions of light can be established. This technique is called flicker photometry. CFF varies as a function of stimulus intensity, the relationship between the two variables being

$$CFF = a \log L + b$$

where $L$ is stimulus luminance and $a$ and $b$ are constants. This logarithmic relationship between intensity and CFF is known as the Ferry-Porter law.

## PERCEPTION OF MOVEMENT

The external world includes many objects which move relative to the stationary or moving observer so that motion detection and acuity must be counted among the basic perceptual capacities of the individual. Movement is a higher order variable involving changes in the spatial properties of stimulation, *e.g.,* size, shape, position and direction, over time. Movement perception can be conveniently classified into three categories; real movement, apparent movement, and induced movement. The first involves the perception of actually moving objects, *i.e.,* objects which change their spatial characteristics over time. Apparent movement occurs when two or more spatially separated objects, each fixed in position, are presented successively in time. Under this condition an observer frequently reports a single object in movement. Numerous advertising signs and moving films gain their effect from apparent movement. Induced movement occurs when a stationary element of a pattern is judged to move, an effect which is due to movement of another part of the pattern. In this section the perception of real movement and the phenomenon of apparent movement will be discussed. Induced movement is among a group of perceptual effects which will be discussed in a later chapter (see Chapter 4).

Real and apparent movement perception have been studied mainly in the context of visual perception, although both occur with respect to the auditory, tactile and postural senses.

## Visual Movement

Aubert in 1896 found that when an observer fixated a moving object in the context of stationary objects the absolute threshold was 1 or 2 minutes of arc per second. When, however, the stationary elements of the visual display were eliminated the absolute threshold increased to 10–12 minutes per second, an increase of about ten times. More recent work has largely confirmed Aubert's findings although such factors as the time for which the object is exposed and the area of the retina stimulated affect the threshold. At very short exposures, less than about 0·25 sec, the presence of stationary objects has little effect and the threshold is substantially greater when the object's retinal image falls on the periphery of the retina. Further, the threshold for movement decreases in a curvilinear fashion as the luminance of the object increases. The differential threshold for velocity is lowest in the range 1–3° per second after which it increases progressively.

In addition to visual discrimination of movement an observer can also discriminate object displacement. These two aspects of object movement are, of course, the same in physical terms, but they represent different classes of perceptual judgment. In the first place the observer is required to judge whether an object is moving while in the second he is asked to judge whether a change in position has occurred. With very slow movement such as that of the hands of a clock, movement *per se* is not discriminable, but over a period of time an observer can discriminate displacement, *i.e.,* change in position. The displacement threshold for vision in good light is of the order of 20 seconds of arc, substantially less than for movement detection, and it varies as a function of rate of displacement. Recent data suggest that, depending on rate, the displacement threshold approximates that for vernier acuity.

If two objects (lines, lights, dots) are exposed one after the other an observer judges them as being one object in motion between the two positions. The time for which each is exposed, the time interval between offset of one and onset of the other, the distance between them, and their shapes and sizes determine the occurrence of apparent movement. At certain time intervals it is claimed that movement alone occurs (*i.e.,* "unattached" to the objects), a phenomenological event called the phi-phenomenon. The considerable interest which apparent movement has aroused derives from its investigation by Wertheimer who in 1912 pioneered the Gestalt theory. This interpretation of perception rests on the central principle that perception considered in terms of the appearances of things is relationally determined. That is, what is seen, felt or heard is determined not by the individual properties of things but by the temporal, spatial and other relations between them. Korte in 1915 proposed four laws stating the relationships between the separation distance, temporal interval, luminance, and exposure times of the two objects in determining apparent movement.

For example, he proposed that the spatial separation (*s*) increases as luminance (*L*) increases if interval (*p*) and exposure time (*t*) remain constant. In general these laws apply over limited ranges of the four determinants although later work has shown that "subject states" induced by instructions play a considerable role in determining whether two objects presented successively are judged as a single object in movement.

### Auditory and Tactile Movement

An observer can detect the motion of an auditory source, of an object impinging on the skin surface, and movement of his whole body or limbs, without using vision. Early studies of auditory movement carried out under somewhat crude conditions showed that for a "buzzing sound" the least perceptible distance of movement (analogous to the displacement threshold in vision) ranges from 2·5° when the source is more or less straight ahead to 8·7° at right angles to the head. If, however, displacement is simulated by introducing a time difference of about 12 microseconds between the sound at the two ears (an interaural time difference) a displacement of about 1° is reported.

In addition to real movement, apparent movement occurs with inter-mittent and spatially separated stimulation in both hearing and the tactile sense. In the case of skin stimulation the application of short bursts of vibrating stimulation to two skin areas in succession leads to the judgment of a single object in motion. Early studies involving weights dropped on the skin and recovered by an electro-magnet resulted in far less reliable judgment of apparent tactile movement and a wide range of reports as to the nature of the movement. Vibratory stimulation applied to the skin is by far the most effective means of producing apparent movement effects on the skin.

# Bodily Orientation and Movement

The human observer is capable of perceiving the posture and movement of his own body and its parts. Perception of body posture and movement is mediated by systems whose receptors are located in the bony labyrinths of the head (Fig. 1.11) and in the joints and tendons of the limbs. As pointed out in Chapter 1, the sensory structures associated with the discrimination of body posture and movement are collectively referred to as proprioceptive systems and this aspect of perception as proprioception. It is difficult to separate the roles of structures in the non-auditory labyrinth and in the joints and tendons. When an individual changes posture or moves both groups of structures are involved in addition to those in the skin and internal organs. In taking up a supine posture not only is the orientation of the whole body altered but the limbs and internal organs are differently disposed. Further, the distribution of pressures on various areas of the skin is changed as the body changes in overall posture. It is convenient, however, to consider the mechanisms of the non-auditory labyrinth and those of the limb joints and tendons.

## BODY POSTURE AND MOVEMENT

The bilaterally disposed structures sensitive to linear and angular acceleration of head and body are shown in Fig. 1.11. The sac-shaped utricle and the three semicircular canals are mainly responsive to linear and angular motion of the body respectively. Further, since both structures respond to the direction of motion, both can be thought of static as well as dynamic sensory structures. The essential mode of action of utricle and canals is similar. When the body moves parts of the system change position relative to the viscous fluid with which both utricle and canals are filled. In consequence the sensory cells in the form of fine hairs bend thus triggering impulses in the nerve fibres. The sacs and canals are thus hydrodynamic circuits in which the internal structures move relative to the contained fluid. The mode of action is more readily understood by reference to Fig. 1.11.

If an observer is angularly accelerated as smoothly as possible about his own longitudinal axis or, alternatively in a cabin at the end of an extended arm (see Fig. 3.4), it is possible to establish his threshold for acceleration, *i.e.,* the minimum change in angular velocity which can be detected. This value turns out to be about $0.2°$ per $sec^2$. There are wide variations according to the device and psychophysical method used and the duration of the period of acceleration. Thresholds for linear acceleration are more difficult to establish and usually the observer's *visual* judgments of direction and extent of movement are studied during linear acceleration. This is, however, a special perceptual problem which will be considered later (Chapter 4).

It should be mentioned that gravitational force is an instance of acceleration. When the body is tilted in a lateral direction the position of the structures in the utricle change relative to the direction of gravity. Thus lateral body orientation is mediated in part by stimulation of the structures of the utricle. But, of course, when the whole body is tilted changes occur in the distribution of pressure on the skin and usually in the posture of limbs. These sources of stimulation probably provide information for body orientation in addition to that mediated by the non-auditory labyrinth.

## LIMB POSITION AND MOVEMENT

Kinesthesis refers to the sense of position and movement of body parts especially that of the limbs. The tissues in and about the joints and their tendons contain receptors which are stimulated when the surrounding tissue is deformed with movement of the limb. It is mainly the kinesthetic system which confers the capacity to reach out and locate objects in the dark, to perform various skills such as walking and bending without benefit of vision or hearing, and to carry out delicate tasks such as tying a shoe lace and buttoning a shirt. As well as receptors embedded in and about limb joints, the muscles also contain receptors which respond to muscle stretch. Since the force of movement is dependent upon the muscles, and since limb movement and limb position depend upon the force applied, the receptors of joints and muscles must be nicely coordinated in achieving a particular position or movement. Limb position and movement can, however, be discriminated without involvement of the muscles. A limb can be passively moved by an external force while the relevant muscles are either completely relaxed or even eliminated by the injections of drugs. Under such conditions an observer can still discriminate where a limb is in relation to his body and whether or not it is being moved.

# Summary

The absolute amount and degree of change in energy to which the various sensory systems of the organism are sensitive impose limits on perception and define the organism's basic perceptual capacities. The perceptual thresholds for minimum amounts and changes of stimulus energy serve as indexes of perceptual capacity.

In this chapter the perceptual capacities of the human observer are reviewed. The main stimulus dimensions dealt with are stimulus intensities, qualities (such as wavelength of light and frequency of sound vibration), spatial characteristics, and temporal features. In general, the term "sensitivity" is used in connection with intensity judgments, and "acuity" in connection with spatial features of stimulation.

Basic perceptual capacities in vision, hearing, the skin senses, taste, and smell are discussed and compared. Movement perception and perception of orientation are also discussed in terms of threshold functions.

# 3. Perceptual Stability : Static Space

AS THE observer moves about and changes posture in relation to environmental objects the projections of the objects at the receptors undergo considerable change. For example, when an observer moves away from a stationary object, say, a tree, the object's retinal image progressively diminishes in size as shown in Fig. 3.1. Analogous changes occur in the shape of the retinal image when the observer changes his angular bearing from the object. Likewise, the orientation of an object's retinal projection undergoes change as the observer's body tilts laterally to right and left (Fig. 3.1).

Although the size, shape and orientation of the visual image vary as a function of observer distance, angular bearing, and lateral tilt respectively, the observer's *judgments* of object size, shape and orientation vary slightly. Judgments remain relatively constant. This *relative* stability of perceptual judgments of object characteristics with variation in their sensory representations is called perceptual constancy. As will be seen later, similar effects occur in relation to object movement, reflectance, and colour, with change in the sensory image. The term perceptual constancy is, however, slightly misleading; for the most part judgments *do* vary as the sensory projections of object characteristics change but the variation is very much less than would be predicted from the degree of change occurring at the sense organ. In some instances the change in judgment with variation in the sensory representation is in the same direction as the latter, a phenomenon referred to as underconstancy. In other situations the judgmental change is in the *opposite* direction, an effect called overconstancy.

Here, then, is the central problem of perception; sensory representations of environmental object properties undergo gross change but judgments vary only slightly. In alternative terms, the observer maintains contact with object properties even though sensory information about them varies widely as the observer moves and changes posture. In the following pages the nature and basis of perceptual constancy will be examined in some detail. It will be shown that perceptual illusions, apparent distortions of object characteristics, are essentially in the same class of events as perceptual constancy and represent another form of stable perception.

Perceptual constancy of size, shape, orientation and other object properties with variation in stimulation is an instance of biological adaptation. If an object were perceived as smaller and smaller as distance progressively increased, and thinner and thinner as its angular bearing changed, maintenance of contact indicated by detection, discriminatory and recognition responses would be difficult or impossible. Imagine a situation in which a

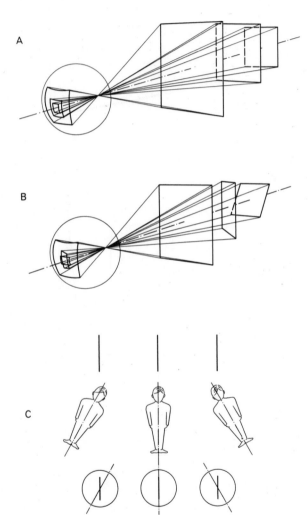

**Figure 3.1** Variation in the projection of an object at the retina of the eye. *A* The size of the retinal image decreases as object-observer distance increases. *B* The shape of the retinal image changes as the object slants. *C* The orientation of the retinal image changes relative to the normal vertical meridian of the eye as observer orientation changes.

person appeared 6 ft tall at 1 yd, 3 ft at 2 yd, and 1·5 ft at 3 yd. How could appropriate responses be made if such variations occurred in perception? But such variations do occur in the projected information about object size as can be seen from Fig. 3.1.

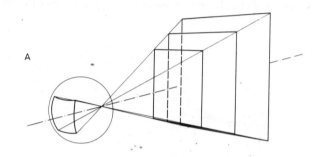

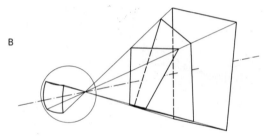

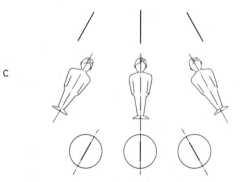

**Figure 3.2** Stimulus equivocality which follows from the situations depicted in Fig. 3.1. *A* Identical size of retinal image for objects of different size at different distances. *B* identical shape of retinal image for objects of different shapes at different slants. *C* Identical orientations of retinal image (relative to the normally vertical meridian of the eye) for objects at different tilts with different body postures.

# Stimulus Equivocality and Perceptual Resolution of Orientation, Size and Shape

The fact that the retinal image changes in size with changes in observer-object distance, in shape with observer-object angular bearing, and in orientation with observer-object orientation has consequences which render constant perception even more perplexing. If the retinal image of an object varies with distance as shown in Fig. 3.1 it follows that different sized objects at different distances will project the *same* image size if the relationship between size and distance is maintained. Identical image sizes for different sizes of object and different observer-object distances are shown in Fig. 3.2. In like fashion the same shape of retinal image and the same relative orientation of retinal image may occur for different object shapes viewed from different angles and for different object orientations with different observer tilts. In brief, identical sensory projections may occur for a wide range of object dimensions providing that size-distance, shape-bearing and orientation-tilt relationships are constant. The range of such conditions which give rise to the same image at the eye is infinite. Put in different terms, the projection of an object property at the visual receptors is equivocal in that it is representative of an infinite range of object sizes, shapes and orientations. It will be shown that stimulus equivocality also occurs in connection with a wide variety of object properties including those of reflectance, surface colour and motion.

The fact that sensory projections or images of external object properties are equivocal but that properties are perceived with relative accuracy implies that perception is essentially a process of resolving equivocalities in stimulation. The processes whereby equivocal stimuli are resolved in the interests of accurate and stable perception will be called perceptual resolution.

## PERCEPTION OF OBJECT ORIENTATION

The human observer adopts a variety of postures between the vertical and horizontal with the consequence that the retinal projections of external objects change their orientations relative to the visual receptors. The principles underlying perceptual resolution on a continuum between perceptual constancy and illusion will emerge clearly in the context of visual orientation perception.

### Visual Orientation with Body Tilt

It has been noted (Fig. 3.1) that as the body is laterally tilted the orientation of the retinal image of an object varies relative to the retina. When the observer is upright a hypothetical line passing vertically through the centre of the retina is called the vertical meridian. If the body (or head) is tilted laterally through 30° this hypothetical line also tilts. It does not, however, tilt to the same degree as head or body since a reflex action causes the eye to rotate slightly in the opposite direction, a phenomenon referred to as ocular countertorsion or counterrolling. For a body tilt of 30° this counterrolling is about 5° in the opposite direction so that the normally vertical meridian of the eye is tilted at about 25° for a 30° tilt of head or body. Thus when the head or body is tilted 30° left or right the retinal image of say, a vertical object, tilts about 25° in the opposite direction relative to the normally vertical meridian of the eye. An infinite range of object tilts and observer tilts can result in the same orientation of the object's retinal image considered in relation to the meridian.

Aubert in 1861, Müller in 1916, and many others since, have shown that if a gravitationally vertical bar of light is the only visible object in an otherwise dark room and the head or body is laterally tilted, the vertical bar is judged to be tilted slightly. Between body upright and about 50–60° lateral body tilt the bar is judged to be tilted in the *same* direction as body tilt and beyond about 60°, slightly in the opposite direction to body tilt. The complete function which is shown in Fig. 3.3 is referred to as the Aubert-Müller effect. When the body is tilted to the right up to about 60–70° the retinal image of the line rotates to the *left* of the normally vertical meridian but is judged as tilted to the right. Thus, not only do judgments of line orientation fail to follow the changes in the relative orientation of the retinal image but, on the contrary, tend in the direction opposite to what would be anticipated from the changed orientation of the image. This is an example of overconstancy in the visual perception of orientation. The slight tilt of the bar in the opposite direction to body tilt when the body is tilted beyond about 70° is a case of underconstancy in that the judged orientation is slightly in the direction of the changed direction of the object's retinal representation.

The Aubert-Müller phenomenon can be summarized briefly as follows. When the body is tilted the orientation of the retinal image of a vertical bar shifts relative to the retina. That is, there is change in relative retinal orientation which, due to ocular counterrolling, is slightly less than the angle of lateral body tilt. But despite large changes in retinal orientation, judged orientation of an object changes only slightly. For smaller angles of body tilt the object is judged to be tilted slightly in the *same* direction as body tilt (overconstancy) and for larger angles in the *opposite* direction (underconstancy).

We have noted that the orientation of an object's retinal image is equivocal in that a particular orientation can result from an infinite range of object and body tilts (Fig. 3.2C). For this reason the retinal projection alone cannot serve as a reliable source of information about the orientation of the object. The equivocal retinal representation of an object can be resolved provided that there is information for lateral body tilt. As noted earlier,

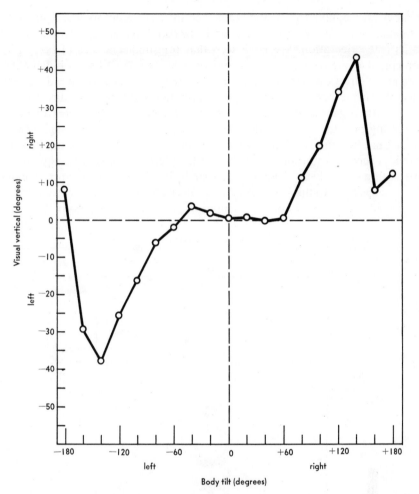

**Figure 3.3** The visual vertical as a function of body tilt between 0° (body upright) and 180° (body upside down). When the body is tilted between 0° and 50–60° the visual vertical is tilted in the opposite direction; at greater angles the visual vertical is in the same direction to body tilt. (From N.J. Wade, The effect of body posture on visual orientation. Unpublished PhD thesis, Monash University, 1968.)

information for body tilt is provided partly by the response of the otolith organs situated in the utricle of the labyrinth (Fig. 1.11). As the body is tilted the weighted otolith organs roll in the direction of tilt thus bending or shearing the hair-like structures. In the case of head tilt there is evidence that kinesthetic receptors in the cervical joints signal tilt and it is also probable that receptors in the skin and internal receptors provide information for body tilt. With sensory information for body tilt provided by stimulation of labyrinthine, kinesthetic, and tactile and internal receptors, the equivocal retinal image of an external object can be resolved to a close approximation to its true orientation. We have seen that for smaller angles of body tilt perceptual overconstancy occurs and only at extreme tilts do judgments tend in the direction of the retinal image. The point can be made in a different way. When the body is tilted laterally, gravitational force acts directly on the otolith organs and indirectly on the receptors of the skin (through increasing pressure on one side) and the internal receptors (through shifts in internal structures). This direct and indirect gravitational stimulation provides sensory information for body tilt in terms of which the equivocal orientation of an object's retinal image can be resolved to a close approximation to object tilt. In this way visual orientation constancy is achieved despite the considerable changes in the orientation of the image with body tilt.

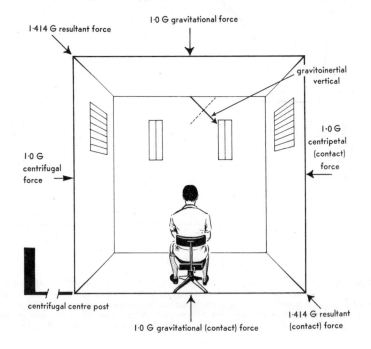

**Figure 3.4** Diagram of a human certrifuge. The gravitoinertial force is 1.414 G at 45 degrees if the centripetal force is 1 G.

Since perceptual resolution of object orientation is dependent upon information for body tilt provided mainly by the action of gravity on various sensory systems, it follows that changes in the direction of force acting on the body would result in changes in visual judgments of orientation. The normal force of 1G acting vertically can be changed to a force of greater magnitude acting obliquely by rotating the observer in the closed cabin at the end of a pivoted arm. This arrangement is called a human centrifuge (Fig. 3.4). The direction of force under centrifugation is the resultant of gravity and the applied force, a direction referred to as the gravitoinertial vertical. When a truly (*i.e.,* gravitationally) vertical line is viewed under these conditions it is judged to be tilted at about the same angle as the force acting on the body, an effect termed the oculogravic illusion. Thus as the direction of force which through stimulation provides the sensory information necessary to resolve the equivocal visual image is varied, visual judgments of object orientation undergo change.

**Perceptual Illusion and Perceptual Constancy**

It is now possible to consider perceptual constancy (as exemplified in the Aubert-Müller effect) and perceptual illusion (as exemplified by the oculogravic effect) and show that they represent points along a continuum of stable judgments ranging from constancy to varying degrees of illusion. The orientation of the retinal projection of an external object in the absence of any visual framework is entirely ambiguous since it can result from an infinite range of body (or head) and object tilts. The orientation of the object can be perceptually resolved, however, if there is sensory information for body (or head) tilt. This information is provided in large part by gravitational force acting directly on the otolith organs of the labyrinth and indirectly on skin and internal receptors. Under normal gravitational conditions, even at extreme angles of tilt, judgments of object orientation approximate to objective orientation exhibiting overconstancy at the smaller angles and underconstancy at the greater. If by artificial means (centrifugation) the direction of force on the body is altered (thus changing information for body tilt) visual judgments of object orientation depart from true object orientation. The greater the change in direction of force, the greater the discrepancy between judged and objective orientation.

Under normal conditions of gravity various sensory systems signal body orientation thus permitting resolution of the entirely equivocal visual image of an external object. The gross changes in retinal orientation do not lead to gross changes in judgment of orientation since information for body posture permits perceptual resolution. For normal gravitational conditions constancy is high and illusion is small as can be seen from Fig. 3.3. On the other hand, under abnormal conditions of force direction such as occur in a human centrifuge (Fig. 3.4) the equivocal retinal projection is resolved differently. That is, when information for body tilt is changed by varying the direction of force on the body, visual judgments of orientation also change. Under these conditions constancy is low and illusion is great. Depending on the nature of information on the basis of which the equivocal sensory image is resolved, judgments vary between a close approximation to object properties (high constancy, low illusion) and poor approximations (low constancy, high illusion). In this sense a constancy-illusion dimension represents a continuum of judgments and the position of a particular judgment on the continuum is a function of the information available for resolution of the visual image.

In the situation in which a force different in direction from gravity is applied to the observer, a gravitationally vertical bar is judged as slanted. This illusory effect is measured in terms of the gravitational vertical. Within the centrifuge, however, in which the direction of force is the resultant of gravity and the applied force, the judgment is expected. A plumb-line suspended in the centrifuge would lie at the same angle as the resultant. An illusion can only be said to have occurred if the observer's judgment is compared with the state of affairs outside the centrifuge, *i.e.,* the direction of normal gravity, which defines verticality.

### Visual Orientation with Field Tilt

The judgmental conditions just considered involve a single object, usually a dimly lighted bar, in an otherwise dark environment. When, however, judgments of object orientation are made in good light with other visible objects in the field of view, body tilt has little or no effect on judgments of orientation. Object orientation is largely determined by visual information relating to the uprightness or tilt of the environment.

In a now classical series of experiments, Asch and Witkin in the 1940s required observers to adjust a bar 1 metre in length to the vertical. The bar was pivoted about its centre on the rear wall of a miniature room which was tilted sideways at an angle of 22°. In one condition the observer stood close up to the room so that only its tilted interior was visible. The average judged vertical for a large group of observers was about 15° off true (gravitational) vertical in the direction of room tilt. Even when the observer stood well back from the tilted room so that the walls and other vertical features of the laboratory were visible, the pivoted rod was adjusted on the average to 8–9° in the direction of room tilt. It can be inferred from these results that had the rod been viewed when it was fixed in the gravitationally vertical position, it would have been judged as slanted at about 15° in the opposite direction to room tilt under the first condition and about 8–9° under the second.

The orientation of the retinal representation or image of the rod is equivocal for the reasons pointed out in the previous section. Under normal viewing conditions perceptual resolution of this equivocality is determined by visual projections of other features in the visual field. In a natural environment this information is derived from vertical walls, windows, trees, the horizon and numerous other features. If, however, the whole visual field is tilted, as in Asch and Witkin's experiment, perceptual resolution of the equivocal projection of an object can only be made in terms of visual information from the tilted environment. The illusion, however, is not complete. The fact that with room tilted at 22° and constituting the whole visual field, the apparent vertical is only 15° off true vertical, suggests that there is alternative information available for the true vertical. It is reasonable to suppose that this information is provided by stimulation of labyrinthine, tactile and possibly internal sensory systems. But it is clear that this source of information is dominated by the visual framework or field. With the observer standing back from the tilted room the difference between the apparent and true vertical is less (8–9°) than when the slanted room occupies the total field of view when it is about 15°. In this condition the vertical features of the laboratory in addition to gravity provide information for orientation. In consequence orientation constancy is greater or, alternatively, the illusion is less. It can be noted again that orientation judgments made with the tilted room as background can be treated either as constancy or illusion. It is possible to describe any given judgment as exhibiting slight constancy (or great illusion) or *vice versa*.

Perceptual resolution of the equivocally oriented visual stimulus in terms of visual information for orientation provided by the surround is by no means confined to tilted rooms. Essentially similar visual resolving information is provided by a field of tilted lines in various patterns. The apparent tilt of an upright line presented in a field of tilted lines is the well-known Zöllner's illusion. In the same way as the tilted contours of a room serve as resolving information so does a pattern of tilted lines. The tilted room together with numerous patterns which provide visual resolving information for object orientation are shown in Fig. 3.5. It should be noted that in the patterns shown in Fig. 3.5 information for resolving object tilt is also available from the straight contours of the book, the table on which the book rests and other visible contours so that the illusory effect is less than when the total field is tilted.

The effect of visual field tilt on perceptual resolution of object orientation can be observed in a "trick" room often seen in amusement parks. Inside the room water is judged to be running uphill and a ball will run *up* the slope of a table. So far there have been no investigations of the magnitude of constancy (which is undoubtedly low) or, alternatively, illusion (which is undoubtedly high) in this enclosed tilted environment.

## VISUAL PERCEPTION OF SIZE AND DISTANCE

The size of an object's retinal representation varies as a function of observer-object distance (Fig. 3.1) so that an infinite range of object sizes and distances can give rise to images of identical size (Fig. 3.2). Thus the retinal image alone is ambiguous as a source of information for object size. In essentially the same manner as information for body or field tilt is necessary to resolve object orientation, information for observer-object distance is necessary to resolve object size.

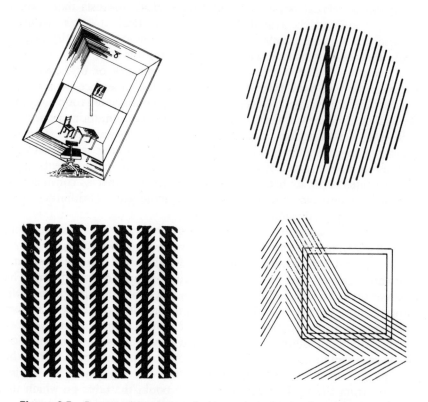

**Figure 3.5** Perceptual resolution of object orientation by the orientation or tilt of the background. *A* A vertical bar in a tilted room is judged to be tilted in the opposite direction to room tilt. *B* A similar effect with a field of tilted lines. *C* A variant known as Zöllner's illusion. *D* A more complex effect in which the orientation of the background lines determines the judged orientation of the lines forming a square. (*A* after M. Austin, Studies in perceptual spatial adaptation and its aftereffect. Unpublished PhD thesis, University of Sydney, 1968.)

### Information for Distance

Sensory information for distance falls in three broad classes; proprioceptive stimulation from the muscles controlling the accommodation and convergence of the two eyes, the slight difference between the images of an object at the two eyes, and the characteristic images of the ground plane at the eye. The two eyes must converge at an angle determined by the distance of an object in order to produce singleness of vision. At the same time, the lens of the eye must change focus in order to produce a sharp clear image of the object at the retina. Although the precise manner in which the reflexly linked accommodation-convergence process provides distance information is not known, there is evidence which strongly suggests that up to distances of about 1 metre these ocular adjustments signal distance. The two eyes are separated by about 60 mm so that each eye receives a slightly different projection of an object than the other. The geometry of retinal disparity can be seen in Figs 1.10 and 2.10.

Information for distance projected from the ground plane or terrain extending before the observer requires somewhat more detailed treatment. There are numerous sources of ground plane information which derives in the main from the sheer geometry of three-dimensional space projected on to a plane, in this case the retinal surface. Because the same geometry applies when extended distance is projected on to the film of a camera, most of these sources of information can be demonstrated photographically. The ground plane information for distance shown in Fig. 3.6 is essentially an enlarged version of the retinal pattern.

In viewing over extended indoor surfaces or outdoor terrain, features of more or less constant size (flagstones, lamp poles, furrows, floor planks) project smaller and smaller images in both the vertical and horizontal dimensions of the retina. A lamp pole 100 yards away projects an image twice the size of one 200 yards away. The outcome of the projection of regular features is a gradient of perspective and texture from large to small vertically and horizontally on the retina. Examples are shown photographically in Fig. 3.6.

As the head and eyes are moved from side to side the projection of stationary environmental features on the retina move laterally. The further away a feature the less is its displacement. Thus in surveying an extended horizontal surface with regularly arranged features there is a gradient of lateral image displacement at the eye. This source of information is called motion parallax.

If a near object is in the same line of sight as a far object, as a lamp pole might be along the same line of regard as a building, then the image of the first must overlay the image of the second object on the retina. This is referred to as overlay or inter-position. Some examples are shown in Fig. 3.6.

Because an object usually rests on a surface, its lower edges form a contour where they intercept the ground surface. This interception of an object with a surface is another important source of information (see Figs 3.6 and 3.7).

The four sources briefly described here are probably only a few of many subtle characteristics of the retinal image which signal distance. The role of ground projection characteristics in providing information for distance can be demonstrated in two ways; by a sort of laboratory "trickery" in which these sources of information are presented in a "misleading" fashion, and by including them in a two-dimensional drawing or painting.

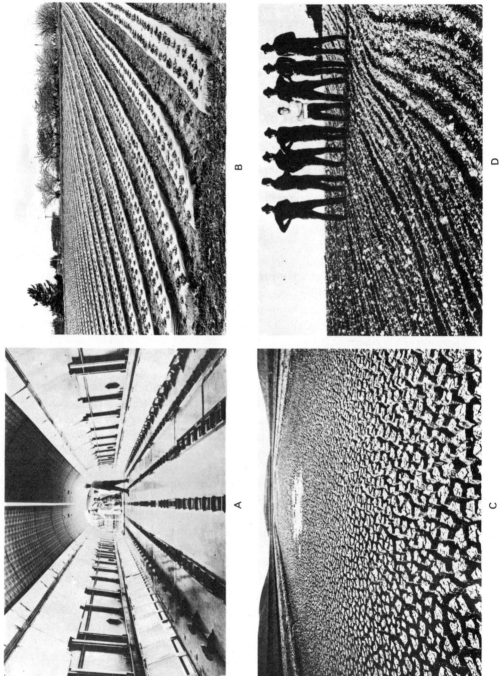

E

F

G

H

**Figure 3.6** Four classes of stimulus information for distance provided by the projection of terrain characteristics. In *A*, *B*, *C* and *D* the vertical and horizontal dimensions decrease with distance to produce texture and perspective effects. In *E* and *F* near objects overlay far objects, and in *G* and *H* the lower edges of near objects intercept the surface pattern lower in the field than do those of far objects. Illusory effects from overlay and intercept information are shown in Fig. 3.7. (*A* by courtesy of Qantas, *C* by courtesy of *The Australian* and *D* by courtesy of Greenleaf Fertilizers Ltd.)

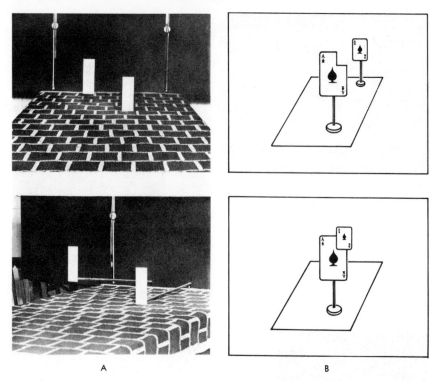

A                    B

**Figure 3.7** Apparent distance determined by "false" or "misleading" interception and overlay. *A* By raising one object above another the interception of its lower edge with the ground is further away than the other. *B* By cutting out one corner of a card and aligning another card so that its corner fills the cut-out, the latter appears nearer than the former. (*A* from J.J. Gibson, *Perception of the Visual World*, Boston, Houghton Mifflin Co., 1950. By courtesy of Houghton Mifflin Co. *B* adapted from F. P. Kilpatrick (Ed.), *Human Behavior from the Transactional Point of View*, Washington, Office of Naval Research, 1953. By courtesy of the Office of Naval Research.)

In Fig. 3.7 are shown two situations in which overlay and intercept information are simulated so as to lead to errors in monocular judgments of distance. By cutting out the corners of cards in an appropriate fashion a near card is judged as further, and by raising a near object higher above the ground plane than a far object, the first is judged further away. In the second case the object's lower edge is seen as intercepting the surface further away.

The three-dimensional environment is projected on the eye as a two-dimensional image. If the characteristic ground projection information is included in a two-dimensional array it would be expected that the array would be judged as three-dimensional. This technique is used, often with great skill, in the art-form known as *trompe l'oeil* to convey the impression of depth and distance in a drawing. An example of *trompe l'oeil* is shown in Fig. 3.8. Using overlay and gradients of texture and shading as would normally occur from the projection of a three-dimensional array on the retina the artist has produced an "illusion" of depth.

**Figure 3.8** Trompe l'oeil art; the use of distance information, especially overlay, to convey impression of three dimensions on two; *Still-Life* by Edwart Collier dated 1702.

By far the most dramatic use of distance information to produce apparent distance in a two-dimensional representation is found in the stereogram. Wheatstone in the nineteenth century constructed representations of objects as they would be projected at the left and right eyes *i.e.*, with the same retinal disparity (Figs 1.10 and 2.10) as in normal vision. These were then presented to the two eyes separately but simultaneously in a stereoscope with optical channels such as to project one diagram to the left eye and another to the right. The outcome is a compelling apparent depth or distance effect. Examples of stereograms and a simple prism stereoscope are shown in Fig. 3.9.

In summary, then, distance information which is essential for perceptual resolution of the equivocal retinal representation of object size derives from three sources; the accommodation-convergence mechanism of the binocular visual system, disparity between the two retinal images, and the geometrical characteristics of projected surfaces extending before the observer. In the next section it will be seen that whether size is resolved perceptually in accord with object size (size constancy) or in varying degrees of non-correspondence (size illusion) is a function of the nature of distance information.

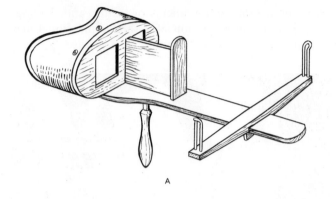

A

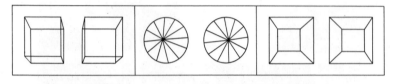

B

**Figure 3.9** Apparent depth varied by manipulating retinal disparity. *A* prism stereoscope designed to present disparite images separately to each eye. *B* Typical stereograms used by Wheatstone; during sterescopic viewing each pair of drawings is seen as single and three-dimensional.

### Perceptual Resolution of Object Size

Perceptual resolution of object size as a function of information for distance was demonstrated in a series of classical experiments by Holway and Boring in the 1940s. Observers were required to match the size of a small circular area of light located at progressively greater distances up to 120 ft in a long corridor. Four conditions were used; unrestricted binocular vision in good light with free head movement, monocular vision under the same conditions, monocular vision through a small aperture, and monocular vision with the lights in the corridor turned off. The effect of these four conditions was to eliminate progressively information for distance. Monocular viewing eliminates retinal disparity, the small aperture obscures intervening surfaces and restricts motion parallax, and darkness leaves only the disk of light in view. The results of this study are shown in Fig. 3.10. As distance information was progressively reduced judged size departed increasingly from objective size in the direction of retinal image expectancies.

If distance information is necessary for the resolution of the ambiguous visual representation of object size (Fig. 3.2) in terms of the true size of the object, *i.e.,* for size constancy, "artificial" manipulation of distance information would be expected to result in variations in judged size. This is so in respect of the three sources of distance information reviewed in the last section. For example, the muscular exertion required to converge and accommodate the eyes can be controlled by means of a system of prisms and lenses of variable power. While the size of the retinal image and the distance of the object àre constant, the prism-lens system called a phorometer permits variation of muscular involvement such as would be required if the object were located at different distances from the eyes. Using this optical system Leibowitz and Moore (1966) increased the amount of convergence and accommodation necessary to view an object whose retinal image remained

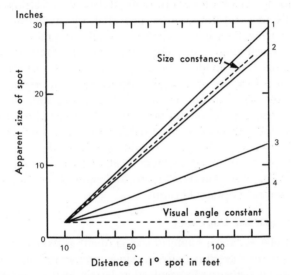

**Figure 3.10** Apparent size of a one-degree spot of light as a function of viewing distance and conditions of observation. Plot 1 binocular vision, 2 unrestricted monocular vision, 3 monocular vision through a small aperture, and 4 monocular vision with most of the background obscured by viewing the spot through a dark tunnel. (From A.H. Holway and E.G. Boring, Determinants of apparent visual size with distance variant. In *Amer. J. Psychol.*, 1941, 54, 21–37.)

constant in size. Up to a convergence-accommodation-distance of about 1 metre the apparent or judged size of the object increased, even though the retinal image remained constant. In somewhat similar fashion Gogel, Wist and Harker (1963) used an optical system to increase retinal disparity. This was achieved by means of a device which in effect increased the distance between the two eyes—the inter-pupillary distance or "base" (it is not difficult to see that if the distance between the eyes is increased retinal disparity would also increase). Gogel, Wist and Harker showed in general that an increase in retinal disparity made objects apparently closer and smaller and a decrease in retinal disparity apparently further and larger.

In both experiments, that of Leibowitz and Moore and that of Gogel, Wist and Harker, the retinal images of objects were constant. Optical devices varied muscular contraction and retinal disparity consonant with greater or less distance and, in consequence, the objects appeared smaller and larger respectively. It follows that if the retinal projection is constant in size, and the object appears closer, it must also be smaller. Likewise, if the object appears further, it must also appear larger. At a great distance an object must be large to project a retinal image of a certain size, and, at a small distance it must be small to project the same retinal image.

In addition to oculomotor adjustments of the eyes and retinal or binocular disparity, distance information is provided by numerous geometrical features of extended surfaces including retinal size gradients and overlay (Fig. 3.6). In considering the effect on size judgments of retinal size gradients, one point needs to be made quite clear. Features of surfaces and terrain extending out before the observer are projected at the retina as gradients of *size*. The further a ground feature such as a flagstone, a furrow, or a lamp pole, the smaller its retinal projection. Distance along the ground is essentially size along the ground, although the sizes involved are usually greater than those in the fronto-parallel plane. It would be expected that if size gradient information were systematically varied, the apparent sizes of objects would vary also. This is in fact so, and many of the effects are referred to as the geometrical optical illusions.

### Size Illusions and Size Constancy

In Fig. 3.11A is shown a typical size gradient as would be projected on the retina by natural extended terrain. Since the two logs are the same size, the further one is perceptually resolved as larger, as it would have to be to project the same retinal projection if actually at a greater distance. By including distance information in the form of a size gradient an illusion of size occurs. In other words there is a departure from size constancy, the degree of departure presumably depending on the characteristics of the size gradient. The other two figures in Fig. 3.11A, variants of the Ponzo illusion, are similar to the first except that the essential rather than "naturalistic" features of a size gradient as might be projected by extended terrain are included. It is clear from Fig. 3.11 that far objects occur in the context of ground features with small retinal projections and near objects in the context of those with large projections. If, then, these small and large features are abstracted, as in Fig. 3.11B, an object in the context of small elements would be expected to be judged larger than an objectively equal object in the context of large elements. That such is the case can be observed in Fig. 3.11B. There are many variants of the effect of surround element size on the apparent size of an object. In Fig. 3.11C are shown four well-known instances. In each case, surround information which, under normal visual

**Figure 3.11** Perceptual resolution of object size by size of background features. *A* Three variants of Ponzo's illusion in which size or width of elements determine apparent size. *B* Size of elements determine overall size of squares. *C* Some well-known illusions of size in which the size of background or field elements determine size of circles (Titchener and Delboeuf illusions) and lines (Müller-Lyer and dumbell illusions.)

conditions, is simply part of the extended size gradient, is abstracted in various arrangements of elements of different sizes. Since the size of an object's retinal projection is equivocal and its resolution dependent upon distance information, which in these instances takes the form of a *size* gradient or pattern, the size of surrounding elements determines apparent object size.

In viewing Fig. 3.11 on the page of a book there are many other features of various sizes in the field of view, the page itself, the print, the table, and so on. If the various patterns in Fig. 3.11 are drawn in luminous paint and viewed in a dark room, the effects (differences in apparent size of equal objects) are considerably enhanced. In the natural, physically extended, environment the retinal size gradient is a linear function with features extending to a vanishing point on the retina. The retinal gradient of size is geometrically determined. Artists and draughtsmen simulate this gradient in depicting three dimensions in two. The linear size gradient projected by man-made and natural surfaces (floors, fields, roads) is a source of information for distance which results in perceptual resolution of the ambiguous projection of an object. The perceptual outcome is that apparent size approximates true size. That is, constancy of size obtains and contact with the true features of the environment is maintained. But if this resolving information is manipulated and abstracted as shown in Fig. 3.11, constancy is reduced and illusion increases. The point can be demonstrated by drawing the three patterns shown in Fig. 3.12 on large sheets of stiff cardboard and

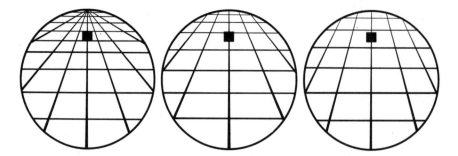

**Figure 3.12** Three size gradients which result in different apparent sizes of an object. The different gradients lead to different perceptual resolutions of the equivocal retinal projection of object size.

placing upright squares of cardboard on the surfaces as indicated. When held horizontally at about eye-level the pattern with parallel lines projects the "natural" retinal gradient and size constancy of the upright object obtains. In the other two patterns, projecting patterns which would not normally occur, there is a departure from constancy, the objects being apparently larger in each case. An experiment similar in principle to that outlined has recently been reported by Blessing, Landauer and Colt-heart (1967).

### The Judged Size of the Moon

When the full moon is just above the horizon it is usually judged to be greater than when at its zenith, the ratio of judged horizon size to judged zenith size being about 1·3 : 1. The moon's distance is about 240,000 miles and its visual subtense about 0·5° irrespective of its position relative to the earth. Photographs of the moon at horizon and at zenith show that there is no physical basis for the apparent difference in perceived size. The moon illusion, as it is popularly called, is a good example of the resolution of equivocal retinal size in terms of distance information. The Greek philo-sopher Ptolemy suggested over 2000 years ago that the apparently greater size of the moon at the horizon is due to the apparently greater distance of the horizon compared with the distance of the "celestial dome". Since the retinal projection of the moon is the same size in the two positions then it follows that when apparently further away it must be perceived as larger. At a greater distance the object must be larger to project a retinal image of a certain size. Ptolemy's ancient explanation has been supported by a series of observations by Rock and Kaufman (1962) using artificial "moons", spots of light viewed at optical infinity. Why horizon distance is apparently greater than "dome" distance (the inside of the "celestial dome") is not clear. So far we are compelled to accept the fact that the two distances are apparently different, and consequently the size of the moon in the two positions, without knowing the reason.

### Apparent Size of Afterimages

Following stimulation by an intense light an observer reports an after-image, a persistent visual effect which outlasts the period of stimulation (see Chapter 7, especially Fig. 7.2). It also retains the shape and size of the original object if visual fixation at the original distance is maintained. The more intense the original stimulus the greater the duration of the after-image. Since the size of the afterimage is entirely ambiguous, it would be expected that its judged size would depend upon distance information. The judged size of the afterimage is an excellent example of the manner in which visual size resolution is dependent upon distance information. Emmert in 1881 first drew attention to the increase in the apparent size of the after-image with increase in the distance of the surface on which it is projected. This near-linear relationship is referred to as Emmert's law.

It can be noted also that if following induction of a sharp circular afterimage, the observer directs his gaze first above the horizon the image is apparently substantially larger than when he gazes upwards to the sky. That is, the effect noted in connection with the resolution of the size of the moon occurs also in the perceptual resolution of the afterimage.

## Haptic Judgments of Size

It has just been noted that in vision much of the information for distance which serves to resolve the ambiguous retinal projection of object size is in the form of size gradients. As a matter of sheer geometry, distant objects occur in the context of small surrounding elements and near objects in the context of large elements (Fig. 3.11A). If two objects are of the same size at the retina, but one is surrounded by small elements (a cue for greater distance) and the other by large, the former appears to be much the larger. Size of element is a basis for distance information.

It would be expected that size of surrounding elements would also determine apparent object size in other sensory modalities. This is, in fact, so. Révész (1953) showed that most of the well-known illusions of size occur with "haptic" judgments; judgments which involve the combined kinesthetic and tactile senses. For example, if the horizontal line of the Müller-Lyer figure (Fig. 3.11B) in the form of a raised pattern is judged in length by moving the hand or finger to and fro across it taking in the outward extended "arrowleads", it is judged as longer. The arrowleads, the surrounding size elements, also determine the apparent size of the haptically judged object.

The occurrence of haptic illusions of size and length has been confirmed more recently by Rudel and Teuber (1963) and Over (1967).

## The Perspective Theory of Illusions

The basic principle of a theory originally proposed by Volkmann and by Thiéry in the nineteenth century and recently revived separately by Gregory, von Holst and Tausch is that the well-known visual illusions (some of which are shown in Figs 3.5 and 3.11) involve apparent distance effects or perspective and other features associated with distance. At first sight this view appears similar to that set out in the last two sections. In fact there are important differences between the "perspective" type theories and that outlined above. First, the perspective theories make no distinction between those visual effects determined by information for orientation (Fig. 3.5), of which the tilted room effect is the most dramatic, and those due to size gradients (Fig. 3.13). Second, what is commonly described as perspective is, as emphasized above, one aspect of the variation in size of spatial features as projected at the eye. The projection of extended distance at the retina takes the form of variations in the size of elements in the visual image. Finally, the perspective theory of visual illusions involves an explanation of illusion in terms of size constancy. The view adopted here is that information for the resolution of equivocal sensory projections of object properties such as orientation, size and shape varies. Depending on the nature of this information so the apparent property agrees or disagrees with the objective property. These size gradients at the retina are one source of information for the resolution of object size. When certain features of these gradients are abstracted and presented as in Fig. 3.11 size judgments depart from constancy. It will be seen in Chapters 4 and 5 that essentially the same departures from object constancy occur with object movement, reflectance, and colour as the resolving information is varied. Constancy-illusion is a perceptual continuum. The point on the continuum of a particular judgment is a function of the information available to resolve the equivocal projection of the object property.

## VISUAL PERCEPTION OF SHAPE

Like orientation and size, the retinal representation of object shape is equivocal since the same projection or image may occur for a variety of shapes at a variety of slants. If while facing inwards an observer moves in a circular path around a square of cardboard with black and white stripes on its surface and suspended by a string from the ceiling, the square's retinal image undergoes a continuous shape change. When the square is fronto-parallel to the observer its retinal image is square but as the observer moves around, the image becomes trapezium shaped and narrow and the black and white elements project a texture gradient ranging from large to small. Another way of putting this point is to say that as the observer changes his angular bearing to the stationary square the slant of the square relative to the observer changes. Much the same state of affairs occurs if the observer remains stationary and the square is rotated about its vertical axis. Whether the observer moves around the stationary object or the object moves relative to the observer the outcome is the same; the shape of the object's retinal image varies from a square through a continuous series of trapezium shapes (Fig. 3.13). Put in the same terms as that for retinal orientation and size, the same retinal projection may occur for an infinite range of object shapes and slants (Fig. 3.2). A certain trapezium at a certain slant projects the same retinal image as a square at another slant. In consequence the true shape of the object can be perceptually resolved only if there is information for object slant. Without such information the perceived shape of an object can only be that of its retinal projection which, as has been noted, varies with slant.

In a well-lit environment, however, judgments of object shape are relatively constant as the object's visual projection varies as a function of observer-object angular bearing. This is the phenomenon of shape constancy. If in an otherwise dark room, however, the object is presented in the form of a stationary luminous outline, its apparent shape changes in accord with changes in its retinal projection. Much the same occurs if an observer is required to judge the shape of an object with a plain surface against a black velvet background, using one eye so that retinal disparity is eliminated.

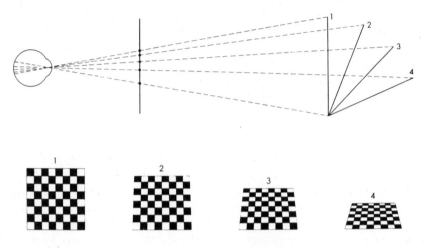

**Figure 3.13**   Information for object slant in depth; as the slant of a patterned rectangular object changes, the outline and texture of the visual image undergoes change also. (From J.J. Gibson, *Perception of the Visual World*, Boston, Houghton Mifflin Co., 1950. By courtesy of Houghton Mifflin Co.)

The sources of information for object slant are by no means as clear as they are for distance. It is known that the outline of an object, and gradients of surface texture serve as sources of slant information as shown in Fig. 3.13. A considerable body of research has demonstrated that a trapezium shape placed fronto-parallel to an observer is judged as slanted with its short vertical edge further away than its long edge. A clue to another basis for slant information is provided by experiments in which the shape of an object is judged in rooms or spaces of different overall shapes. Langdon in 1955 and Beck and Gibson in the same year, presented shapes in a distorted room and against a slanted background. The slants of the objects were judged in terms of these surroundings or frameworks and their shapes were also misjudged.

The role of the surrounding terrain has been almost wholly overlooked in experiments on shape and slant. We observe a particular object against the background of the floor, walls, buildings, etc. For example, we observe a table against the background of floor and walls. Its orientation can be judged in terms of its relationship to characteristic features of the floor such as carpet, floor-boards and so on. There is an analogy here with distance information discussed in the last section. Information for distance is partly provided by interception of object contours with surfaces (Fig. 3.6). Similarly the edges of viewed objects intercept characteristic features on the ground, floor and elsewhere, and their angles of interception as represented in the visual projection may well provide information for object slant, in turn permitting perceptual resolution of shape. It is significant that many studies of shape constancy have been conducted with the surrounding environment plainly visible. The question as to which features of the environment are primarily involved in providing information for object slant (apart from outline and texture of the object itself) remains open.

Since shape at the retina is equivocal and slant information is necessary for the resolution of object shape, it follows that the nature of the slant information will determine the judged shape. The experiments by Langdon and by Beck and Gibson bring out this point clearly. Information for slant was provided by the projection of the background slant, so that the object's judged shape differed from its true shape. Presumably it would be possible to vary slant information and to note the variations in judged shape from near accord with true shape (constancy) to a marked discrepancy between them (illusion) as the object was slanted in depth relative to the observer.

# Stimulus Equivocality in Auditory Space

To this point the discussion has been confined to problems of visual space perception. Far less is known about auditory spatial resolution, although in at least one situation stimulus equivocality can be shown to occur.

It was noted in Chapter 2 that perception of the direction of a sound source derives from the different intensity, arrival time and phase of the sound at the two ears. If the sound is located to the observer's right the sound is more intense at the right ear, reaches it slightly ahead of the left, and usually differs in phase. Depending on the direction in which the observer's head is turned, however, identical binaural conditions may obtain for different source locations. It can be seen from Fig. 3.14 that as the head is rotated the binaural stimulus varies markedly.

Recent experiments by the author indicate that with variations in the binaural stimulus (intensity, arrival time and phase) with lateral head rotation there is a high degree of direction constancy; the judged direction of a source changes much less than would be expected from changes in the binaural stimulus. Presumably this constancy is due to information for head position relative to the body provided by kinesthetic receptors in the neck. The situation is essentially similar to that of visual orientation constancy with body tilt.

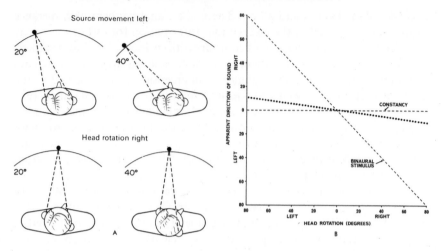

**Figure 3.14** Perceptual resolution of auditory direction. *A* As the head is turned left or right with the sound source stationary the binaural stimulus changes in the same manner as when the source is moved right or left with head stationary. *B* Even though the binaural stimulus changes greatly with head turn the apparent location of the source is relatively constant. This effect is called perceptual constancy of auditory direction. (From R.H. Day, Perceptual constancy of auditory direction. *Nature*, 1968, 219, 501-502.

# Perceptual Stability and Perceptual Constancy

As the sensory projection of an object varies, observer size, shape and orientation judgments tend to remain constant. Brunswik in 1929 and Thouless in 1931 proposed similar indices for the expression of perceptual constancy. The Brunswik ratio is $(P-R)/(C-R)$ where $P$ is the judged property, $C$ is the objective property and $R$ is the relative sensory representation. The Thouless ratio is the same as Brunswik's except that the logarithms of $P$, $C$ and $R$ are used. When the ratio is unity perfect correspondence between the judged and true property is indicated and values greater and less than unity indicate over- and underconstancy respectively. Both ratios are designed to measure the extent to which the observer's judgment of size, orientation, shape, etc., approximates the value of the object property. The use of the Brunswik ratio can be illustrated by examples of judgments of size at a distance and judgments of orientation with body tilt.

An observer is required to judge the size of a 10 cm diameter disk placed 500 cm away by adjusting a spot of light located 100 cm away so that the latter appears to be the same size as the former. With the disk at 500 cm its retinal projection would be one-fifth its size at 100 cm, so that if judgments were made in terms of the retinal image it would be judged to be one-fifth of 10 cm, *i.e.,* 2 cm, in diameter and the light spot matched accordingly. If, on the other hand, perfect constancy obtains, the light spot would be adjusted to 10 cm even though the retinal image is one-fifth the size. Let us assume that the observer adjusts the light spot to 9 cm to match the 10 cm disk at 500 cm. The Brunswik ratio $(P-R)/(C-R)$ is then $(9-2)/(10-2)$ $= 0.875$, which indicates underconstancy of size.

In applying the ratio to orientation judgments it is necessary to relate orientation to a hypothetical retinal reference. The most convenient is the vertical meridian, a line falling vertically across the retina when the observer is upright. If this meridian is called $0°$ and points to the left given a negative sign and those to the right a positive sign it is possible to compute a Brunswik ratio for visual orientation constancy when the body is tilted. When the head is tilted $40°$ right the eyes counterroll about $5°$ in the opposite direction so that the normally vertical meridian is tilted about $35°$ to the right. The projection of a vertical line on the retina thus falls at $35°$ to the left $(-35°)$ of the retinal reference. This is the relative retinal orientation. If the objectively vertical $(0°)$ line is judged to be slanted $6°$ to the right then the Brunswik ratio becomes $[6-(-35)]/[0-(-35)] = 1.17$, an instance of overconstancy.

Since Thouless found that there was a strong tendency to judge object size, shape, and brightness in terms of the objective property, he used the term "phenomenal regression to the real object" to describe the effects. In the previous sections we have seen that this tendency is a function of information additional to that available from the variable retinal projection of the particular object property. Distance information is essential for the visual resolution of object size, body tilt information is necessary for the resolution of object orientation, and slant information is required for the resolution of object shape. If this information is "natural" in the sense that it is the information normally available from extended distance, slanted surfaces, and gravitational force, objective and judged properties tend to correspond. If the information is altered from that which is normally available, as happens when the direction of force acting on the body is changed by centrifugation, or when the exertion necessary to converge and accommodate the eyes is changed by a phorometer, judgments undergo change. Perceptual constancy can, therefore, be considered as a special case of perceptual stability, one which occurs when appropriate normally available resolving information is present to resolve the equivocal sensory projection of an object property. The Brunswik and Thouless ratios have been developed to measure this special instance of perceptual stability. If, however, resolving information other than that normally available from extended distance, gravitational force, slanted surfaces, etc., is presented, then although judgments are relatively stable they do not correspond with the true object size, orientation or shape. The geometrical visual illusions, the oculogravic effect and many other "illusory" phenomena are instances of stable perception determined by resolving information or "cues" different from those normally provided by the natural environment.

# Summary

Orientation, size, and shape are properties of external objects. The projections of these properties at the eye are equivocal or ambiguous. The same orientation of the retinal image occurs for a range of object tilts and body tilts; the same size of retinal image occurs for a range of object sizes and object distances; the same retinal image shape occurs for a range of object shapes and object bearings. To resolve perceptually the true orientation of an object the observer must have information for his own tilt; to resolve its size, information for its distance; to resolve its shape, information for its bearing (or slant in depth). If the information for body tilt, distance of object, and slant of object is valid, judged object orientation, size and shape approximate closely to true orientation, size and shape. If this information is rendered invalid, *i.e.,* "distorted", judgments depart from true orientation, size, and shape. When the ambiguous visual image is resolved to a close approximation to the object property on the basis of valid resolving information, the term perceptual constancy is used to describe the outcome. When, however, the ambiguous image is resolved to a poor approximation (*i.e.,* when there is a marked discrepancy between the judged and physical property) the term perceptual illusion is used in describing the effect. In other words, perceptual constancy and perceptual illusion are points on a judgmental continuum determined by the nature of the resolving information required for the resolution of ambiguous visual representations of orientation, size and shape.

# 4. Perceptual Stability : Occurrence, Velocity and Direction of Motion

THE HUMAN observer moves about in the environment and environmental objects move in relation to him. Both the head and eyes are moved frequently in visual scanning and listening. The movement of objects can take a variety of forms including approach and recession relative to the observer, rotary motion, transverse movement in the observer's fronto-parallel plane, and angular movement. Since both observer and objects move in various ways the same patterns of movement can occur at the retina of the eye for different external situations. In much the same manner as static object properties such as orientation, size, and shape are equivocal, in that they are representative of an infinite range of conditions, the projected motion characteristics of objects are ambiguous. In order to perceive (*i.e.,* maintain contact with) the external state of affairs, information additional to that provided by the projected motion pattern is necessary. Depending on the nature of this resolving information so the observer's judgment accords closely with the objective motion characteristics of the object in space (motion constancy) or departs from it (motion illusion). A particular judgment may be located at any point on the constancy-illusion continuum.

Equivocality in the retinal representation of object motion may occur in relation to its occurrence, velocity, and direction.

## Observer and Object Movement

### VISUAL MOTION AND BODY MOVEMENT

When the head or eyes are moved from side to side the retinal projections of stationary environmental objects move in the opposite direction. This pattern of retinal motion may be the same as that which occurs when the head and eyes are stationary and the object moves. For any particular pattern of motion at the eye, including the limiting case of stationariness, there is an infinite range of head-eye and object movements which could produce it. Nevertheless, a stationary light observed in an otherwise dark room is judged as more or less stationary when the head is rotated. Perceptual motion constancy of a single object viewed in the dark has been cleverly demonstrated by Wallach and Kravitz using a connecting link between an observer's head and the light. By manipulating a system of gears between head and light the latter could be varied from stationariness to varying velocities of movement as the head rotated left and right. If the light was seen to move to the right as the head rotated to the left, then it would presumably be judged stationary if during left head movement it were moved left. In fact almost perfect constancy of visual motion (or, more properly in this situation, visual position) occurred. As the head rotated, with consequent movement of the light's retinal image, the object was judged as nearly stationary.

The motion of an object's retinal projection, including its stationariness, is ambiguous since it is jointly determined by head-eye and object movement. For this reason information for the rotary acceleratory movement of the head and lateral eye movements must be available if perceptual resolution of object motion is to obtain. Without such information it would not be possible to judge the occurrence, velocity or direction of movement.

The eyes are suspended and controlled by three pairs of muscles. In considering information for eye movement alone it would seem reasonable to suppose that as these muscles contract, stretch receptors would be stimulated, thus signalling the extent and direction of ocular movement. Although the extraocular muscles (Fig. 1.7C) are richly supplied with receptors, especially at their termini, the nature of the information which controls eye movements, some of which are extremely fine and rapid, is by no means agreed upon. Since the external environment is seen to move when the eye is moved "involuntarily" with the finger (which presumably involves the stretch and contraction of muscles), it has been argued that proprioceptive information fed back into the system is not the basis of ocular control. Rather it has been suggested that the *intention* of moving the eyes into a certain position provides the necessary information. The validity of neither the "inflow" nor "outflow" theory has yet been finally established. It is clear, however, that information for ocular posture and movement is necessary to resolve object movement, including its stationariness.

It is possible to be more definite about the sources of information for head movement which result in visual motion constancy. Positive and negative angular accelerations of head and body are signalled through stimulation of the organs contained in the semicircular canal system of the labyrinth (Fig. 1.11) and possibly the receptors of the neck region. The cupulae of the three canals operate in the manner of loaded pendulums and swing from their bases when angular head and body motion occurs. It is conceivable, of course, that other sensory mechanisms associated with skin, joints, and internal organs are also involved in signalling body movements, but very little is known about these possible sources of information.

Considering the head alone as it is rotated left and right, the movement is one of acceleration and deceleration. During this movement the cupulae of the horizontal canals (Fig. 1.11) discharge and signal direction and rate of acceleration.

If information for normal movements of the head derives from the fluid circuits of the semicircular canal system and their associated structures, thus resulting in perceptual resolution of object movement, it can be predicted that "artificial" stimulation of this system would give rise to illusory movement. There is an interesting analogy here with judgments of object tilt in the absence of a visual field (Chapter 3). It was noted that under normal gravitational conditions visual orientation constancy is high, but that when "unnatural" force directions occasioned by rotary movement of the body stimulate the various receptor organs, there is a departure from constancy, the oculogravic effect. The receptor organs of the semicircular canals can also be stimulated by acceleration in a centrifuge. If seated in the dark cabin of a centrifuge (Fig. 3.4) the observer, while viewing a stationary point of light, is subjected to acceleration the light is reported as moving in the direction of rotation. Rotary acceleration results in displacement of the cupulae and stimulation of the sensory cells as would occur when the head or body are rotated naturally during normal movement. Since the resultant information is consonant with that for rotary motion and the stationary light remains in front of the observer, the light can only be perceived as moving. This apparent movement of a stationary light (*i.e.,* stationary relative to the observer) is called the oculogyral effect. It should be noted that explanations of this illusory motion in terms of nystagmatic movements of the eyes during acceleration (so-called vestibular nystagmus) are difficult to sustain. Apart from any other consideration a visual after-image, which is stationary relative to the moving eye, is also judged to move during rotary acceleration.

A necessary outcome of angular acceleration in a centrifuge with consequent stimulation of the semicircular canal structure is apparent rotary movement of the body itself. Although the body is stationary relative to the rotating environment, stimulation of the semicircular canals must result in apparent body rotation. The light, since it remains in the same position relative to the observer, must also exhibit apparent movement in the same direction. Since motion (including stationariness) of the object's retinal image is ambiguous and stimulation of the semicircular canals results in apparent body rotation, the light must also appear to move.

The retinal projection of object motion is ambiguous because it may occur with innumerable combinations of head-eye and object motions. To resolve perceptually the ambiguous image of a moving (including the limiting case of a stationary) object there must necessarily be information for movement of the eyes, head and body. The basis of information for eye movement is still not clear but that for angular acceleration of head and body is provided in part by stimulation of the receptors in the fluid circuits of the semicircular canals. Under normal conditions of angular body motion this information results in a close agreement between judged and objective movement, *i.e.,* in visual movement (or position) constancy. If by means of acceleratory centrifugation the receptors of the canals are "artificially" stimulated then illusory motion of the object occurs, a phenomenon called the oculogyral effect or illusion. There is a continuum of judgment from motion constancy to illusion, the nature of a particular judgment being dependent upon the nature of the resolving information for body movement.

## OBJECT MOTION AND FIELD MOVEMENT

For the most part visual judgments of motion are made in the context of a visual framework such as is provided by natural terrain and man-made environments. As with perception of orientation, the visual field seems to be dominant in determining object motion perception. During angular acceleration in a well-lighted cabin the oculogyral effect is either markedly reduced or absent, presumably because of the visual framework of the cabin interior, which is stationary relative to the observer.

The visual environment in which various objects move is largely stationary. The extended terrain of ground, hills and valleys, the floors and walls of rooms, and numerous objects such as trees, buildings, and rocks are stationary. Objects move in this stationary environment. The essential stimulus for movement is, therefore, motion of an object's retinal image relative to the stationary retinal projection of the visual field. These are the more or less "natural" or "normal" conditions under which visual movement perception occurs. The equivocal retinal projection of a moving object is perceptually resolved by information provided by the stationary background. Since the stationary features of the visual array constitute the basis of information which gives rise to motion constancy, it is to be expected that if under appropriate conditions the background is moved a stationary object will be judged as moving. Induced movement of this kind occurs and it has many points in common with the induced apparent tilt of a vertical object in a tilted environment (Fig. 3.5). Since the visual framework or background provides the information in terms of which object orientation is involved, a vertical object is perceived as tilted in a tilted environment. Similarly, a stationary object is perceived as moving in a moving environment.

There are numerous anecdotal accounts of induced visual movement. The moon appears to move across the clouds even though the clouds are actually moving relative to the observer and the moon is stationary. The train in which one is seated appears to move while that at the opposite platform appears stationary. An old but effective trick for lending the appearance of movement to a rider on a movie screen is to move the rider up and down while moving the background scenery horizontally. The total effect is that of a rider moving in a direction opposite to the background and rising and falling as on horse-back. In each of these conditions the object is stationary and the background is moving. The normally stationary surround which provides the information necessary for perceptual resolution of object movement is in motion, so that the stationary object is judged to be moving.

Qualitative studies of induced movement have been conducted by Duncker and Rubin in the 1920s and more recently by Wallach. Among the few quantitative investigations are those of Brosgole (1966) whose observers viewed and controlled a small luminous sphere surrounded by a large (40 in × 23 in) luminous frame (Fig. 4.1) in a dark room. When the frame

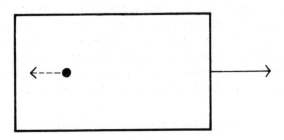

**Figure 4.1** Induced movement; perceptual resolution of object movement by movement of background. As the surrounding frame moves right the stationary dot is judged to move left but through a shorter distance than the actual movement of the background frame.

was moved 20 cm to the left the sphere, which remained stationary, was judged as moving about 8 cm to the right. With a smaller surrounding frame judged movement of the sphere was less. If the stationary sphere was judged as moving in the opposite direction to the background, then it would have to be moved in the *same* direction in order to be perceived as stationary.

Since in Brosgole's experiments the extent of apparent movement of the sphere was only 8 cm for 20 cm of background movement, some degree of motion (position) constancy occurred. Presumably information for the stationariness of the observer himself from labyrinthine, kinesthetic and internal sources reduced the degree of illusory motion of the sphere or, alternately, maintained a degree of constancy.

Most studies of visual motion have been done with a frame as surround or background. So far as is known there have been no investigations of visual motion perception of an object under conditions in which the total background moves. This could be achieved by placing the observer inside a large rotating cylinder while he judged the movement of a stationary object viewed against the moving background. This situation would be similar in principle to that of the tilted room of Asch and Witkin and, under such conditions, it would be expected that the degree of constancy would be small and illusion great.

The equivocal retinal projection of a moving or stationary object is perceptually resolved to an approximation of the objective state of affairs. In darkness, perceptual motion constancy probably derives from information available for head and body movement through stimulation of the semicircular canal receptors. In lighted conditions motion occurs relative to a largely stationary visual background. If, however, the perceptual resolving information is artificially modified by angular acceleration in a centrifuge or by means of a moving background, constancy diminishes and illusion increases. The first of these effects is the oculogyral effect and the second induced visual movement. A judgment of object motion can be located at a point on a constancy-illusion continuum, the particular location depending on the nature of the sensory information available for resolution of the ambiguous retinal representation of a moving object.

# Rotary Motion in Depth

When a flat (planar) object made of thin cardboard or metal rotates in depth relative to an observer its retinal motion pattern is one of expansion and contraction. It can be seen from Fig. 4.2 that this retinal expansion-contraction occurs for both clockwise and counterclockwise motion of the object. A three-dimensional object made by bending a piece of cardboard or metal symmetrically about its centre line also projects a pattern of expansion-contraction at the retina as it rotates before the observer. In this case an object with its centre edge near (and outer edges far) projects nearly the same motion pattern at the retina when rotating clockwise as an object with its centre edge far (and outer edges near) rotating counterclockwise as shown in Fig. 4.2. Since near-identical patterns of retinal motion occur with both the planar and three-dimensional objects for clockwise and counterclockwise rotation, the retinal representations are equivocal. To resolve perceptually these ambiguities of retinal motion additional information is clearly necessary.

A point that needs to be noted in connection with the retinal projections of clockwise and counterclockwise motion in depth concerns the degree of similarity between the two projections as a function of observer-object distance and object size. Consideration of Fig. 4.2 shows that if observer-object distance is small or if the object is large, there is a marked difference between the relative velocities of the projections of points (including those on the edge of the object) at the retina. When one part of the object is far and the other near the difference in the velocity of points projected from the surface would increase with decreases in viewing distance and with increases in the lateral extent of the object. In fact there would be a slight difference no matter what the size and distance of the object. With relatively small objects and relatively great distances, however, the difference in velocity of points projected from near and far parts of the rotating object would be below threshold. Under such conditions the retinal projections of clockwise and counterclockwise motion would be *functionally* or psychophysically equivalent.

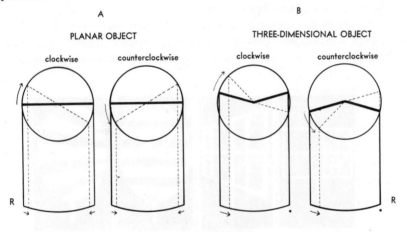

**Figure 4.2** Equivocal retinal projection of two planar and two three-dimensional objects moving clockwise and counterclockwise. The retinal images of object movement are psychophysically equivalent for the two directions of movement.

## PLANAR OBJECTS

Although the flat objects depicted in Fig. 4.2 have thickness they can be considered as planes or surfaces. It can be seen from Fig. 4.2 that when the flat object is rotating it is slanted relative to the observer except when fronto-parallel or "edge-on". Although the retinal expansion-contraction pattern of motion is nearly identical for the two directions of rotation the object is slanted with the right edge far in counterclockwise motion and with the left edge far in clockwise motion. In other words, the direction of slant in depth is different for the two directions of motion when the expansion-contraction at the retina is functionally identical. Thus information for slant direction in depth would serve to resolve perceptually the ambiguous retinal motion pattern. Information for slant, as noted in the last chapter (Fig. 3.13), is provided partly by gradients of outline and texture. It would be expected, therefore, that were information for object slant available the equivocal retinal projection for object motion would be resolved, and such is the case. A rectangular object whose outline at the retina becomes more and more sharply trapezium shaped as it rotates is judged as travelling in the same direction as its true motion direction. That is, information for slant as conveyed by outline results in resolution of motion direction in accord with the object's actual motion direction, an outcome which can be called constancy of rotary motion direction. A regular pattern of stripes or bars which provides texture gradient information for slant at the retina serves equally well in using an elliptical object.

If, however, the information for slant is such that when the object is slanted one way, say with the right edge far, it is apparently slanted the other, with the left edge far, then for half its rotary cycle it should be judged as

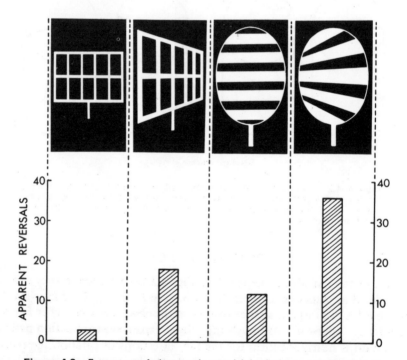

**Figure 4.3** Frequency of changes (reversals) in the apparent direction of rotary motion as a function of information for object slant. Since the retinal images of the clockwise and counterclockwise motion of planar objects are psychophysically equivalent (Fig. 4.2) apparent direction is resolved by information for object slant in depth. If "false" slant information is presented apparent direction is opposite to true direction for half of the complete revolution.

rotating in one direction and for the remaining half in the other. Since perceptual resolution of motion direction is dependent on information for slant, "false" or "misleading" information will result in the judged motion direction being opposed to the actual direction for half a cycle (for the other half cycle the slant information will accord with the actual direction of slant). Cutting the planar object in the shape of a trapezium with an exaggerated texture gradient on its surface causes it to be judged as slanted in one direction for half a cycle when in fact it is slanted in the other direction (Fig. 4.3). When set rotating it is judged as travelling clockwise for half and counterclockwise for the other half of its cycle. The effect is one of apparent "flapping" or oscillation.

A convenient manner of recording these effects is to have the observer report each time an apparent reversal in motion direction occurs. In Fig. 4.3 are shown the frequencies of reversals during 20 revolution trials for two objects with valid slant information available from outline and texture and for two with invalid or misleading information. An illusion of motion direction occurs on many half cycles as a result of the false slant information.

## THREE-DIMENSIONAL OBJECTS

In the case of the three-dimensional objects shown in Fig. 4.2 information for relative depth (*i.e.* centre ridge near or far) is necessary to resolve the equivocal information for motion direction given by the asymmetrical retinal projection of rotary motion. Much the same state of affairs applies in this case as with the planar objects. If the information for centre ridge near or

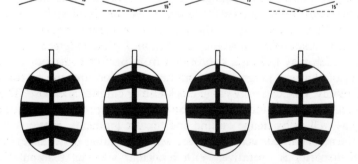

**Figure 4.4** Patterns used to establish that apparent direction of rotary motion in depth of three-dimensional objects is dependent on information for depth. With "false" information for depth (objects 2 and 4) apparent direction is opposite to true direction. (From R.P. Power, Studies in the apparent reversal of rotary motion in depth. Unpublished doctoral dissertation, University of Sydney, 1966.)

far accords with its actual depth relative to the edges, apparent motion direction during about 30° of rotation corresponds with objective direction, *i.e.,* constancy of motion direction obtains. If, on the other hand, the information for the relative distances of centre edge or "ridge" and outer edges is falsified by means of inappropriate surface patterns as shown in Fig. 4.4, apparent motion direction is opposite to true motion direction, *i.e.,* an illusion of motion direction occurs.

## CONSTANCY AND ILLUSION OF ROTARY MOTION DIRECTION

Day and Power (1963, 1965) and Power (1966) in a series of studies systematically varied the information for object slant using both planar and three-dimensional objects and showed that perceptual resolution of motion direction is a function of this information. In situations where the information validly indicated slant, constancy of motion direction obtained, but where the information conflicted with the objective slant the apparent direction of motion was opposed to the true direction. The latter perception is an illusion of motion direction which results in the apparent oscillation or "flapping" effect of a continuously rotating object. Power has shown that by arranging slant information on both sides of planar objects made of thin metal such that slant direction is out of accord with true slant when either side is towards the observer, apparent motion direction is also dictated by slant information, giving rise to a different pattern of apparent movement.

The perceptual resolution of the direction of rotary motion is essentially similar in principle to the resolution of object size and shape. In all situations the visual representation is ambiguous and additional sensory information is necessary. If the information is "natural" in the sense that it is what is normally available, then the judgment exhibits constancy. If the information is rendered misleading or false the judgment exhibits illusion. It can be noted, however, that in the case of the direction of rotary motion, perceptual resolution must exhibit constancy *or* illusion. Unlike judgments of size and shape, which may fall on a continuum from perfect constancy to various degrees of illusion, judgments of motion direction are one or the other; a dichotomy. One can only judge clockwise or counterclockwise. There are no points between. Since information for slant is provided by retinal disparity as well as by image outline and texture gradients, motion direction is for the most part correctly perceived within the range of distances in which retinal disparity is operative. With binocular viewing, manipulations of outline and texture gradients affect judgments of motion direction only at relatively great distances.

The curious reversals of the apparent direction of rotary motion, which are due to misleading information for object slant, were originally noted by Kenyon in 1898 who observed that a "two-winged pendant fan" appeared to rotate in a direction opposite to that of its physical movement. The wings of the fan were presumably roughly trapezium shaped with rounded ends, thus providing the outline usually given by an object slanted in depth. The problem was later taken up by Adelbert Ames in 1951, who made many observations of the effect using a trapezium-shape cut and painted to resemble a window slanted in depth (Fig. 4.3). He attributed the changes in apparent direction not so much to the availability of stimulus information for slant in depth as to assumptions about the shapes of familiar objects such as windows. He therefore used an object cut out and painted to resemble a window slanted relative to the observer, As it turns out, however, familiar objects with the appearance of slant are not the only objects which exhibit apparent reversals of rotary motion. Reversals occur when outline and texture gradient information for slant conflicts with the true slant of the object.

# Visual Perception of Velocity

It was noted in Chapter 3 that the greater the distance of an object the smaller its retinal image, but that with information for distance from retinal disparity, ocular muscles, and the visual field, judged object size tends towards constancy. For the same geometrical reason that an object's retinal projection decreases with increasing observer-object distance, the velocity of the retinal image decreases in the case of a moving object at a distance.

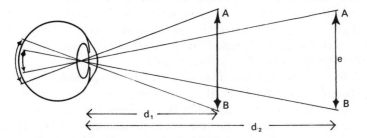

**Figure 4.5** Retinal velocity depends on distance of object. The velocity of the retinal projection of an object oscillating through distance $e$ in time $t$ at distance $d_2$ from the eye is less than when it oscillates through $e$ in time $t$ at distance $d_1$.

In Fig. 4.5 is depicted a small object moving through a distance $e$ between points $A$ and $B$ in time $t$ at two distances $d^1$ and $d^2$ from the observer. The retinal distance traversed by the object's representation is greater for the shorter distance $d^1$ than for $d^2$. Since the time $t$ taken for the movement is the same in each case and retinal velocity is distance divided by time, the retinal velocity is greater for the shorter viewing distance.

In terms of an everyday situation, the retinal velocity of the image of a car travelling at 30 mph is greater when the car is 10 yards away than when it is 20 yards away, and travelling laterally across the field of view. As with the retinal projection of object size, the velocity of the retinal projection can represent a range of different velocities at a range of distances from the observer.

Since the retinal representation of object velocity is ambiguous, and since as the distance between observer and object increases retinal velocity diminishes, the question arises as to whether velocity constancy occurs with variations in viewing distance. This question was first taken up by Porterfield in 1759 who reported that objects moving at constant velocity varied in their apparent velocities inversely as their distances from the observer, an observation which suggests underconstancy. It was J. F. Brown in the 1930s, however, who conducted the most comprehensive studies of this question. Brown used two moving patterns, a standard placed at 3·3, 6·6 and 10·0 metres from the observer and a variable located at a distance of 1 metre. The experiment took place with normal room lighting, and the observer was required to state when the velocity of the variable was equal to that of the standard at the three distances. The average apparent velocities of the standard at 3·3, 6·6, and 10·0 metres for three observers were 8·7, 8·7 and 8·3 cm per second respectively. If the judgments had been made in terms of retinal velocities the variable would have been judged as equal in velocity at 1·0, 1·6 and 3·3 cm per second for the 10, 6·6 and 3·3 distances respectively. Brown's data show that there is a considerable tendency towards velocity constancy, even though retinal velocity declines with distance. Since at 10·0 metres the judged velocity $P$ was 8·3, the objective velocity $C$ was 10, and the relative retinal velocity $R$ was 1, then the Brunswik index of constancy (Chapter 3) is $(8·3—1)/(10—1)$ which is 0·81.

The visual representation of velocity is a function of both object velocity and object distance. It seems likely, therefore, that, like size constancy, velocity constancy as demonstrated by Brown depends on distance information. Unfortunately there is no relevant experimental evidence. It can be predicted, for example, that in darkness with intervening terrain invisible to the observer, judged velocity will decrease with distance if all other factors such as visual size and movement extent are held constant. It can also be predicted that, if false or misleading information for distance is made available, judgments of object velocity will vary accordingly. In Fig. 3.12 are shown three line patterns which, if reproduced as luminous lines in a darkened environment, would presumably lead to different estimates of distance. If under these three conditions of distance information a luminous object is oscillated from side to side with the same velocity and extent, its judged velocity would vary according to the nature of the distance information. Since with the pattern on the right the object would be judged closer for a given distance, its apparent velocity should be least, and with that on the right greatest. Under all these conditions the velocity of the retinal image is the same.

In discussing the information for distance projected by the visual field to the eye (Chapter 3) it was seen that as the distances of terrain features increase the retinal representations decrease in size. Consequently the visual surround is projected at the retina in the form of gradients. The retinal representation of a distant object occurs therefore in the context of the fine texture and that of a near object in the coarse texture of the retinal gradient. The significant point is that distance information as presented in the retinal image of the extended terrain is essentially variation in *size*. In the absence of alternative distance information, therefore, an object will be judged as larger when surrounded by fine texture and smaller when surrounded by coarse texture. The same should apply in the case of judged velocity. An object moving with a certain velocity in a large field or surround should be judged as moving more slowly than one in a small field when both objects are located at the same distance from the observer. The small field is part of the retinal coding for greater distance, so that to achieve a particular retinal velocity it must have a greater apparent velocity. This is what Brown demonstrated. He arranged two apertures, one twice the size of the other in all its linear dimensions, each at a distance of 2 metres from the observer.

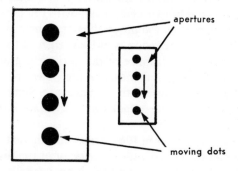

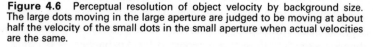

**Figure 4.6** Perceptual resolution of object velocity by background size. The large dots moving in the large aperture are judged to be moving at about half the velocity of the small dots in the small aperture when actual velocities are the same.

Objects in the form of moving dots, also with a size ratio of 2 : 1 (Fig. 4.6) were moved across these apertures which with the dots, constituted the only visible objects in a darkened room. The dots in the larger aperture were judged as moving at about one half the velocity of those moving with the same velocity in the smaller aperture.

Brown's experiments have shown that with a decrease in retinal velocity with distance, judged velocity tends to remain constant. They have also demonstrated that if distance information in the form of background size is varied, judged velocity varies accordingly. That is, illusions of velocity occur when elements of information for distance are modified. Velocity judgments vary along a continuum from accordance (constancy) to discordance (illusion) with object velocity as a function of distance information.

## THE ANSBACHER-BROWN SIZE EFFECT

Consideration of variation in velocity of an object's retinal image with increases in observer-object distance leads to a further prediction. As object distance increases its retinal velocity and size decrease. If, then, an object were located at a fixed distance from an observer in an otherwise dark environment (so that all distance information is eliminated) and its velocity progressively increased, its apparent size would be expected to decrease. Increases in velocity occur with decreases in distance, so that if retinal size is fixed and velocity increased, apparent size must diminish. Increasing retinal velocity occurs as an object approaches the observer, so that if retinal size is invariant the object should appear to grow smaller. With decreasing velocity, an object whose retinal size is fixed should appear to expand. Without a visual surround, and in the absence of information for distance, perceptual resolution of the entirely equivocal retinal image in terms of object size would be expected to vary with velocity. The situation is similar in principle to that of the moon illusion, where the moon's retinal projection is invariant but the moon is judged larger at the horizon than at zenith because the apparent distance of the horizon is greater than that of the zenith. At a greater apparent distance the object must be apparently larger in order to project a given retinal image size. Similarly, with greater retinal velocity an object whose retinal size is invariant must be apparently smaller.

Brown, and later Ansbacher in 1944, arranged a lighted arc near the edge of a disk and rotated it. As the angular velocity of the disk was increased from 0·5 to 1·3 revolutions per second the judged length of the 13 cm arc decreased from 10 to 5·2 cm. This change in judged size with variation in velocity was later confirmed by Marshall and Stanley (1964) although the size changes were less than those reported by Ansbacher. It is conceivable that differences in room illumination between the two studies, with consequent differences in the availability of distance information, may have resulted in the inconsistency.

It would also be expected that changes in apparent distances should occur with variations in object velocity. Increases in velocity occur as an object approaches so that, in addition to an object appearing smaller as velocity is increased, it should also appear nearer. If, then, a point of light in the dark is moved from side to side with a greater velocity in one direction than in the other it should be judged nearer while moving in the first than in the second direction. Kilpatrick in 1951 arranged a point of light so that it could be moved with a different velocity while travelling from right to left than when travelling left to right. It was reported as moving through an elliptical path in depth relative to the observer, presumably because its apparent distance was different for the two directions.

## Mechanisms of Visual Motion Perception

In discussing perceptual resolution of equivocal projections of the movement of objects in the environment the term "resolving information" has been frequently used. In the case of head and body movement this information derives at least partly from stimulation of the semicircular canals. The resolution of the direction of circular motion in depth is dependent on information for slant and the resolution of velocity at a distance on distance information. In each of these situations manipulations of resolving information may result in conflict between judged and objective movement. The actual manner in which the patterns of stimulation referred to as resolving information are encoded and interact with those deriving from the judged object property is so far unknown. Doubtless there are processes in the central nervous system which are associated with the stabilization of motion perception either in the direction of correspondence or non-correspondence between apparent and objective movement. In the present state of knowledge, however, it is only possible to speculate on the processes which might be involved in the constancy (or illusion) of motion direction and velocity. It is conceivable, for example, that changes in apparent velocity as a function of surround size, as demonstrated by Brown, may be mediated by inhibitory effects which the background elements exercise on the receptors responding to movement. Such a mechanism would be of significance in the maintenance of motion constancy with variation in distance. Although at the level of psychophysics the term "resolving information" can be used in referring to sensory stimulation necessary to maintain perceptual stability of movement, perceptual resolution probably has correlates in neurophysiological processes.

There is much recent evidence from neurophysiology to indicate that neurones both in the retina and cortex respond to movement and that, in some instances, these cells are specifically sensitive to one direction of movement. If the rate at which such cells respond is affected by adjacent contours then a mechanism for Brown's observations would exist. Such a mechanism would effectively serve perceptual constancy of velocity by maintaining constant rates of neural motion activity even though the retinal image of velocity varied with distance. It is also conceivable that cells specific to particular directions of movement are controlled by the typical stimulus patterns. A slanted surface with regular features projects a typical outline and typical gradients of texture on the retina. These may possibly differentially affect the direction specific cells of retina or cortex.

The question of the mechanisms involved in the perceptual resolution of the equivocal stimulus for motion direction and velocity remains open. In the present state of knowledge we can only speak with conviction of resolving information at the level of psychophysics. It is likely, however, that psychophysical events have their neurophysiological correlates and that perceptual resolution is a function of interactions in the central nervous system.

# Summary

As with the visual projection of stationary objects, the visual projections of the properties of movement are frequently ambiguous. This ambiguity occurs in connection with the sheer occurrence of movement, its direction in depth relative to the observer, and its velocity. To resolve perceptually the ambiguous retinal image of occurrence, direction and velocity, information for head and eye movement and field movement, the slant of the object in depth, and the distance of the object, respectively, is necessary. Depending on the characteristics of this resolving information, so apparent occurrence, direction and velocity of movement corresponds with objective occurrence, direction, and velocity (perceptual constancy) or does not correspond (perceptual illusion).

The Ansbacher-Brown effect is the apparent shrinkage of a moving object. This effect can be interpreted in terms of retinal velocity serving as a cue to distance in the absence of the usual cues to distance. Increases in velocity for an object of constant retinal projection results in the latter being judged as closer with consequent apparent shrinkage in size.

Recent experiments have shown that certain neurones are sensitive to movement of an object in one direction but not to movement in another. It is conceivable that motion constancy and illusions may eventually be explained in terms of neurophysiological processes in the nervous system.

# 5. Perceptual Stability, Lightness, Brightness and Colour

THE PROPERTIES of light reaching the eye from surrounding objects and sources are determined jointly by the reflecting and emitting properties of surfaces and sources, and the intensity and spectral composition of the light illuminating them. The light reflected from a surface of constant reflectance varies with the intensity and composition of incident illumination. Correspondingly, surfaces of different reflectances may reflect the same level and composition of light to the eye. A surface of low reflectance under high illumination may result in the same amount of light falling on the retina as a surface of high reflectance under low illumination. In addition, equivocalities occur in connection with the wavelength composition of the retinal stimulus, since it is determined by the selective absorption and reflectance of the surface for different wavelengths and the spectral composition of the incident light.

Despite these ambiguities the human observer is capable of perceptually resolving object lightness and colour to a close approximation to object reflectance and colour. In this chapter lightness, brightness and colour constancy will be described and considered along with lightness, brightness and colour contrast. It will be seen that, as with the spatial properties of objects, perceptual resolution of the equivocal retinal projection of these surface characteristics is determined by information additional to that contained in the retinal image. Depending on the nature of this information the observer's judgments vary along a continuum between agreement and disagreement with the objective property.

## Perception of Lightness and Brightness

### TERMINOLOGY

Light can be specified in radiometric, photometric or psychological terms; *i.e.*, from the viewpoint of physics, vision or subjective experience, the latter being indicated by the observer's responses. Radiant energy from the spectrum of electromagnetic energy is usually expressed in watts; power in ergs per second. In the visible region of the electromagnetic spectrum

(Fig. 1.1) energy is considered in terms of vision, and the term "luminous flux" rather than "radiant flux" is used to designate energy transmitted from a source to an intercepting surface. Further, in referring to the emission of energy from a spatially extended source, the photometric term *luminance* is used instead of radiance. Luminance is expressed as candles per square centimetre (a candle being a standard measure of luminous intensity) or, more commonly, as millilamberts. Light falling on a surface is measured as *illuminance*. Since, as pointed out above, a surface absorbs a proportion of the light falling on it, luminance and illuminance differ except in the case of a perfect reflecting surface. Finally, the light falling on the retina of the eye is referred to as *retinal illuminance* and is frequently measured in *trolands*, a troland being the intensity of light at the retina from an external source of 1 candle per square millimetre passing through an aperture (an artificial pupil) of 1 square millimetre. Retinal illuminance, a measure of the effective visual stimulus, varies according to pupil size, the direction of light rays passing through the pupil, and the density of the ocular media. Because of the obvious difficulties involved in arriving at a measure of retinal illuminance it is usual to express visual stimulation in terms of source luminance.

In describing sources of light on reflecting surfaces the human observer refers to their brightness or lightness. Brightness derives from observer judgments or estimates of light intensity expressed photometrically as luminance. Lightness refers to the reflectance of a surface. For example, two pieces of paper, one dark grey and the other light grey, may be differently illuminated, the first by intense light and the second by dim light. Although their brightnesses (the judged luminance of their surfaces) may be the same, their lightnesses (their judged reflectances) may be quite different.

## LIGHTNESS AND BRIGHTNESS CONSTANCY AND CONTRAST

### Lightness and Brightness Constancy

Before proceeding to describe some typical experimental studies of lightness constancy, a distinction needs to be made between lightness and brightness constancy, and the term constancy clarified. As already pointed out, lightness refers to apparent or judged reflectance of a surface. Reflectance is a relatively stable object property. When the intensity of illumination on a surface from a source varies so does the luminance of the surface. If the intensity of light incident on the surface increases, the luminance of the surface increases. But despite this increase in the light reaching the eye from the surface, judgments of lightness change only slightly compared with changes in luminance. This is *lightness constancy*. Imagine, however, light of constant intensity transmitted through a transparency. This source has a certain luminance and is, therefore, of a certain *brightness*. If now the intensity of an overhead source is increased so that its light is reflected also from the surface of the transparency to the eye, the luminance of the target would increase since both its transmitted and incident light (from the overhead source) determine its luminance. If judgments of the brightness of the transparency were to change either slightly compared with the luminance change or not at all we would use the term *brightness constancy*. Lightness constancy refers to the relative stability of apparent reflectance with changes in luminance, and brightness constancy should be used only to refer to apparent transmission or luminance of a source with changes in its total luminance from another source.

Unfortunately, the terms lightness and brightness constancy are frequently used interchangeably leading to considerable confusion. The term constancy is also somewhat misleading in that perfect constancy, complete invariance, of surface lightness or source brightness with changes in incident illumination is rare, as is the case with spatial and movement constancies. More commonly the changes in lightness and brightness vary less than would be predicted from the total luminance changes, which in turn determines retinal illuminance. Almost all the work in this area on constancy has been concerned with lightness constancy and much of the work on contrast has been concerned with brightness.

## Studies of Lightness Constancy

Although lightness constancy has already been described, a recent account by Graham and Brown (1965) is worth quoting. Although they use the term brightness constancy, they are really referring to lightness constancy:

> "Under any illumination, the best white paper reflects only 60 times as much light as the deepest black paper. Consequently by placing the black paper in an illumination that is 60 times greater than the illumination of the white paper one can make the two surfaces—black and white—reflect into the eye the *same amount of light* and thus stimulate the retina with equal intensity. Nevertheless we know that the two surfaces will not look alike. The black surface will be seen as black in a high illumination, the other surface as white in a lower illumination. The black surface retains its characteristic constant brightness in spite of the change in illumination."*

Lightness constancy is commonly investigated using the arrangement shown in Fig. 5.1, originally developed by Katz in 1911. In one compartment of the box under fixed illumination is a grey disk (sometimes composed of black and white sectors), which when rotated at high speed results in a uniform grey appearance. This disk is called the standard. In the other

---

*Vision and Visual Perception*, by C.H. Graham *et al.* (page 453). Copyright 1965 John Wiley & Sons Inc., N.Y.

compartment is a disk composed of black and white sectors but adjustable so that the proportions of black and white can be varied while the disk is rotating to give a uniform grey. By operating a simple control this disk can be varied from almost all white through progressively darker shades of grey to almost all black. That is, during rotation the disk's reflectance, the proportion of incident light it reflects, can be varied. The illumination on this disk is also variable, usually from an overhead source concealed from the observer's view.

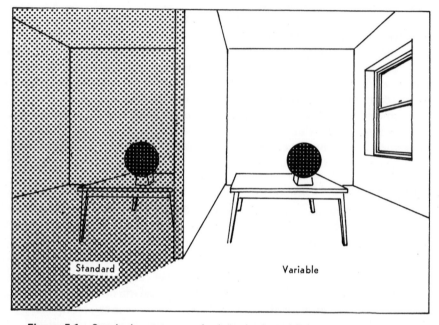

**Figure 5.1** Standard arrangement for investigation of lightness constancy. The observer's task is that of adjusting the lightness of the variable disk in the lighter chamber to match that of the standard disk in the darker.

An observer seated in front of the two compartments can view both disks at the same time. His task is to vary the proportions of black and white (*i.e.,* the reflectance) of the rapidly spinning variable disk so that it is judged to be of the same lightness as the standard in the other compartment. Consider the situation in which the illumination in each compartment is the same and the observer has varied the reflectance of the variable disk so that it is judged to be the same as that of the standard. Now the illumination on the variable disk is increased by increasing the intensity of the overhead source. As a result of this greater illumination, the luminance of the variable disk is increased. If the lightness of the variable disk remains constant with changes in the amount of light reaching the eye (*i.e.,* with variations in retinal illuminance), the observer would make no change in the proportions of black and white. In fact the observer normally reduces the reflectance slightly as the illumination on the disk is increased, but by no means enough to equalize the luminance of the two disks. That is, with changes in luminance the judged lightness of a surface varies only slightly; while the amount of light reaching the eye from a surface changes markedly, its lightness tends towards constancy.

The Brunswik ratio discussed in the last chapter is also applicable to the measurement of the degree of lightness constancy. Suppose that the standard disk reflects 40 percent of the incident light and is illuminated by 12 foot-candles of incident light. The variable has an illumination of, say, 24 foot-candles, twice as intense as the standard. In order to match the lightness of the variable disk under high illumination to that of the standard under low illumination, assume that the observer adjusts the reflectance of the variable to 30 percent (rather than to 20 percent, which would give retinal illuminance equal to the standard). The Brunswik ratio is $(P-R)/(C-R)$ where $P$ is the judged reflectance or lightness of the standard, $C$ its actual reflectance, and $R$ the reflectance that would be required in terms of luminance equality. In the example $P$ is 30, $C$ is 40 and $R$ is 20 and the Brunswik ratio is $(30-20)/(40-20) = 0.5$. Perfect constancy would be indicated by a value of 1 and zero constancy (*i.e.,* a judgment made in accord with luminance) by a value of 0.

Frequently ignored features of the experimental arrangement shown in Fig. 5.1 are the surrounds or backgrounds to the standard and variable disks. The standard disk is viewed under a fixed illumination which lights the background as well as the disk. Likewise, when the illumination of the compartment containing the variable disk is increased or decreased the luminance of both disk *and* background is altered. After the amounts of black and white in the variable disk have been adjusted by the observer to match the lightness of the standard, and the observer views the two disks through black tubes so that only the disk surfaces are in view, the disks appear different in lightness. This observation will shortly acquire some importance when perceptual lightness constancy and simultaneous lightness contrast are considered together.

### Lightness and Brightness Contrast

In Fig. 5.2 are shown two circular patches of the same reflectance each surrounded by an area of greater reflectance. Below these are shown two identical patches, one surrounded by an area of low reflectance (black) and the other by an area of higher reflectance (white). Whereas the two upper patches appear similar in lightness, those below are apparently different. The patch surrounded by black is judged to be substantially lighter than that surrounded by white. The apparent change in reflectance as a function of variation in surround luminance as shown in Fig. 5.2 is referred to as simultaneous lightness contrast or, more simply, as lightness contrast. If the patterns in Fig. 5.2 were transparencies through which light were transmitted, much the same variations in brightness would occur. We would refer in such à case to brightness contrast.

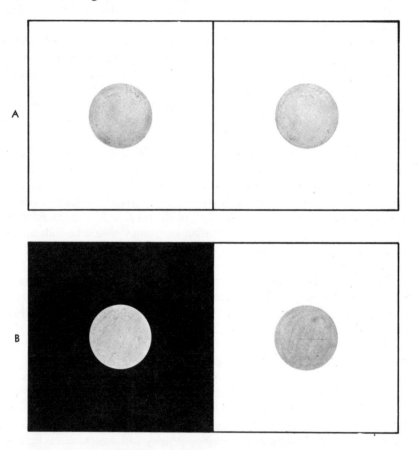

**Figure 5.2** Simultaneous lightness contrast. All disks reflect the same amount of light to the eye. *A* When the backgrounds are of the same lightness disks appear equal in lightness. *B* A disk on a dark background is judged lighter than one of the same reflectance on a light background.

As in experiments on lightness constancy, investigations of contrast usually involve a test and a comparison target. The test target is usually maintained at constant luminance and that of its surround varied. The observer may then match the comparison patch so that it is judged to be the same as the test or standard patch. Any of the psychophysical procedures described in Chapter 1 can be used. If the luminance of the surround is increased by steps starting well below the test patch luminance, the test patch is judged slightly *lighter* as the surround luminance approaches that of the test patch. When the surround luminance exceeds that of the test target the latter is judged progressively darker as the former increases, an effect which can be observed in Fig. 5.2. Factors such as the area of the surround (or background) and its distance from the target also affect the degree of lightness change.

In the experiment now to be described the patterns were produced by projecting areas of light on a screen and the observers were required to judge the lightness of the targets. Using more complex targets a relationship between the test target and background luminances emerges.

Wallach in 1948 arranged four projectors which cast two circular targets each surrounded by an annulus of different luminance to its target. For one condition the luminances of the standard target and its background had a ratio of 1 : 2. The background of the other combinations, the variable, was then set at *half* that of the standard background and the observer was required to report when the variable target matched the standard target luminance. Apparent equality between standard and variable targets was achieved when the luminance ratio of the variable target to its background was also 1 : 2. Even though the absolute luminance of the standard was double that of the variable target, the two targets were judged equal when each had the same luminance relationship to its background.

In Wallach's experiment the range of luminance used and the range of target-background ratios were restricted. A wider range of these two factors were used in an experiment by Jameson and Hurvich in 1961 and the data

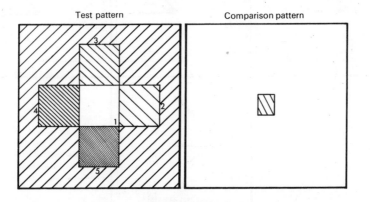

**Figure 5.3** Test and comparison areas used in the experiment by Jameson and Hurvich (1961). The luminance of the five parts of the test area decrease from 1 (the brightest) to 5 (dimmest). (From D. Jameson and L.M. Hurvich, Complexities of perceived brightness. In *Science*, 1961, 133, 174–179. By courtesy of *Science*, Copyright, 1961, by American Association for the Advancement of Science.)

are more revealing. This study was similar in principle to a much earlier investigation by Hess and Pretori in 1894. The test pattern, consisting of five areas of different luminance, was arranged in the form of a cross as shown in Fig. 5.3. The area of greatest luminance was at the centre of the cross followed in decreasing order by those at the right, above, left, and below. While the luminance relationships between these five areas was fixed, the *overall* luminance was varied in three steps of increasing luminance. The observer's task was that of matching a variable comparison pattern (Fig. 5.3) to each of the five areas at each of the three luminance levels. The results are shown in Fig. 5.4. The graphs are arranged so that the observer's brightness judgments (transmitted light was used) can be compared with those which would have occurred had there been no change in brightness with increases in luminance and those which would have occurred had

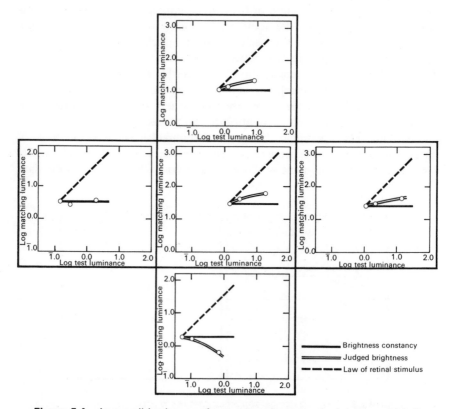

**Figure 5.4** As overall luminance of test pattern increases the brightness of 1, 2 and 3 increase slightly, that of 4 does not change noticeably, and that of 5 (the darkest) decreases. (From D. Jameson and L.M. Hurvich, Complexities of perceived brightness. In *Science*, 1961, 133, 174–179. By courtesy of *Science*, Copyright, 1961, by American Association for the Advancement of Science.)

judgments been made in terms of retinal illuminance. This experiment is important in showing that the judged brightness of an area is not only determined by that of its background, but that Wallach's finding of brightness equality with invariant relationships between target and surround applies only to a limited range of ratios and luminances.

## The Gelb Effect

Gelb in 1929 drew attention to a special case of lightness contrast which was later investigated quantitatively by Stewart in 1959. Gelb set up a black disk in a dark room and rotated it so that its surface texture at the eye was homogeneous. He then illuminated the disk's surface with a beam from a concealed projector. The observer perceived the illuminated black surface as light grey or whitish. When, however, a small piece of white paper was introduced in front of the disk and in the beam, the disk turned much darker. That is, although the luminance of the disk was unchanged its lightness changed from white to black (or light to dark) with the intro-duction of the piece of white paper. Stewart, using an apparatus similar to that shown in Fig. 5.1, required his observers to match the lightness of the disk by means of a variable disk with black and white variable sectors. He changed both the area and position of the white object in front of the black disk and found that variations in judged lightness were a function of both factors. The black disk was judged darkest with the greater area of white object in front and less and less dark as the area was reduced. The darkest appearance occurred when the white object was placed in front of the disk's centre.

When the Gelb disk is illuminated by a projector beam with no other object or surface visible, it can only be judged in terms of its luminance. The situation is essentially the same as that of viewing an illuminated surface through a blackened tube so that only the surface occupies the field of view. In both the Gelb situation and that of the "reduction" tunnel all information for incident illumination is eliminated, so that judgments are determined entirely by luminance. We shall see later that there is some neurophysiological evidence for the manner in which the information necessary for the resolution of object reflectance operates.

## Constancy and Contrast

In general there are two points of difference between investigations of constancy and contrast. First, while studies of constancy have been mainly concerned with lightness, studies of contrast have concentrated on bright-ness. As far as is known there has so far been no attempt to study lightness and brightness constancy using the conditions and apparatus depicted i Fig. 5.1. Nor have lightness and brightness contrast been compared und the same conditions. Second, investigations of brightness contrast have be marked generally by much greater precision and more careful attention to control of such factors as visual fixation, pupil diameter, state of adaptation of the eye and systematic variation of stimulus conditions. Despite these differences it is worthwhile comparing constancy and contrast in an attempt to relate them. In so doing it is useful to consider again the human observer in a natural environment.

In the natural environment (as opposed to the artificial or man-made environment) objects vary widely in reflectance, from highly reflectant snow and ice to surfaces such as dark soil and rocks which reflect only a small proportion of incident light. Reflectance is a stable object property like size and shape. Also like size and shape, reflectance is a property in terms of which an object may be identified or recognized. But reflectance can only be perceived by the light reaching the retina of the eye from the object's surface and the intensity of this light varies with both object reflectance and incident illumination. Thus the retinal projection of reflectance, again like size, shape, motion and other properties, is equivocal. Information for incident illumination is necessary for perceptual resolution of reflectance, the perceptual correlate of which is lightness. That perceptual resolution does occur is evidenced by the numerous studies of lightness constancy in which close approximations to object reflectance are achieved with variations in incident illuminations.

In situations involving both reflected and transmitted light, the relative stability of lightness and brightness with changes in illumination is dependent upon the object's background or surround. If background is obscured from view by using a reduction screen or a blackened tube with which to view the target, judgments are made largely in terms of total luminance rather than reflectance. Constancy and contrast constitute a continuum of perceptual judgments. Lightness (or brightness) is a function of background luminance. When illumination incident on object and background changes, lightness remains relatively stable in that changes are substantially less than would be expected from the total luminance change. When the background is varied, lightness undergoes change. The relationship between surround and target luminance is a critical determinant of lightness and brightness constancy. Jameson and Hurvich have demonstrated that the occurrence of underconstancy, perfect constancy or overconstancy depends on this relationship.

At this point it is sufficient to note that as incident illumination on an object changes so background luminance provides the information necessary to resolve perceptually the ambiguous retinal representation of object lightness and brightness. Depending on the nature of this information the retinal image, which itself is equivocal, is resolved in terms of a close (constancy) or poor (illusion) approximation to the object's lightness or brightness. The material to be dealt with in the following two sections is suggestive of the way in which luminance information from the surround determines contrast effects at the level of neurophysiological interactions.

### Border Contrast: The Mach Effect

In viewing a surface like that in Fig. 5.5, on which there is a gradient of luminance, the observer does not report that white shades gradually into grey and grey into black. In fact he reports that at the point where white

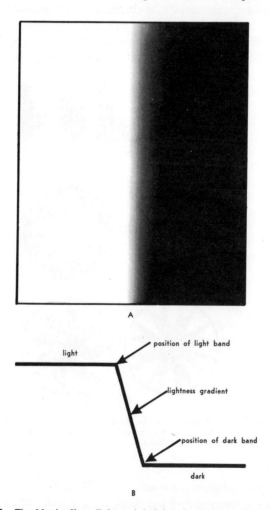

**Figure 5.5** The Mach effect; light and dark bands appear at the boundaries between uniformly light and dark areas and the lightness gradient joining them. In *A* only the light band can be seen clearly. In *B* is shown the approximate distribution of luminance across *A* and the approximate location of the light and dark bands. (The advice of Dr Tom N. Cornsweet, Stanford Research Institute, in the production of *A* is gratefully acknowledged.)

appears to shade into grey there is a band of greater apparent lightness than the white, while at the apparent point of change from dark grey to black there is a band apparently darker than the black. A photometer reveals that these apparently lighter and darker bands are not physically but only apparently present in the pattern. Such gradients can be produced by varying either the reflectance of a surface, or by varying luminance with a suitable transparency. The apparently lighter and darker bands which occur at the points of greatest change in rate of change in luminance are referred to as Mach bands or border contrast. Ernst Mach first reported this visual effect in the nineteenth century using various black-white patterns. When patterns such as those shown in Fig. 5.6 are set in motion to the point of fusion of

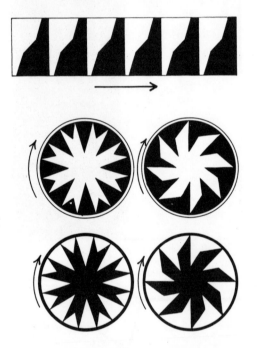

**Figure 5.6** Typical patterns used by Mach for producing lightness gradients. When in motion in the direction shown uniform areas and gradients occur and bands appear at the boundaries.

black and white, there appear gradients of luminance in the form of Mach bands. It is as if there is a visual mechanism which serves to enhance or sharpen blurred or fuzzy contours. It is generally held that the Mach effect, so obvious with luminance gradients such as that shown in Fig. 5.5, does in fact serve to enhance contours which are rendered blurred by various optical properties of the eye.

The retinal representation of a sharp contour between areas of different luminance (as, for example, the contour of a silhouette drawing) loses its sharpness. The optical system of the eye is by no means perfect. As a result of dispersion or scattering of light in the eye itself and defects such as chromatic and spherical aberrations of the lens system a sharp contour is imaged at the retina as a blur or gradient of light. But despite this blurring of the retinal image due to deficiencies of the visual optical system we judge a sharp clear contour to be sharp and clear. It is suggested that Mach bands which are obvious in a contour whose luminance gradient is markedly exaggerated (Fig. 5.6) are a result of the same visual mechanism which has as its principal function the "sharpening" of the blurred retinal representation of an objectively sharp contour.

### A Possible Basis for Contrast Effects

It will be recalled that the frequency of neural impulses generated by a stimulus is a function of stimulus intensity. The more intense the light falling on the retina the greater the frequency of impulses within limits. In a series of outstanding investigations Hartline, Ratliff, and various collaborators have studied the ways in which the frequency of impulses generated by stimulating one area of the retina are affected by stimulating adjacent areas. Much of this work has been conducted on the relatively simple compound eye of the horse-shoe crab *Limulus*. The *Limulus* eye contains about one thousand ommatidia receptors in small bundles. The individual bundles are interconnected by a plexus of nerve fibres.

If a single ommatidium is stimulated by focusing on it light of fixed intensity it will discharge impulses with a characteristic frequency. If now while this ommatidium continues to discharge, adjacent ommatidia are stimulated by light, the discharge frequency of the first one diminishes. The degree to which the activity of one cell is diminished by stimulation of adjacent cells is a function of the intensity, area, and configuration of the adjacent stimulation. The further removed the adjacent cells from the test cell, the less the degree to which the frequency of discharge of the former is reduced. Hartline and Ratliff have referred to this influence of one group of cells on another as lateral inhibition.

Great caution needs to be exercised in correlating neural inhibitory effects associated with the compound eye of an arthropod with perceptual effects reported by a human observer. Nevertheless, there is a compelling similarity between the apparent diminution in brightness of a test area when an adjacent area is stimulated as in Fig. 5.2, and reduction in impulse frequency from a receptor element when adjacent elements are stimulated. The exact manner in which lateral inhibition across a mosaic of receptors operates still remains to be fully established, but it is known to occur in the mammalian visual system as well as in compound systems.

Lateral inhibition of one stimulated retinal area by another is mutual. If a number of receptor elements are stimulated simultaneously they exert a mutual inhibitory effect on each other, the degree of inhibition being a function of light intensity. Further, if one group of cells when stimulated inhibits another, then inhibition of the latter by the stimulation of a third group will lessen the inhibitory influence of the second group on the first. The mutual inhibitory effect of a pattern of stimulation such as that shown in Fig. 5.5 would be expected to be greatest among those receptors stimulated by the "lighter" or more intense area of luminance. The group of cells lying across the contour between white and the commencement of the gradient would be strongly influenced on one side by the intense stimulation, and progressively less so by the gradient region. It could be expected therefore that the cells stimulated by the gradient would respond with greater impulse frequency than those in the more strongly stimulated area to the left (Fig. 5.5). The retinal representation of the contour would be characterized then by a region of higher impulse frequency, an event normally correlated with more intense stimulation. The opposite state of affairs would be expected to apply in the case of the retinal contour between the gradient and the dark area or area of weak stimulation. This differential inhibitory effect could serve then as a physiological basis for the bright and dark regions associated with Mach bands or border contrast generated by patterns like those shown in Fig. 5.6.

In Fig. 5.7 are shown the frequency of impulses from receptors when the *Limulus* eye is stimulated by a gradient like that in Fig. 5.5 and the apparent brightness of such a pattern obtained psychophysically with a human observer. Although, as already emphasized, similarities between neurophysiological and psychophysical data need to be treated with considerable caution, especially when the species are so widely separated, there is a possibility that simultaneous and border contrast are correlated with lateral inhibitory processes in the visual system.

While the data concerning lateral inhibition and lightness contrast do not bear directly on lightness constancy, they do suggest the manner in which resolving information from the surround may function to maintain perceptual constancy as illumination varies. It is conceivable that as overall illumination varies in the manner of Fig. 5.1 the increased luminance of the surround serves to maintain impulse frequency in the area stimulated by the target at levels consonant with the effects found by Wallach and by Jameson and Hurvich (Fig. 5.3, 5.4). In the same fashion as increased surround luminance reduces impulse frequency in the target region, so maintaining the same ratio of luminance between target and surround (but increasing overall luminance) may control impulse frequency over a limited range. This relationship at the level of neurophysiology has not, however, been established.

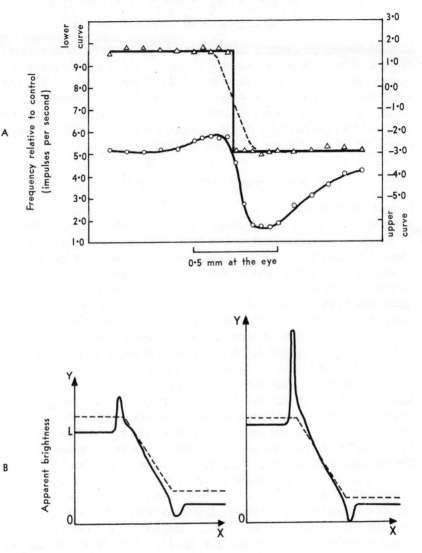

**Figure 5.7** A possible basis for the Mach effect. *A* The response of a single element in the retina of a horse-shoe crab (*Limulus*) to a simple step pattern of illumination. The frequency of response varies according to the position of the step pattern relative to the receptor element. *B* Judgments of the brightness of a Mach pattern made by two skilled observers. (*A* adapted from F. Ratliff and H.K. Hartline, The responses of *Limulus* optic nerve fibers to patterns of illumination on the receptor mosaic. In *J. gen. Physiol.*, 1959, 42, 1241–1255. By courtesy of *J. gen. Physiol.*, Rockefeller University Press. *B* adapted from A. Fiorentini and T. Radici, Binocular measurements of brightness on a field presenting a luminance gradient. In *Atti Fond. G. Ronchi*, 1957, 12, 453–461. By courtesy of *Atti. Fond. G. Ronchi.*)

# Perception of Colour

Like luminance, the spectral composition of light at the retina of the eye is determined by both the wavelength characteristics of light incident on a surface, and the selective reflectance of the object surface. If hue were determined solely by the wavelengths constituting the stimulus, objects would change hue as the composition of the illumination changed. In fact object hue changes relatively slightly as the composition of incident illumination varies. This is the phenomenon of colour constancy.

## COLOUR CONSTANCY AND CONTRAST

In an experiment reported in 1938 Helson arranged 19 achromatic (grey) paper samples varying in reflectance from 0·03 to 0·81 (*i.e.,* reflecting 3 to 81 percent of incident light) against three backgrounds, white, grey, and black. The samples and backgrounds were then illuminated by light with wavelengths in the red, green, yellow and blue regions. In general, the samples of high reflectance were judged as being the same colour as the illuminant, those of intermediate reflectance were judged achromatic, and those of low reflectance were judged as near-complementary in colour to that of the illuminant. In addition, the samples which were judged achromatic in the red, green, yellow and blue illumination varied with the reflectance of the background. Thus in an analogous fashion to lightness constancy, colour constancy is maintained for a limited range of background and background-target conditions. Outside this range, and for the surfaces of greater reflectance, underconstancy of hue occurs, and for the surfaces of lower reflectance, overconstancy. If, however, the surround is eliminated by viewing the target through an aperture or blackened tunnel its hue is that predictable from the wavelength composition of the stimulus.

Since colour constancy under different wavelengths of illumination is a function of information from the object's background, independent variation of surround colour should result in departures from colour constancy. This effect is obtained and is called colour contrast. If a small grey target is surrounded by an area of say, red, the hue of the target changes. For targets of high luminance the change is towards red, but for intermediate and lower luminances the target is judged to be near-complementary in hue to the surround, *i.e.,* bluish green. The extent of hue and saturation shift is a function of numerous variables. The greater the area of the background colour the greater the contrast effect, and the greater the separation between target and surround the less the contrast effect. Colour contrast also varies with luminance differences between target and surround. Precise measurements of colour contrast have been made in recent years by MacAdam (1950) and Akita, Graham and Hsia (1964).

# LIGHTNESS, BRIGHTNESS AND COLOUR PERCEPTION

The reflectance of achromatic and chromatic light by a surface is a more or less fixed object property. Like size, shape, orientation, and motion, reflectance is among those properties of the environment which serve as a basis for object identification. But the representation of surface reflectance at the eye is ambiguous in that it is a function of both reflectance and the intensity and composition of incident illumination on the surface. Provided that there is information for the luminance and colour of the object's background, the equivocal stimulus can be resolved to a close approximation to object reflectance and colour.

Perfect agreement between objective and judged reflectance is the exception rather than the rule. Under certain conditions of illumination and target-background luminance relationships, there may be such agreement, but for the most part, depending on the stimulus conditions, discrepancies of various magnitudes occur between the judged and objective property. In this sense lightness and colour constancy are misnomers.

In using the term "perceptual resolution" to refer to the processes involved in these effects it is not implied that there are conscious or unconscious inferring activities whereby illumination is "taken into account" in order to arrive at surface lightness and colour. In fact, the recent data from the study of the eye of the horse-shoe crab, although by no means conclusive, do suggest that the retinal stimulus from background luminance modulates the processes generated by the focal stimulus. In other words, there is evidence, albeit tenuous, to indicate that there may be a visual mechanism involving lateral inhibitory effects which operates to maintain lightness constancy. One wonders whether there might not be analogous neural interactions in the visual system which serve to resolve perceptually the ambiguous projections at the eye of spatial properties and so maintain space and motion constancy. Considering the biological significance of perceptual resolution and constancy such a conjecture is not entirely unjustified.

In the natural daylight environment light is reflected by object surfaces which are illuminated by a single source, the sun. The luminance of the numerous surfaces of varying reflectance is the main source of information for illumination necessary to resolve perceptually the reflectance of a particular object surface. There is an analogy with perceptual resolution of object size. We saw earlier (Chapter 3) that distance information is provided in part by a retinal size gradient which derives from objects and features at increasing distance from the observer. It is the retinal projection of numerous environmental features of differing reflectance which provides the information for incident illumination. It seems reasonable to suggest that under natural environmental conditions it is object *reflectance* that the visual system is primarily adapted to resolve. In the laboratory it is possible to simulate these natural conditions by sources of controlled light transmittance. The use of transparencies and neutral density filters through which light of known intensity can be projected to the eye gives much the same effects as surfaces of different reflectance. The perceptual effect of transmitted light is referred to as brightness to distinguish it from lightness, the perceptual correlate of reflected light. Both, however, give rise to constancy under the conditions discussed.

In recent years there have been numerous attempts to explain lightness and brightness constancy in terms of lightness and brightness contrast. The most parsimonious view would seem to be that constancy and contrast represent points on a continuum of perceptual effects determined by the information for incident illumination derived from the object background. If background is varied independently of the focal surface so lightness (or brightness) varies. If background reflectance is invariant while incident illumination changes, the perceived lightness (or brightness) of the object surface varies only slightly compared with the degree of change at the retina.

# Summary

Because the terms used in describing the physical and apparent properties of light tend to confuse, in the first part of this chapter definitions and terms, including definitions of lightness and brightness, are given together with units of measurement.

The intensity and wavelength of light reaching the eye from a surface are jointly determined by the intensity and wavelength of incident light on the surface, and by the reflecting properties of the surface itself. For this reason, the light at the eye varies as the incident light changes on a surface of constant reflectance. Lightness and colour constancy refer to the fact that the apparent lightness and colour of a surface is relatively stable as the light falling on it (and, therefore, on the eye) varies widely.

Experimental evidence suggests that lightness and colour constancy depend on the intensity and colour characteristics of surrounding surfaces, *i.e.,* the background to the particular surface which is judged. On the basis of information from the background judgments of lightness and colour correspond with physical reflectance (lightness and colour constancy) or fail to correspond (lightness and colour contrast or illusion). As with the apparent spatial properties of objects, there is a continuum of judgment of lightness and colour from perfect constancy to varying degrees of illusion.

In the final sections of this chapter on lightness and colour the mechanisms involved in and which control lightness constancy and contrast are discussed. Inhibitory processes in the nervous system may serve as a basis for both constancy and contrast and offer a clue to the basis of constancy and illusion in regard to spatial properties.

# 6. Perceptual Instability

COMMON features of the perceptual effects dealt with in Chapters 3, 4 and 5 are equivocality of the sensory representations of object properties and resolution of the representation to stability. Correspondence between apparent and objective size, shape, orientation, motion and lightness depends on the characteristics of the resolving information. Correspondence and non-correspondence between apparent and objective properties, effects commonly referred to as constancy and illusion respectively, constitute a continuum of stable perceptual outcomes. The point on this continuum of a particular judgment is determined by the resolving information. What is the perceptual outcome if information necessary for resolution of the equivocal sensory projection is either markedly reduced or completely eliminated? It is this question which will be taken up in the following pages.

There is a range of perceptual effects which are characterized by "reversals", "fluctuations" and "wanderings". For the most part these effects occur when the sensory projection of an object property is representative of more than a single external state of affairs and when resolving information is either absent or reduced so that the apparent shape, orientation, direction of movement and other properties fluctuate; *i.e.,* perceptual instability occurs.

"Assumptions" derived from prior experience play a major role in perception under stimulus conditions marked by reduced information for perceptual resolution. Although numerous instances of perceptual stability have aroused curiosity since the early years of experimental psychology, there has been no attempt to consider them in general terms. Each instance has been regarded as a problem in itself and investigated without regard for others. This piecemeal approach to the problem of perceptual instability has not only tended to obscure issues but has led to a degree of confusion.

## Perceptual Instability and Static Space

### OBJECT AND FIGURE INSTABILITY

Although objects have three dimensions they project a two-dimensional representation at the retina of the eye. For the most part retinal disparity between right and left images, motion parallax, ocular convergence-accommodation, and characteristics of the image itself (overlay, size gradients) provide information for the relative distance or depth of the object parts (Chapter 3). Under certain conditions, however, these sources of depth information are absent.

## Object Fluctuation

In Fig. 6.1 is shown an object in the form of a truncated pyramid constructed of thin wire. If the object is placed large base down and viewed with one eye from a point vertically above the centre of the base its retinal image will be that shown in Fig. 6.1. Turned upside down so that the smaller end rests on the table and again viewed monocularly from a point directly above, the retinal representation will also be as shown in Fig. 6.1. If viewing distance is such that slight discrepancies between the images due to differences in the distances of object parts are slight, the two orientations of the object (large base near, large base far) project the same retinal image. This would apply if the objects were constructed of thin metal or cardboard and evenly illuminated.

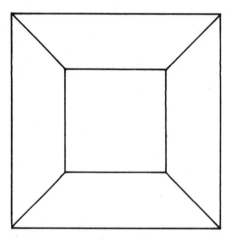

**Figure. 6.1** Plan view of a truncated pyramid; the image at the eye is the same whether the pyramid is viewed with large square near or small square near.

When viewed binocularly from a few feet above, the object shown in Fig. 6.1 is perceptually stable and the observer correctly judges its depth features. But when viewed monocularly the observer judges it part of the time with large base near and part of the time with small base near regardless of its true depth characteristics. Perceptually, the object alternates or fluctuates between the two. Such variation in the apparent depth relations of the object is an instance of perceptual instability. With binocular vision, retinal disparity is presumably a source of information for the relative distances of the large and small base, but with monocular vision there is no such basis for distance discrimination. In the absence of information for relative depth the object is judged as alternating between the two depth relations of which its retinal projections are equally representative.

There are numerous classes of object with depth characteristics such that when placed in one orientation they cast the same retinal image as another object in a different orientation. During a period of monocular inspection they are reported as fluctuating between an object with certain depth relationships in one orientation and another object with different depth relationships in a second orientation. If a piece of cardboard about 3 × 2 in is folded to a V-shape about its centre, placed on a table and viewed with one eye, apparent reversals occur. The bent card is reported either as a V with the centre ridge near lying flat on the table or a V with the ridge far standing on end but tilted backward. It can be shown by projective drawing that two objects, one with its apex near and the other with apex far, placed flat and on end respectively give rise to the same projection on a plane. As the depth relationships, V apex near and far, fluctuate so must the card's apparent orientation. Sanford in his book *Experimental Psychology* (1897) referred to this perceptual instability of a V-shaped object.

For the most part, information for the resolution of equivocal sensory projections is available simultaneously with the equivocal image itself. This is the case with size at a distance, shape at a slant and orientation at a body tilt. In the cases of the bent card and the object shown in Fig. 6.1 there is little or no information for depth when they are viewed with one eye. The result of this reduction in, or elimination of, resolving information for object depth is fluctuation from one set of depth characteristics to the other, so that perceived object orientation must also fluctuate.

### Figure Fluctuation

The identical two-dimensional representation which occurs at the eye for two or more combinations of depth features and of orientations can be projected on to surfaces other than the retina of the eye. The retinal image of a two-dimensional projection of a three-dimensional object is essentially the same as the retinal projection of the three-dimensional object itself. It would be expected, therefore, that if the identical projection of an object in two or more orientations relative to the observer were first presented on a surface, this two-dimensional version would also exhibit fluctuations. Drawings representing three-dimensional objects in more than one orientation do exhibit instability. Because the drawings have no objective depth and do not, therefore, give rise to retinal disparity, fluctuations occur with both binocular and monocular viewing.

Fluctuations of plane projections of three-dimensional objects are among the earliest investigated phenomena in experimental psychology. In 1832 Necker, a Swiss naturalist, described the apparent reversals in perspective or orientation of a diagram of rhomboid crystal (Fig. 6.2) and, in 1858, Schroeder remarked on the same effect with a projective drawing of a staircase (Fig. 6.2). From time to time other figures have been used such as the Mach "book" and a tube composed of rings, both of which are shown in Fig. 6.2. With all these drawings apparent reversals or fluctuations of orientation occur during an observation period. It can be noted that if the objects shown as plane projections in Fig. 6.2 are constructed as three-dimensional models, oriented as shown, and observed monocularly, they are also reported as fluctuating between the orientations which their retinal projections represent.

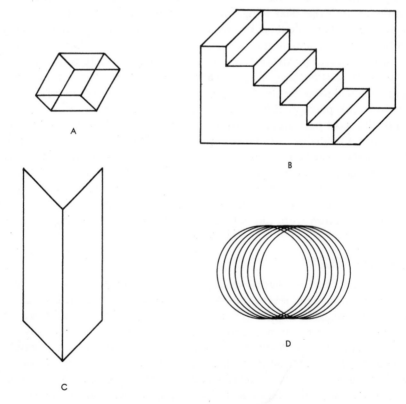

**Figure 6.2** Typical unstable figures which undergo apparent reversals or fluctuations. *A* Necker rhomboid. *B* Schroeder staircase. *C* Mach book. *D* Interlacing circles forming a cylinder. The four figures also exhibit reversals from one apparent orientation to another if they are presented as three-dimensional models and viewed monocularly.

## Basis of Object and Figure Fluctuations

Two main issues concerning object and figure fluctuations deserve further consideration. The first concerns the determinants of rate of reversal from one orientation to the other and the second stabilization of a perceptually unstable stimulus. While there is now a considerable body of data relating to the first there is very little concerned with the second issue.

Rate of reversal has been studied as a function of a variety of figure and subject variables using versions of a cube projection. This figure is commonly referred to as the "Necker" cube although Necker himself did not comment on it. Figure characteristics such as width of lines, length of diagonals (*i.e.,* "depth") and size do not have any marked effect on rate of reversal from one apparent depth relationship to the other. Orientation of the figure to the left or right does, however, affect reversal rate slightly. Over a period of viewing the cube figure there is an initial increase in rate of reversal which gradually falls off to give a negatively accelerated function.

Necker himself originally suggested that the point on the figure fixated by the observer is a factor in determining whether it is judged to have one or the other apparent depth. Accordingly there has been interest in the role of eye movements in the apparent reversal from one to the other. As the eyes move the point of fixation on the figure changes. Recent studies have demonstrated conclusively that eye movement is not a major source of figural fluctuations. Pheiffer and his associates in 1956 recorded both eye movements and times of reported reversals and showed that eye movements tended to *follow* rather than precede reversals. Perhaps more convincingly Pritchard in 1958 stabilized the retinal image (see Fig. 1.6) so that there was no movement of the image relative to the retina and found that apparent reversals of depth still occurred.

The question of what causes the reversal of apparent depth with a perceptually unstable figure will be considered further below. At this point it is worthwhile considering possible ways in which stabilization of the object or figure might be achieved. With three-dimensional objects and binocular vision apparent reversals of depth are infrequent. Presumably information for the relative depth of the object parts is provided by retinal disparity (Chapter 3). It is likely, therefore, that the object or its plane projection would be perceptually stabilized by other sources of depth information.

In Fig. 6.3 are shown versions of the Mach figure with a size gradient consonant with two depth relationships. So far data on the rate of reversal of this and the Schroeder figure are incomplete but it seems that reversal rate is markedly diminished. The figure is judged to have depth characteristics according with the gradient for a substantially longer period than for the alternative characteristics. Experiments by the author and associates have confirmed that perceptual stabilization occurs when information for depth as in Fig. 6.3 is provided.

It can be expected that resolving information for depth in the form of texture gradients shown in Fig. 6.3 will serve to stabilize the depth characteristics of objects as well as their two-dimensional figural equivalents. If the depth information is in accord with the true depth of the object, then presumably apparent and true depths would be in agreement. If the information provided by information such as surface gradients and overlay were opposed to that normally available from the particular depth characteristic of the object then apparent and objective would be in disagreement. The constancy-illusion continuum probably applies equally to judged object depth as to the classical constancy-illusion stimulus patterns.

**Figure 6.3** Stabilization of Mach book. Both apparent depth and orientation are stabilized by adding texture corresponding to central ridge near (left) or far (right) compared with the unstable figure in the centre.

In summary, certain combinations of object depth characteristics and orientations result in identical or near-identical sensory images. In the absence of information for depth the apparent depth and orientation of such objects fluctuate perceptually between the combinations which their sensory projections represent. Essentially the same perceptual instability is observable in line drawings which are plane projections of the equivocal combinations of object depth and orientation. They would be perceptually resolved in terms of their objective orientation (constancy) or opposite to it (illusion). So far this point has not been thoroughly checked experimentally. In short, information for depth relations stabilizes this property and since two or more depth relations and two or more orientations project the same image at the eye, information for depth determines apparent orientation.

## DEPTH AT A DISTANCE

Environmental features are seldom flat and even. For the most part they include undulations, depressions, protuberances, holes and cavities. For example, a rock at a distance of 100 yards may include surface irregularities such as bumps, cavities and folds. At the eye these surface features occur as luminance gradients, the direction of the gradient depending on the position of the light source relative to the feature. In certain instances the representation of the object feature is equivocal since both a surface protuberance and a depression can result in nearly the same retinal illuminance gradient. This state of affairs is shown in Fig. 6.4. A circular protuberance illuminated from the left results in a similar pattern of light as a depression illuminated from the right. In isolation such a pattern exhibits similar perceptual instability to that associated with the objects and figures discussed in the last section.

There are remarkably few experimental data on the perceptual resolution of surface features represented at the eye by ambiguous gradients or patterns of light. If, as in Fig. 6.4, the feature is a rounded protuberance illuminated from the left, information for the direction from which the light derives should serve to stabilize the equivocal projection. It can be predicted, therefore, that a gradient of luminance across the surface from light on the left to dim on the right would resolve the image as a protuberance. A similar gradient running from right to left would be expected to resolve the ambiguous projection of the feature as a depression in the surface. Recent experiments by the author and associates have tended to confirm that perceptual stabilization of the direction of depth (protuberance or depression) is achieved by means of a gradient of the sort shown in Fig. 6.4 B and C. In the absence of a gradient, however, there is evidence to suggest that the assumption that the source of light is above determines whether or not the ambiguous pattern is judged as a protuberance or a depression. This effect can be observed in Fig. 6.7. If the book is right side up the circular areas appear as depressions, a judgment which accords with the assumption that light is above the pattern. When the book is turned upside down, however, the same areas appear as depressions, again in agreement with the assumption that the light source is above*. The role of such assumptions based on prior learning will be examined in further detail in Chapter 8.

# Perceptual Instability of Motion

In Chapter 4 it was shown that the stimulus correlates of the occurrence, direction, and velocity of object motion are by themselves equivocal and additional sensory information is necessary for their resolution. In essentially the same fashion as with static objects and figures, where apparent depths and orientations are unstable without the necessary resolving information, both the direction and occurrence of movement are unstable under certain conditions.

---

*Burns, R. Shadow-gradient Invarience in the Monocular Perception of Depth. Unpublished MSc thesis, Monash University, 1968.

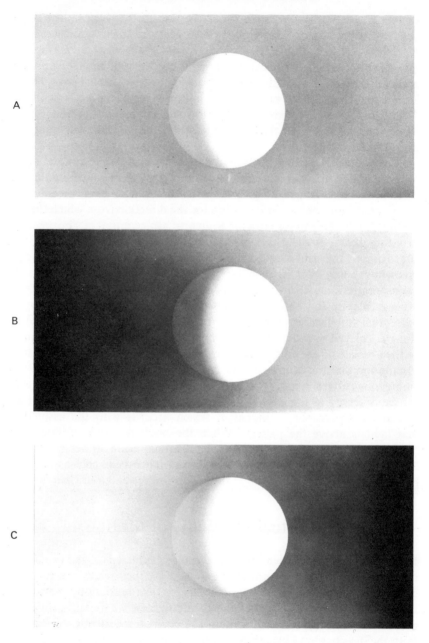

**Figure 6.4** Perceptual resolution of depth by direction of light gradient. In *A*, the pattern fluctuates between a protuberance and a depression. In *B*, the direction of the gradient stabilizes the pattern as a protuberance, and in *C*, as a depression.

## INSTABILITY OF MOTION DIRECTION

### Object Motion Fluctuation

Consider an object like that shown in Fig. 6.1, mounted on a vertical rod so that it can be rotated in depth relative to the observer. Let us assume that the small base is initially near and fronto-parallel to the observer. If now with binocular viewing the object is rotated clockwise, the retinal image of the near base will move left and that of the far base right. The observer will report clockwise rotation. But if the object is viewed monocularly a perceptual reversal is likely to occur so that the small base (which is near) seems far and the large base (which is far) seems near. When rotated clockwise while apparently reversed, the object will be judged as rotating counterclockwise. This must be the outcome since the far base which is apparently near is moving right and the near base which is apparently far is moving left. Movement of a near side of a three-dimensional object to the right occurs when an object moves counterclockwise. Since the far side is *judged* near and moves *right* the object must be judged in counterclockwise motion even though it is rotating clockwise.

Apparent reversals in the direction of rotary motion with objects of the class shown in Fig. 6.1 are a necessary perceptual consequence of reversal in depth. The retinal motion pattern of a near part of the object moving clockwise is identical with that of a far part of the figure moving counter-clockwise. If, in the absence of information for relative depth (*e.g.,* overlay, size gradients, retinal disparity), a perceptual reversal occurs in relative nearness and farness, the apparent direction of rotary motion must also change. Skeletal objects such as that shown in Fig. 6.1 do not project sensory information for the relative depth of their various parts. As a result they are perceived as unstable and fluctuating from one depth relationship to another. The outcome of this instability of depth while they are in motion is apparent reversal in direction of movement.

Much less data has been collected in connection with fluctuations in apparent direction of motion than with fluctuations in apparent orientation using stationary objects. What data exist are concerned mainly with the causes of reversals rather than with the nature of the sensory information necessary to stabilize perceptually motion direction. Using a skeletal cube mounted and rotating about one corner, Howard in 1961 conducted a series of observations intended to throw some light on the processes involved in reversals. But apart from the finding that binocular viewing involving retinal disparity information for depth results in a reduction in reversals no experiments have examined the effects of overlay (an obvious source of depth information with skeletal objects), size gradients, or other retinal information for depth. Overlay could be enhanced by painting near and far parts of a skeletal object in different colours.

In summary, the retinal stimulus for motion direction is ambiguous in that a far part of the object moving clockwise projects the same motion pattern as a near part moving counterclockwise. In the absence of information which resolves object depth, apparent depth fluctuations and motion direction reverses. The situation is similar in principle to object depth and orientation. An object with certain depth characteristics in one orientation projects the same visual image as an object with different depth characteristics in another orientation. If apparent depth fluctuates so does orientation.

### Figure Motion: The Kinetic Depth Effect

Since actual three-dimensional objects whose depth information is either reduced or absent exhibit apparent reversals of movement direction, it is to be expected that, like static objects, their two-dimensional projections will give rise to similar perceptual instability. Such effects with the plane projections of objects moving in depth do occur, being variously known as stereokinetic phenomena and kinetic depth effects.

A detailed introspective account of these effects was given by Metzger in 1934. Metzger arranged upright rods on a horizontal rotating turntable (similar to a phonograph turntable) which in turn was placed between a light source and a translucent screen. The observer viewed the moving shadows of the rotating upright rods from the opposite side of the translucent screen. The plane projection of rotary motion is a sine function so that the velocity of the rods' projection is greatest at one point in their path, falling off in a sine function. This motion pattern is nearly identical with that of the rods' retinal images without the screen. It is not surprising, therefore, that the shadows were occasionally reported as moving in depth (since their two-dimensional motion patterns were the same as those of the retinal image of a rotating object) and reversing their apparent direction of motion. The apparent reversals of motion direction derive from the fact that the retinal projection of clockwise motion in depth is nearly identical with counterclockwise motion (Fig. 4.2). Like two-dimensional stationary objects which are representative of three-dimensional objects, two-dimensional moving patterns with the same motion characteristics as the retinal projection of an object moving in depth are judged as having depth characteristics. Since, however, the pattern is equally representative of two directions of motion, perception of direction is unstable, the pattern giving rise to frequent reversals of motion.

If the projection of three-dimensional motion on a surface is non-ambiguous in that it is representative of but one direction in depth, it will still be judged as three-dimensional motion but reversals will be infrequent or absent. Many of the kinetic depth phenomena reported in recent years and reviewed in detail by Braunstein in 1962 are of this class. The resolving information for motion direction in depth can be present in a two-dimensional projection of three-dimensional motion, as is frequently the case with the retinal projection of motion. The only essential effect of projecting the motion onto a screen before it is projected to the eye is that it is first rendered in a two-dimensional form. All the characteristics of motion as they occur in the retinal image are retained.

The characteristics of motion in depth can be produced as two-dimensional projections by various means other than placing the moving object between a light source and a screen. One method is that of connecting oscillators to the vertical and horizontal inputs of an oscilloscope and adjusting the frequencies of oscillation in simple numerical ratios. The result is an effect called Lissajous patterns, which by slight mistuning are judged as moving in depth, such as apparent rotation about vertical or horizontal axes. Not only does the apparent direction of rotation in depth of these figures vary but also the direction of the axes about which they appear to move.

Two-dimensional projections of motion in depth, however produced, are frequently (but not invariably) ambiguous in terms of their direction or axes of movement. A single pattern may be equally representative of two or more directions of motion or two or more motion axes. In consequence, and in the absence of the necessary resolving information for these qualities, perceptual instability characterized by apparent reversals occurs. The basis of such instability is essentially the same as that of shape and orientation in depth for stationary projections.

## INSTABILITY OF MOTION OCCURRENCE: AUTOKINETIC EFFECTS

The visual correlate of object motion, like those of orientation, size, and lightness is equivocal, since a movement of the retinal image is jointly determined by both observer (body, head, eyes) and object movement. In Chapter 4 it was noted that in the absence of a visible surround or background, information for body, head and probably eye, movement is necessary to resolve the motion (including the stationariness) of an object. With a visible field the stationary environment is the basis of the perceptual resolution of movement. In both situations illusions of movement occur if the resolving information is manipulated by centrifuging the observer in darkness (oculogyral effect) or by moving the visual field (induced movement). It was also noted in Chapter 4 that judgments of velocity are dependent upon information for observer-object distance. What is the perceptual outcome if resolving information for object movement (including the limiting case of object stationariness) is reduced or eliminated?

### Visual Autokinetic Effect

Information for the occurrence of object movement is supplied in part by the extensive stationary visual field of the observer. A slight movement occurs against a background of stationary features. An object is stationary in relation to an extended stationary surround. What then is the perceptual outcome if this visual information for object movement and stationariness is eliminated? Such a state of affairs can be simply achieved by arranging a single dim light in an otherwise completely darkened environment.

In 1799 the astronomer Von Humboldt reported apparent movement of a stationary point of light in the dark, an effect which Aubert in 1887 called the autokinetic effect or autokinesis. Since these early reports a vast body of research on autokinetic phenomena has been published. In considering the various data and theories of visual autokinesis one salient point should be emphasized; autokinetic movement occurs in the absence of a structural visual surround. In a well-lighted environment with other objects and features in the field of view, a stationary object is judged as stationary. It is only when this structural visual surround is severely reduced or eliminated that apparent motion of the object is reported by an observer.

Experiments concerned with visual autokinesis have concentrated largely on two problems; the possible involvement of eye movements and the ocular muscles in the effect, and the effect of various object and surround properties. Since autokinetic movement poses many problems in accurate recording and measurement, considerable effort has been devoted to the development of acceptable techniques for its observation.

In phenomenal terms visual autokinesis takes the form of what seems to be random wandering of the object, usually a dim light, after an initial period of stationariness called the latency period. Now, since the stationary surround of an object serves to render an object in space perceptually stable, and since the eyes tremble and drift even when fixated, eye movement would seem an obvious explanation of visual autokinesis. As the eyes drift in the largely dark environment, the retinal projection of a stationary object moves. Evidence supporting this obvious explanation is, however, very mixed indeed. Various psychophysical and physiological techniques have been developed for the recording of eye movements. Not infrequently there is little relationship between the direction of apparent movement and that of eye movement. On the other hand, some recent experiments suggest that ocular motion may be involved to some degree. For example, Matin and MacKinnon in an elegant experiment in 1964 showed that if the retinal image is stabilized so that it remains stationary on the retina with horizontal eye movements, apparent horizontal movement is reduced. There is also evidence to suggest that both the onset and direction of autokinetic movement are related to eye movements.

Since the stationary visual field is a source of information for object movement (including object stationariness), the gradual provision of this information should decrease the amount of apparent movement of a stationary point. If the number of visible elements in the visual field is increased the extent of movement does generally decrease. In broad terms, autokinetic movement of a point is reduced by information from the stationary surround.

It has been noted (Chapter 5) that information for head and body movement is involved in the perceptual resolution of object movement. If this information is falsified by rotating the observer in a centrifuge, a point of light which remains in a fixed location relative to the observer undergoes apparent movement. If, in addition to visual field information, that for head and body were also reduced or eliminated, the extent of autokinetic movement would be expected to increase. Defects of the semicircular canals and other labyrinthine structures 'frequently occur following certain diseases such as meningitis. Since the semicircular canals are critically involved in signalling head and body movement, such individuals would be expected to report greater extents of autokinetic motion. In 1962 Miller and Graybiel measured the extent of autokinetic movement for nine observers with defects of the labyrinthine systems and compared these measures with those of nine normal observers. A typical result is shown in Fig. 6.5. The extent of movement reported by those observers with defective labyrinthine systems is substantially greater than the normal observers.

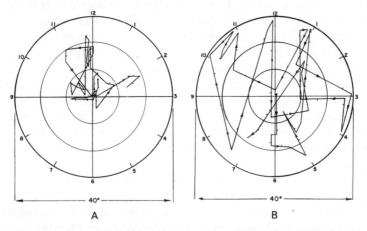

**Figure 6.5** Extent of apparent movement of a stationary point of light in the dark (autokinetic movement) reported by a normal (*A*) and labyrinthine defective (*B*) observer. (From E.F. Miller and A. Graybiel, Comparison of autokinetic movement perceived by normal persons and deaf subjects with bilateral labyrinthine defects. In *Aerospace Med.*, 1962, 33, 1077–1080. By courtesy of *J. of Aerospace Med.*)

Beginning with observations made by Charpentier in 1886, it has often been suggested that autokinetic movement is associated with muscle strain. If the muscles controlling the movements of the eye are strained in one direction, apparent movement of a stationary point might be expected to occur. This aspect of visual autokinesis, however, fits more properly into perceptual effects associated with sensory adaptation and aftereffects, which will be taken up in Chapter 7.

### Auditory and Tactile Autokinesis

In 1937 Kleint described perceptual instability of the spatial location of an auditory source and points of stimulation on the skin. Since this early report, very few investigations of the determinants and characteristics of these non-visual autokinetic effects have been undertaken. The occurrence of auditory and tactile autokinesis is important in demonstrating that perceptual instability of object position and movement cannot be fully explained in terms of mechanisms and processes associated with the visual system alone.

## Perceptual Instability and Learning: Assumptions, Set and Instructions

The perceptual resolution of ambiguous sensory projections of external objects and events does not necessarily depend upon information inherent in the total stimulus. So far, however, we have considered only those situations in which resolving information for such properties as object size, shape and lightness occurs simultaneously with the projection of the object property itself. Resolving information may be carried over or "stored" from prior experience and thus play a role in resolving stimulus equivocalities. In so far as the individual's perceptual behaviour is modified by previous events, we can refer to *learned* perceptual resolution. The involvement of prior experience in perceptual resolution is particularly marked in the type of situation which has been considered in the last few sections, situations in which information is not immediately available from the total stimulus complex.

The effect of past experience on the perceptual resolution of equivocal stimuli has been variously attributed to assumptions, expectancies or "sets" which the prior experience is said to invoke. In general terms, prior experience may be experimentally controlled by subjecting the observer to certain conditions prior to the presentation of an unstable stimulus of the classes discussed above, or invoked through instructions. Instructions, like experimentally controlled conditions, serve to "tune" or prepare the observer to respond in a particular way to equivocal stimulation.

The role of prior experience can be seen in visual autokinesis. For example, if prior to observing the stationary point of light in a dark room the observer is shown a light which is actually moving, stationary light is judged to move in a similar path to the previously-viewed moving light.

Again, if instead of a light the stationary object is in the form of an object which normally moves, such as an arrow, a running animal, or a moving vehicle, the direction of autokinetic movement conforms with the expected direction of movement for such objects. An object in the form of an arrow is judged to move in the direction of the arrow-head and a running animal in the direction of depicted movement. In a now well-known series of experiments Sherif, in 1935, demonstrated that social factors considerably affect the extent of autokinetic movement. If other observers were in the room and called out the extent of judged movement after an exposure of the light, the judgments of a particular observer tended to agree more and more closely with those of the group.

The sensory projection of a point of light in a featureless field is ambiguous, since any motion is a joint function of observer and object movement. There is no visual surround in terms of which object movement may be resolved. For this reason prior experience, whether introduced in a controlled manner or deriving from the back-log of the observer's experiences of moving objects, has a considerable effect on perceptual resolution. Furthermore, it is likely that such prior experience considerably affects other unstable stimuli such as the Mach "book", Schroeder staircase, and Necker rhomboid. It would be of considerable interest to establish whether presentation of an actual staircase (or its obverse in the form of a structure projecting out from a wall with steps upside down) prior to presentation of the line drawing (Fig. 6.2) determines the amount of time the figure is perceived with one depth relationship or the other. Alternatively, the Mach book figure (Fig. 6.2) is the projection of a three-dimensional object with centre ridge near and the same object with centre ridge far in a different orientation. Would the presentation of an actual three-dimensional object in a particular orientation and with centre ridge, say, near, determine how the line figure would be judged when presented subsequently? Such prior exposure would probably have a marked effect.

In Fig. 6.6 is a slightly different class of figure which, as can be seen, is equally representative of a human profile and of a rat. Alampay and Bugelski in a clever experiment in 1961 presented this figure to observers after they had viewed a series of pictures of either human or animal figures. Those observers who had previously viewed human figures tended on the whole to judge Fig. 6.6 as a profiile of a man and those who had previously seen animal drawings judged it to be a rat. The ambiguity was resolved in terms of immediately prior experience. It seems likely that the presentation of a three-dimensional object with certain depth characteristics and in a certain orientation would have a determining effect on judgments of ambiguous and perceptually unstable line drawings. But this has yet to be put to an experimental test.

It is reasonable to suppose that most human observers are much more

**Figure 6.6** An ambiguous figure; the figure fluctuates between the appearance of a rat and a human profile. (From B.R. Bugelski and D.A. Alampay, The rule of frequency in developing perceptual sets. In *Canad. J. Psychol.*, 1961, 15, 206–212. By courtesy of B.R. Bugelski.)

familiar with staircases than with the upside down stairs of which the Schroeder figure (Fig. 6.2) is equally representative. That is, observers have probably been exposed to one situation far more frequently than the other. It is likely, therefore, that when shown the Schroeder figure they will report it as a staircase more frequently and for larger periods than they will the obverse structure which is relatively uncommon. As already pointed out, the tendency to judge a pattern as a hollow or a protuberance when the pattern is turned upside down (Fig. 6.7) is probably due to expectancies concerning the direction from which light normally falls, *i.e.,* from above. In Fig. 6.7 the pattern is ambiguous in the absence of a light gradient as in Fig. 6.4. Unfortunately, little or no attention has been given to the role of uncontrolled prior stimulation in determining either reversal rate or time of reporting certain depth relationships with unstable figures or objects.

The problem of perceptual instability can be summarized in the following way. There are numerous static and moving stimulus conditions in which the ambiguous sensory projection of object properties occur in the absence of resolving information. For this reason the projection is perceptually unstable and, in the case of various objects and figures, fluctuations occur between the various objects of which the projection is representative. Prior experience in the form of either experimentally controlled or chance exposures to certain objects and situations play a significant role in determining the perceptual outcome when resolving information is reduced or absent. The effects of experience are often referred to as assumptions, expectancies or sets.

Finally, it should not be thought that prior experience plays a part in resolving the equivocal sensory image only when resolving information is absent or reduced. As will be seen in Chapter 8, past experience also exerts an effect when information is available. The effect of learning is merely greater when there are no other means of perceptually coping with an ambiguous state of affairs.

**Figure 6.7** Telescopic view of moon craters; when the photograph is inverted the craters appear as hillocks. (Photograph from the Mount Wilson and Palomar Observatories.)

# Summary

Numerous perceptual effects are characterized by instability; apparent reversals and fluctuations in the perceived properties of objects. Reversals occur in the apparent depth of two and three-dimensional figures and objects. The basis of this instability seems to be the absence of information for depth. Since the retinal image of the figure or object is equally representative of two more objects with different depth characteristics in different orientations, and since there is no information for depth, the perceptual outcome is one of fluctuation between the depths and orientations which the retinal image represents.

Similar instability characterized by reversals occurs in the direction of movement of figures and objects. The retinal image equally represents two depth relationships in the figure or object and two directions of movement. In the absence of information for depth, fluctuations in apparent depth and apparent motion direction occur.

A point of light in the dark appears to wander, an effect called visual autokinesis. Since movement (including stationariness) occurs in relation to a usually stationary background, absence of background renders the retinal image of the point of light ambiguous; it sometimes appears to move.

Fluctuations in apparent depth and orientation can be reduced or eliminated by providing depth information. Similarly, fluctuations and reversals of motion direction can be eliminated by appropriate depth information. Autokinesis does not occur when the background is visible.

Perceptual instability is due to the reduction in or absence of information necessary to resolve perceptually an object property. Provision of this information renders the effect stable. Past experience plays an important role in the perception of unstable figures and objects.

# 7.  Perceptual Adaptation and Aftereffect

IN CHAPTER 1 it was noted that, during the course of constant stimulation, "washing out" of visual and tactile sensations and progressive increases in detection thresholds occur. A steadily-fixated point disappears if its retinal image is stabilized, and slight pressure on the skin is no longer detectable after a minute or so. These changes correlated with diminution in the frequency of impulses generated in the nervous system are aspects of a general phenomenon consequent upon stimulation called sensory or perceptual adaptation. The terms perceptual adaptation and perceptual aftereffect refer to different procedures for revealing the same process. While adaptation is said to occur when judgments of a particular stimulus change over time, aftereffect refers to changes in the judgment of one stimulus following stimulation by another. Continuous stimulation not only affects judgments of that stimulus but also other values of it.

Adaptation and aftereffect can be observed in relation to such properties as intensity, wavelength, tonal frequency, taste, smell qualities and spatial features including size, shape, and direction. Under certain conditions, moreover, stimulation of one sensory system may result in changes in judgments associated with another. In general terms, adaptation and aftereffect are characteristic of all sensory systems in relation to judgments of most properties of stimulation. In this chapter greater emphasis will be given to adaptation in relation to spatial features, after a brief review of adaptation to stimulus intensity and certain qualities such as colour and tonal frequency.

## Adaptation and Aftereffect involving Intensity and Quality

Stimuli deriving from external or internal situations vary in intensity, the amount of energy, and in respect of wavelength, frequency and chemical composition. Perception of these features, which takes the form of brightness, loudness, colour, pitch and taste judgments, exhibits adaptive change and aftereffect with continuing stimulation.

**Figure 7.2**  Perceptual adaptation and aftereffect with colour. Place a half-inch circular aperture in a sheet of grey paper over the red square so that the cross is centralized, and stare steadily at the cross for about a minute. On removal of the paper while still regarding the cross, the central area of the red square will appear as "faded" or less saturated (chromatic adaptation). Repeat the procedure but after removal of the paper regard the centre of the green square and note change in colour of central area compared with surround (chromatic aftereffect). Repeat procedure fixating the blue square after staring at the red through the aperture.

described, the observer continues to fixate the point (which would need to be dim and luminous) in darkness, there is a progressive recovery from the adaptive effects of prior stimulation. The recovery function could be established by introducing standard and variable together at certain intervals over a 2 or 3 minute period and requiring the observer to make brightness matches as before.

The effects of stimulation on apparent intensity (brightness) and colour (hue) are inseparable. During a stimulation period both brightness and hue undergo progressive change. Colour adaptation can be clearly demonstrated using Fig. 7.2. Punch a hole about $\frac{1}{2}$ in in diameter in a sheet of preferably mid-grey paper large enough to cover the page of this book. Place the aperture over the red patch in Fig. 7.2. so that the small fixation cross is centred. Fixate the cross steadily for about 1 minute. Quickly remove the grey paper by sliding it away but continue to regard the cross. It will be noticed that the centre area of the red patch, the part which has been exposed through the $\frac{1}{2}$ in hole, is duller, more "washed-out" or greyer than the part surrounding it. This change in the judged or apparent colour of the red patch is an instance of colour adaptation. Repeat the same procedure but this time on removing the grey paper fixate successively the green and blue patches. It will be noticed that the area at the centre of each patch is of a different hue to the surrounding colour. Stimulation by red has resulted in changes in the apparent colours of the green and blue. This is a colour or chromatic aftereffect.

If the procedures were better controlled and the observer manipulated a patch of variable wavelength, composition, and intensity to match a standard at intervals after the onset of stimulation, a functional relationship somewhat similar to that in Fig. 7.1 would be obtained. The change in hue is at first rapid and then declines. Likewise, there is an initial rapid rate of recovery followed by a slowing down to a steady state after removal of the stimulus.

Changes in judged intensity with continued visual stimulation are associated with reduction in the frequency of impulses generated in the nervous system. In the case of chromatic adaptation it would be reasonable to assume that, at the level of the retina itself, neurophysiological changes are associated with those receptors and mechanisms specific to certain wavelengths. When the mechanisms sensitive mainly in the red range adapt, those sensitive in the green and blue ranges determine to a greater degree the judged colour.

## AUDITORY ADAPTATION OF LOUDNESS AND PITCH

In studying auditory adaptation it is possible to induce adaptation of one ear by continuous stimulation with either white noise or pure tones, and to match both loudness and pitch at intervals using the other non-adapted ear. Although with the most efficient head-phones, some sound is transmitted to the other ear through bone conduction, the use of one ear for stimulation and the other for matching gives a reasonably clear indication of the course of adaptation and recovery from it.

The elevation of the auditory detection threshold, and the decrease in loudness of a sound with continuous stimulation are variously called adaptation, stimulation deafness, residual masking, temporary hearing loss and auditory fatigue. The term stimulation deafness is usually confined to long-term or permanent effects following very prolonged stimulation of a sort occasioned by industrial noise.

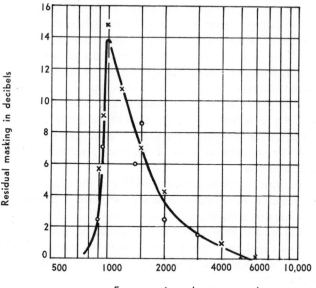

Frequency in cycles per second

**Figure 7.3** Auditory adaptation. The effect produced by a 1000 cps tone is maximal when the test tone is the same frequency (1000 cps) as the adapting tone and falls off in effectiveness for test tones of greater and less frequency. (Adapted from W.A. Munson and M.B. Gardner, Loudness patterns: a new approach. In *J.Acoust. Soc. Amer.*, 1950, 22, 177–190. By courtesy of *J. Acoust. Soc. Amer.*)

Both stimulus intensity and duration affect the degree of auditory adaptation. In general, auditory adaptation occurs with stimulus frequencies above about 1000 cps. The effect of one tonal frequency on another is determined mainly by the separation between the frequency of the stimulating tone and that of the test tone. In Fig. 7.3 is shown the change in *loudness* of tones between 500 and 6000 cps produced by a tone of 1000 cps at a level of 70 decibels. The aftereffect is greatest for a test tone of the same frequency as the stimulating tone and least for those test tones whose frequencies differ most from the stimulating tone.

Essentially similar adaptive and aftereffect phenomena can be observed in connection with intensity and stimulus qualities for other sensory systems. Apparent pressure on the skin changes progressively during constant stimulation. A substance is judged to taste different after a sweet than after a sour solution. A thermal aftereffect can be easily and effectively demonstrated by placing one finger in hot water and the other in cold for about a minute. When both fingers are removed and placed together in warm water the apparent water temperature is greater for the finger previously in cold water.

During prolonged and continuous stimulation, changes occur in the functioning of sensory systems with consequent perceptual effects. The general effects are probably due to inhibitory processes similar to those associated with contrast phenomena. So far, however, it is not possible to state with any precision the nature of the inhibitory processes accompanying extended stimulation.

# Spatial Adaptation and Aftereffect

Verhoeff, in 1902, reported that if a bent line similar to that shown in Fig. 7.4 is fixated for 2 or 3 minutes at the apex and the gaze then shifted to the mid-point of a straight line (Fig. 7.4) the latter is judged to be bent slightly in the opposite direction. The apparent position of the contours of the figures undergoes change during the course of stimulation so that the bent lines appear progressively less bent; when the gaze is shifted to an objectively straight line it appears bent the opposite way. The first effect is called spatial adaptation and the second has been variously referred to as negative, figural and spatial aftereffect. The terms spatial adaptation and spatial aftereffect are the most appropriate since the effect involves the apparent spatial properties of stimulation and is characteristic of the auditory, tactile and kinesthetic systems, where the term "figural" is less applicable than it is in vision.

## VISUAL SPATIAL ADAPTATION AND AFTEREFFECT

Following the early report of a change in apparent direction of lines with prolonged visual stimulation by Verhoeff, two major studies, one by Gibson in the 1930s and another by Köhler and Wallach in 1944, extended the range of observations and established some of the major determinants of the effects.

Gibson first observed adaptation and aftereffect using a prism which when placed over the eye resulted in straight edges of doors, walls, windows etc. appearing curved. This curvature occurred as a result of the refractive properties of the prism. When the prism was removed straight edges seemed to be slightly curved in the opposite direction. Later Gibson dispensed

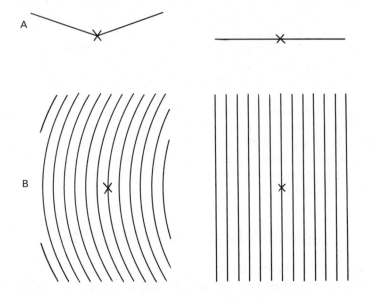

**Figure 7.4** Perceptual spatial adaptation and aftereffect. *A* Pattern similar to that used by Verhoeff to demonstrate a spatial aftereffect. Prolonged fixation of cross in left figure results in the right appearing bent in opposite direction to the first. *B* Pattern similar to those used by Gibson. Prolonged fixation of cross at centre of the left figure results in straight lines on right appearing curved in opposite direction.

with a prism and used instead a field of curved lines essentially similar to that in Fig. 7.4. Following prolonged inspection of this field a series of straight lines falling on the same area of the retina as that previously stimulated by the curved field appeared curved in the opposite direction. Similar effects occur with tilted and bent lines as inducing patterns.

Köhler and Wallach, in addition to observing similar effects with bent and curved lines, found that contours were displaced from the site of previously-presented contours. Typical inducing and test objects used by Köhler and Wallach are shown in Fig. 7.5.

The standard procedure for the measurement of spatial adaptation and aftereffect involves a judgment by the observer prior to stimulation (pre-test), a period of stimulation, and a judgment following stimulation (post-test). The difference between pre and post-tests, which are made under identical conditions, serves as a measure of the adaptive phenomenon. Among the factors which affect the magnitude of the visual spatial aftereffect (and presumably spatial adaptation) are the distance between the inducing and test contours, the luminance contrast between figure and background, and the duration of stimulation.

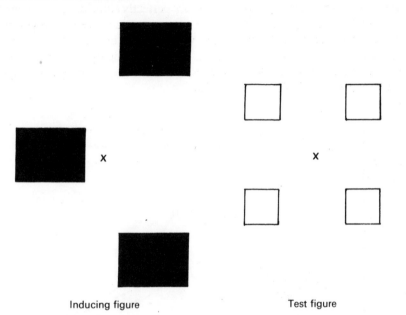

Inducing figure                    Test figure

**Figure 7.5** Inducing (I) and test (T) patterns used by Köhler and Wallach to demonstrate spatial aftereffect. Following fixation of cross in the I figure the two left squares of T figure appear further apart than the two on the right.

## Determinants of Visual Spatial Aftereffects

When one contour is apparently displaced in position following stimulation by another, the spatial aftereffect is often referred to as a displacement effect. The extent of apparent displacement varies with the distance between the stimulating or inducing contour and the test contour. Consider two bars, one above the other, with the lower bar on the opposite side of a fixation point to an area where a black rectangle may be introduced. During the pre-test the observer adjusts the lower bar until it is judged to be in vertical alignment with the upper bar while fixating the point. The two bars are removed, the black rectangle introduced and the observer stares fixedly at the point for 90 seconds, after which the rectangle is removed and the two bars re-introduced. The observer usually reports that after stimulation the lower bar appears to be misaligned or displaced in a direction away from the adjacent contour of the earlier presented rectangle. He thus moves the lower bar towards this earlier contour in order to bring the two bars into vertical alignment. The extent of this apparent displacement or misalignment is greatest when the separation between the inducing and test contours is about 3 minutes of arc, diminishing when the distance is either greater or less. When the two contours are perfectly coincident, *i.e.*, when the edge of the rectangle and lower line are "in contact", a very slight effect occurs. The fact that the maximum visual spatial aftereffect progressively increases up to a certain separation between inducing and test contours is often referred to as the "distance paradox". The function for distance between contours is shown in Fig. 7.6.

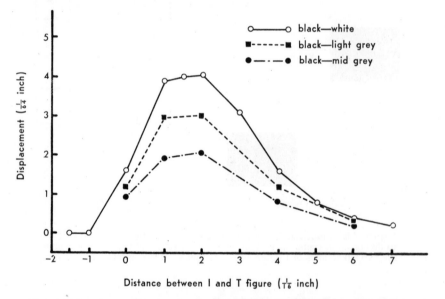

Distance between I and T figure ($\frac{1}{16}$ inch)

**Figure 7.6** The magnitude of a spatial aftereffect similar to that generated by Fig. 7.5 as a function of the distance separating the contours of the inducing and test figures. The magnitude of the aftereffect also varies with the luminance contrast between inducing figure and its background. (Adapted from R.H. Pollack, Figural after-effects: Quantitative studies of displacement. In *Austral. J. Psychol.*, 1958, 10, 269–277. By courtesy of *Austral. J. Psychol.*)

The apparent displacement of one contour following stimulation by another is greatest when the luminance difference or contrast between the inducing figure and its background or surround is large (Fig. 7.6). As the luminance difference decreases the extent of apparent displacement diminishes.

Earlier in this chapter it was noted that the adaptive changes in brightness and other qualities increase rapidly during the first few seconds of stimulation after which the rate of change lessens and eventually levels off. Much the same exponential trend occurs in the case of visual spatial aftereffects, the effect achieving a maximum between 90 and 120 seconds. After cessation of stimulation the effect dissipates, at first rapidly and then more slowly, the total time for recovery depending on the duration of stimulation. The longer the stimulation period the greater the time for dissipation. Although visual spatial aftereffects are usually associated with prolonged stimulation (stimulation periods of a minute or more), they occur after relatively brief stimulation. With precise methods of measurement the effects can be observed after stimulation durations of less than a second.

The direction of displacement for a visual spatial aftereffect is not invariably *away* from the stimulating or inducing contour. Early attempts to explain visual displacement effects were based on the assumption that, following prolonged stimulation by one contour, a contour presented subsequently is apparently displaced away from the first. This is not correct. Depending on the luminance relationships between the figure and its surround the direction of apparent shift varies between towards and away from the inducing figure. When the luminance is low the shift takes the form of an apparent "attraction" between the two successively presented contours and when it is high there is an apparent "repulsion" between them. This "attraction" effect has been demonstrated recently by Ganz and Day (1965).

### Visual Spatial Aftereffects and Afterimages

Stare fixedly at the point at the centre of the red patch in Fig. 7.2 for about a minute and then look at a plain sheet of paper placed adjacent to the book. A blue-green patch of about the same size as the patch will be observed on the surface of the paper. This is the phenomenon of the negative afterimage; its apparent chromatic characteristics are near-complementary to the inducing colour and its apparent size varies directly with the distance of the surface on which it is projected. The afterimage occurs also with achromatic stimuli. Following stimulation by a light object on a dark field the afterimage appears as a dark area on a light field and *vice versa*. The negative afterimage is an instance of perceptual adaptation. It so happens, however, that even with a featureless visual field the afterimage persists and the original spatial characteristics of the stimulating figure remain. The persistence of spatial characteristics with luminance and hue relationships reversed immediately suggests a basis for the visual spatial aftereffect.

When a test figure is introduced following removal of an inducing figure the latter is judged as altered or "distorted" compared with pre-test judgments. This change, as we have seen, is the spatial aftereffect. Now, since the spatial characteristics of prior stimulation persist in the form of the negative afterimage, it can be argued that the spatial aftereffect is really an illusion (Chapter 3), with the afterimage playing the role of the inducing elements of the illusion. That is, the test figure or contour introduced immediately following removal of the inducing or stimulating figure or contour results in a visual image of the latter on which is superimposed the afterimage of the former. The outcome in perception is an illusion, an apparent distortion of test figure characteristics engendered by the simultaneous occurrence of the inducing figure's afterimage. Appealing and simple as this explanation of the visual spatial afterimage may be, it suffers from one major flaw. Consider, for example, the Delboeuf illusion shown in Fig. 7.7. The circumscribed annulus on the left is apparently slightly *larger* than the comparison circle on the right. If, now, the large circle stimulates the retina during fixation of the point in the lower part of Fig. 7.7 and after 2 minutes fixation the gaze is transferred to the point between the two circles

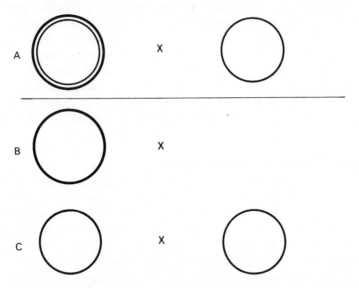

**Figure 7.7** Spatial aftereffect and illusion. In simultaneous presentation the small circle on the left of *A* usually appears slightly *larger* than that on the right when the cross is fixated. In successive presentation prior fixation of cross in *B* for about a minute results in small circle on left of *C* appearing *smaller* than that on the right.

of equal size, the circle on the left is apparently *smaller* than the comparison circle on the right. That is, if the same inducing conditions are used in simultaneous (illusion) and successive (aftereffect) presentation of inducing and test figures, the perceptual effects are opposed to each other. If the spatial aftereffect were essentially an illusory effect, with the afterimage of the large circle serving as inducing figure, it would be expected that the two effects would be in the same direction. In the case of the Delboeuf figure (Fig. 7.7) however, the illusion is an "attraction" effect and the aftereffect one of "repulsion" between the two contours. That this difference is not due to the reversed luminance relationships of the negative afterimage can be shown using a white circle surrounding a black one, both on a mid-grey field. With this arrangement the effect remains one of attraction in the case of the simultaneous presentation and repulsion in the case of the spatial aftereffect.

Although the afterimage-illusion explanation of visual spatial after-effects is simple and parsimonious its validity is suspect, since there are numerous instances where the effects of simultaneous (illusion) and successive (aftereffect) presentation of inducing and test figures are opposed to each other.* In any case, as will be seen below, spatial aftereffects occur following stimulation of the auditory, kinesthetic and tactile systems, systems in connection with which afterimages similar to those in vision are more difficult to imagine. It is to be expected that a general explanation would account for all these effects.

## AUDITORY SPATIAL ADAPTATION AND AFTEREFFECT

Without relying on vision the human observer is capable of discriminating the direction from which sounds reach him, the accuracy of discrimination depending on the relative angular disposition of the sound source. The basis of auditory spatial discrimination is the difference between the arrival time, intensity and phase at the right and left ears (Chapter 2). If following stimulation by a sound in one position relative to the observer, another sound is presented in a different location, the judged position of the latter is different from that prior to stimulation. A series of experiments, one of which investigated the effect of angular difference between inducing and test sources, has recently been conducted by Curthoys.

Curthoys† arranged a speaker emitting intermittent white noise at the end of a long boom which rotated horizontally about a vertical axis directly above the observer's head. The observer's task was to indicate when the sound from the speaker at the end of the motor-driven boom was "straight-ahead". He made this judgment before and after a period during which continuous white noise was emitted from a source placed at progressively greater angles between the "straight-ahead" (0°) and right angles to the head. The position and posture of the observer's head was held constant. The results of this experiment are shown in Fig. 7.8. Following stimulation by a continuous noise judgments of the auditory straight-ahead change, the magnitude of this spatial aftereffect varying with the stimulation angle.

---

*Logan, J.A. An examination of the relationship between visual illusions and figural after-effects. Unpublished PhD thesis, University of Sydney 1962.

†Curthoys, I.S. The Effect of Binaural Adaptation and Masking on Auditory Localization. Unpublished PhD thesis, Monash University 1968.

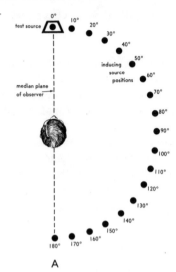

A

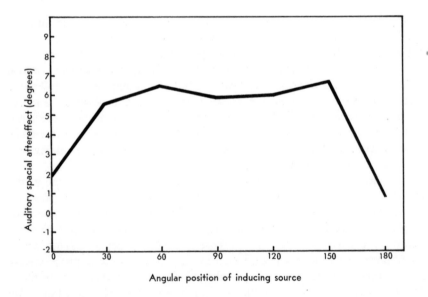

B

**Figure 7.8** *A* An arrangement for measuring an auditory spatial aftereffect. The subject, while blindfolded, is required to judge the position of a noise source following stimulation for 2 minutes by an inducing source placed at positions ranging from 0° to 180° relative to his median plane. *B* The size of the spatial aftereffect as a function of inducing source position. (Adapted from I.S. Curthoys, The effect of binaural adaptation and masking on auditory localisation. Unpublished PhD thesis, Monash University, 1968.)

This auditory spatial aftereffect dissipates exponentially, *i.e.,* at first rapidly and then progressively more slowly.

So far there is no explanation of auditory spatial aftereffects following prolonged stimulation by a sound arriving from a certain direction. It is conceivable that, since the intensity of stimulation of, say, the right ear, is greater when the stimulating source is on the right, the right ear adapts to a greater extent than the left. Thus a subsequent sound located straight-ahead will sound less loud to the right ear than to the left, which is the case for a source on the left. Such an explanation is rendered doubtful, however, by the fact that when the stimulation source is at 90° (where intensity and arrival time differences are greatest) the effect is smaller than when it is at 30°.

## KINESTHETIC AND TACTILE SPATIAL AFTEREFFECTS

Perhaps the most effective way to demonstrate a kinesthetic spatial aftereffect is to close the eyes and raise the arm so that it is judged to be horizontal with respect to the floor. If this is done facing a wall the position can be marked by a pencil held so that it is co-extensive with the outstretched arm and hand. Now raise the arm about another 30° and hold it there outstretched for about a minute. Finally, move the arm again until it seems horizontal to the floor and mark the wall again. The second mark will be about 2 to 3 inches above the first. Had another person moved the arm until it was actually horizontal it would have been judged as slanting down. To compensate for this apparent displacement it is moved upward by an equal angle in the same direction as the stimulation angle.

That this aftereffect is kinesthetic, involving the sensory system signalling limb position, and not muscular can be demonstrated by placing the arm relaxed in a sling and having another person move it until it is judged to be horizontal. Even when the muscles are "passive" and quite relaxed, a positional aftereffect occurs.

There are numerous ways of demonstrating spatial aftereffects in the kinesthetic modality. Gibson first drew attention to the phenomenon in his experiments in the 1930s when he reported that after moving the hand from side to side across a convex edge a subsequently presented straight edge is judged concave. To appear straight the edge must be made slightly convex. An essentially similar kinesthetic aftereffect occurs following side-to-side motion of the extended hand and arm across a slanted edge. Following several minutes of such movement a horizontal edge seems slanted in the opposite direction and must be adjusted in the direction of the stimulation slant to be judged horizontal. By arranging a protractor scale and a bar which can be rotated about a pivot by the observer using the other hand, such determinants of the kinesthetic aftereffect as stimulation time, angle and extent and velocity of side-to-side movement can be studied.

By far the most commonly used method for the study of kinesthetic positional aftereffects involves a wooden block about an inch wide. The observer, while blindfolded, holds this block between thumb and index finger of one hand and slides the same digits of the other hand along a tapering block until they are judged to be the same distance apart. A block either much wider or narrower than the 1 inch block is then held for about 2 minutes and the matching procedure with the 1 inch block and tapering scale repeated. Following the holding of a wider block the inch block is judged narrower than before the stimulation period and following a narrower block it is judged wider.

Although kinesthetic aftereffects occur without their prolonged involvement, muscles may play a role. If a heavy weight is held in the hand while the arm and hand are outstretched at a certain angle the magnitude of the aftereffect is different from the condition with no weight. Effects in which the kinesthetic and muscle sensory systems are involved are more properly referred to as proprioceptive aftereffects.*

So far there have been very few reports of spatial aftereffects in connection with tactile judgments. Day and Singer (1964) showed that the apparent distance apart of two edges pressed into the skin of the inside forearm increase following pressure by an elongated object between them. The effect is similar to that in vision, in that the contours or edges on the skin are displaced away from the area of preceding stimulation.

Explanations in neurophysiological terms of both the kinesthetic and tactile aftereffects must rest on further enquiry. It is clear that during the course of prolonged stimulation the sensory system undergoes some kind of adaptive change which affects subsequent judgments. The kinesthetic receptors are located in the lining of the limb joints and in the tendons to which the muscles are attached. Groups of receptors are triggered when the limb is in a particular position. Presumably gradients of adaptation in receptor groups, with consequent variation in sensory signals reaching the central nervous system result in changes in the apparent position of the limb. In the present state of knowledge it is not wise to speculate further on the neurophysiological correlates of either kinesthetic or tactile spatial aftereffects. The occurrence of such effects, however, stresses their generality and the inadequacy of any explanation based solely on data from vision.

## AN INTERMODAL SPATIAL AFTEREFFECT

From time to time there have been numerous reports of the occurrence of a spatial aftereffect in one sensory modality following stimulation in another. It has been claimed, for example, that visual stimulation by appropriate

*Collins, J.K. Proprioceptive Space Perception: A Study of the Muscular Component in the Position Sense. Unpublished PhD thesis, University of Sydney 1967.

stimulus patterns gives rise to a kinesthetic aftereffect and *vice versa*. Recent experiments, however, have failed to confirm this claimed interaction between vision and kinesthesis following prolonged stimulation.

In Chapter 3 the effects of head and body tilt on visual judgments of object orientation were described. It was noted that, although the visually judged vertical departs systematically from the gravitational vertical as the head or body is tilted, the departure is considerably less than would be expected from variation in orientation of the object's retinal image. Starting from this observation, Day and Wade required observers to adjust a thin bar of light in a dark room to apparent verticality before and after a period of 2 minutes with head tilted 10, 20, 30 and 40 degrees left and right. Following tilt a gravitationally vertical line was judged to be tilted slightly in the opposite direction to previous head tilt. This spatial aftereffect achieved a maximum of about 2 degrees following a head tilt of about 30 degrees.

After a period during which the head is tilted, the upright head is judged to be slightly tilted in the opposite direction, an instance of a proprioceptive spatial aftereffect. This apparent displacement of head position suggests an explanation of the visual aftereffect. Following a period of lateral tilt the upright head is apparently tilted in the opposite direction. A vertical bar is aligned with the upright head. Since the upright head is apparently tilted so must a bar which is aligned with it. But since the visual and kinesthetic aftereffects from head tilt follow quite different functions with variation in the angle of head tilt, this explanation of the visual aftereffect is difficult to sustain (Wade & Day, 1967).

# Motion Adaptation and Aftereffect

During and after visual stimulation by a moving object, and following angular acceleration of the whole body, visual judgments of object motion (including the limiting case of object stationariness) undergo change. The aftereffect of visual motion stimulation is commonly called the "aftereffect of seen movement" and that following angular acceleration the poststimulatory oculogyral effect.

## ADAPTATION AND AFTEREFFECT OF VISUAL MOTION

When any of the patterns shown in Fig. 7.9 are stopped after a period during during which they are viewed while moving they are reported as moving for a short time in the opposite direction. This apparent movement of a stationary object following observation of real movement is not confined to the object itself but occurs when any stationary surface is inspected after movement. Further, during the period of observation the judged velocity of movement progressively decreases. Apparent movement of a stationary surface is the aftereffect and apparent decreases in velocity of movement are adaptation.

**Figure 7.9** Typical patterns for the generation of a visual aftereffect of movement. Following fixation of a stationary point in or near either of the four moving patterns an aftereffect of movement occurs when the pattern is stopped.

The aftereffect of visual motion stimulation is among the oldest problems in the study of visual perception. Aristotle mentioned the effect in his *De Somniis*, and in 1820 the physiologist Johannes Purkinje described apparent movement of stationary objects after viewing a parade. Later R. A. Addams (who is often credited with the first report) described the opposite apparent movement of stationary objects after viewing a waterfall.

Methods of measuring motion adaptation and aftereffect have been unsatisfactory until recently. By far the most common procedure has been to require the observer merely to report apparent movement or to report when apparent movement ceases, using the duration of the aftereffect as the measure. In more recent experiments, notably those of Collins, the observer has been required to match the apparent movement of a stationary object by adjusting the real movement of a similar pattern placed adjacent to the first.

Among the early explanations of the aftereffect of visual motion stimulation was that invoking eye movements as the basis of the phenomenon. Johannes Purkinje wrote:

> "The eye still tended to fixate the stationary surroundings in the fashion to which it had become accustomed to fixating things in motion. Therefore, it unconsciously slipped toward the accustomed direction and the surroundings seemed to slip away in the opposite direction."

Explanations based on eye movements had to be discarded when in 1880 Sylvanus Thompson showed that if two patterns moving in opposite directions were fixated and later stopped, each was reported as moving in the direction opposite to real movement and opposite to the other. The eye could not move in two opposite circular paths at once.

Among the stimulus factors which determine the aftereffect of visual motion are the luminance of the pattern, time of stimulation and the visual angle subtended by the pattern. When measured by matching the movement of a comparison pattern to that of the stationary but apparently moving pattern, the effect increases exponentially with stimulation time, a maximum effect occurring after about 120 seconds of stimulation. A similar increase occurs as a function of the luminance of the brighter areas of a black and white pattern such as a sectored disk. When the difference between the light and dark areas is slight the aftereffect is less marked than for high contrast. Finally, the smaller the retinal projection of a moving stimulus pattern the greater the aftereffect, a result reported originally by Granit in 1929 and recently confirmed by Collins. Neither the velocity nor the direction of movement seems to have a significant effect.

## VISUAL AFTEREFFECT OF BODY ACCELERATION

The oculogyral effect, the apparent movement of a point of light in the dark during rotation of the body, was discussed in Chapter 3. It was noted that the equivocal retinal image of a moving object is perceptually resolved by information for head or body movement. If an object is stationary relative to the observer, stimulation of the semicircular canal system of the labyrinth by rotary acceleration gives rise to apparent movement of the object. After the acceleration phase of body movement, when constant angular velocity is reached, the stationary light point is reported as moving in the *opposite* direction to body rotation.

Like the oculogyral effect, which occurs during angular acceleration of the body, the acceleration aftereffect cannot, on the evidence, be attributed to movements of the eyes induced by body movement. A similar phenomenon occurs with a visual afterimage, which is stationary relative to the retina, and the effect frequently outlasts such eye movements.

# The Basis of Perceptual Adaptation and Aftereffect

During the course of stimulation, judgments of stimulus intensity, qualities such as wavelength, frequency and taste, and spatial features such as size, shape and direction undergo change. If a given stimulus is replaced by one of different value (greater or less intensity, different wavelength or frequency, or greater or less size, etc.), judgments of the newly-introduced stimulus are different from those made prior to any stimulation. These phenomena of adaptation and aftereffect consequent on stimulation are so general both in the range of stimulus properties affected, and the sensory modalities in connection with which they occur, as to raise the question of a general explanation. In the present state of knowledge any such attempt is bound to be speculative. The general form which an explanation might take can be glimpsed by considering the visual aftereffect of motion, visual chromatic aftereffects, and visual spatial aftereffects in terms of sensory specificity, maintained activity, and neural inhibition.

## SENSORY SPECIFICITY, MAINTAINED ACTIVITY AND NEURAL INHIBITION

There are many sensory cells which respond selectively to certain aspects of stimulation. The cells of a sensory system do not necessarily cease their activity when stimulation ceases but exhibit spontaneous or maintained activity. Further, as already observed in connection with lightness contrast (Chapter 5), the activity of one cell or group of cells may inhibit the activity of another.

### Sensory Specificity

Investigations of various species have shown that sensory cells exhibit a high degree of specificity in the stimulus properties to which they are sensitive. For example, in the visual system of the frog there are cells which are primarily responsive to a particular shape of contour. The cells may respond to a curved edge but are unresponsive to a straight edge. The rabbit's retina includes cells which respond to a particular direction of movement while remaining inactive with another. Cells have been found in the cortex of the cat which respond selectively to a narrow range of stimulus orientations. While such cells might, for example, exhibit excitation when the stimulus is vertically oriented they are not responsive to an orientation of 30 degrees. There are numerous instances of sensory elements which respond selectively to a narrow range of wavelengths, motion velocities, temperatures and various spatial properties. Selectively responsive structures have been observed both at the lower and higher levels of the sensory system, occurring in some instances in the sense organ itself and in others at the cortex or in the intermediate sensory structures.

### Maintained Activity and Neural Inhibition

Maintained or spontaneous activity refers to the continuation of activity in sensory structures in the absence of stimulation. This activity is generally characteristic of cells at all levels of the sensory system, so that the effect of onset and offset of stimulation is to alter the level of activity rather than to cause its initiation or cessation.

Sensory cells do not necessarily function entirely independently of each other. As was noted earlier in connection with simultaneous and border contrast (Chapter 5), stimulation of one cell may reduce or inhibit the activity of another. This inhibitory effect is reciprocal or mutual, two cells exhibiting an inhibitory interaction. The extent to which excitation of one cell inhibits (or disinhibits) the activity of another depends on such factors as their spatial separation, relative excitation levels and the total area of stimulation.

## NEURAL CORRELATES OF AFTEREFFECTS

The selectivity of sensory cells to certain aspects of stimulation, their maintained activity and their inhibitory relationship suggests a possible basis for perceptual aftereffects. The general nature of the neural correlates can be seen by considering visual chromatic aftereffects, aftereffects of visual motion and visual spatial aftereffects.

### Visual Chromatic Aftereffects

In 1960 De Valois described cells in the lateral geniculate body in the visual pathway which are selectively responsive to certain wavelengths of light and which, in addition to showing maintained activity in the absence of stimulation, exhibit inhibitory characteristics. These "opponent cells" are not very responsive to changes in light intensity but are sensitive to wavelength changes. Some cells, for example, are excited by blue light but inhibited by yellow, only showing activity when yellow light stimulation ceases. Other cells exhibit the reverse relationship, being excited by yellow light but inhibited by blue.

Consider a number of such cells all in a state of maintained activity in the absence of any stimulus. With the onset of a blue stimulus the activity of one group of cells increases sharply and that of the other decreases. During the course of prolonged stimulation the activity of the first group reduces to a steady level. Now, when blue light stimulation ceases, the maintained activity of the first group is markedly diminished as a result of sensory adaptation, so that the inhibitory effect of the group on other cells is lessened and the spontaneous activity of the second group is increased. The increase in activity of the second group of cells (which normally respond to onset of yellow) over that of the first when blue stimulation ceases is the neural sign for yellow. This change in the relative activity of two groups of cells (one selectively responsive to blue and the other to yellow), on cessation of blue light stimulation, could serve to explain the yellow afterimage from blue light. In short, the "yellow" aftereffect represents a heightened level of activity in cells released temporarily from inhibition.

### Visual Motion Aftereffects

In 1963 Barlow and Hill stimulated the retina of the rabbit with a rotating disk bearing an irregular black and white pattern. By recording from an electrode inserted in the retina they found cells which responded when the disk was rotated clockwise and others which were activated when it rotated counterclockwise. When the disk was stationary both cells exhibited characteristic maintained activity. When the disk was moved clockwise a cell selectively sensitive to clockwise motion showed a marked rise in its frequency of responding, which gradually declined during the course of stimulation. After about a minute the disk was stopped and the cell almost ceased responding. The cell responsive to counterclockwise motion, however, maintained its steady activity.

Consider two cells, one responding to one direction of motion, the other to another direction, and both responding with the same activity in the absence of motion stimulation. When the first cell is appropriately stimulated its activity level rises sharply above that of the second cell which continues responding at a steady level of discharge. This direction of difference in activity level signals a particular direction of motion. But when motion ceases the activity of the hitherto stimulated cell falls below the maintained activity level of the second cell, thus giving rise to the *opposite* direction of difference between the activity levels of the two cells. This latter direction of difference is the signal for movement in the opposite direction. Were a whole population of cells to behave in this way then the *difference* in the activity levels of two groups of cells following directional motion stimulation of one group would serve to explain the aftereffect of visual motion stimulation. This is essentially the explanation proposed by Barlow and Hill.

Although the activity level of the second (non-stimulated) cell, unlike the chromatically-selective cells, does not increase, the basis of the two aftereffects is essentially the same. Motion direction, like colour, is signalled in the nervous system by the direction of difference in the firing rate of two cells, one responding to one aspect (colour, motion direction) of the stimulus property and the other to another value. Following stimulation of the first its activity is depressed and the direction of difference is reversed, giving a neural signal for the opposed stimulus condition.

## Visual Spatial Aftereffects

Among the most widely quoted of all recent experiments associated with the neural correlates of spatial vision are those of Hubel and Wiesel, who have shown among other findings that certain cells in the cerebral cortex of the cat respond selectively to a narrow range of orientations of the stimulus. If a long, narrow stimulus is arranged vertically, the activity level of a certain cell is increased, but when the stimulus is oriented at another angle the cell's activity is unaffected. Adjacent to those cells activated maximally by a particular stimulus orientation are others which respond most actively when stimulation of the first group ceases. The spatial relationships between these two areas of cells varies widely and includes arrangements in which the groups are side by side or one group surrounds the other. Hubel and Wiesel have also shown that there are groups of cells which respond most actively to particular sizes and shapes of stimulus pattern.

If it can be assumed that, following prolonged stimulation of a group of cells by an object of a particular orientation, shape or size, their activity is reduced below the level of their maintained activity, then there is a possible basis for spatial aftereffects. On cessation of stimulation the maintained (as with movement) or enhanced (as with colour) activity of cells is greater than that of the previously stimulated group of cells. This changed direction in the relative levels of activity of different groups of cells may well serve as the signal for another stimulus orientation, shape or size. That is, the altered pattern of excitation occasioned by a depression in the activity of cells previously stimulated may well be that which occurs for stimuli with different spatial properties.

It is too soon to work out this principle in detail. Much of the available evidence, however, suggests strongly that perceptual adaptation and aftereffects result from changes in the relative levels of activity in groups of sensory cells which respond selectively to certain aspects of stimulation. In general, it seems reasonable to suppose, in the present state of knowledge, that the basis of perceptual adaptation is a reduction in the difference of activity levels between two groups of cells, one group signalling one value of a stimulus property and the other another. Perceptual aftereffect is essentially similar in that the difference in activity levels is not only reduced but *reversed*, thus giving rise to the typically opposite aftereffect, the opposite direction of movement, colour, lightness, orientation, curvature, etc. This general principle is illustrated in Fig. 7.10.

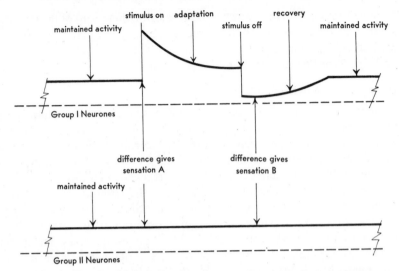

**Figure 7.10** A possible basis for aftereffects. Group I and Group II neurones are spontaneously and equally active in the absence of stimulation. When Group I neurones are stimulated their activity level *rises above* that of Group II thus signalling an event such as clockwise movement, right tilt or red. During stimulation Group I neurones adapt so that on cessation of stimulation their activity level *falls below* that of Group II thus signalling the opposite event such as counterclockwise movement, left tilt or green. The event is signalled by the direction of the difference between Group I and Group II neurones.

# Perceptual Adaptation and Perceptual Resolution

As a final comment on perceptual adaptation and aftereffect their relationship to perceptual resolution discussed in earlier chapters can be briefly reviewed. It will be recalled that prolonged head and body tilt gives rise to a visual orientation aftereffect. Information for head and body tilt is necessary to resolve the equivocal retinal projection of object orientation. Since the orientation of this projection is jointly determined by object *and* observer tilt, information for the latter is essential if object orientation is to be perceived in terms of a close approximation to true or objective orientation, *i.e.*, if perceptual constancy of orientation is to be maintained with body tilt. Prolonged tilt of the head or body presumably results in the adaptation of sensory systems involved in judgments of body tilt. Such adaptation modifies judgments of body tilt. It follows that visual perceptual resolution of an object's orientation will also be affected. Put briefly in different terms, adaptation through prolonged stimulation of those sensory systems involved in the perceptual resolution of the equivocal sensory projections of object properties will modify perceptual resolution. Thus perceptual resolution of equivocal projections is not only changed by the nature of the resolving information but also by modification of those systems involved in the processing of the information. This general link between adaptation and perceptual resolution can be extended to most of the adaptive effects discussed in this chapter.

# Summary

During a period of prolonged stimulation, judgments of object properties undergo change, an effect called adaptation. Furthermore, prolonged stimulation by one value of an object property results in a change in the judgment of another, an outcome referred to as an aftereffect. Adaptation and aftereffect occur with object intensity and colour, tonal intensity and frequency, with taste and smell, and with other forms of stimulation. Both effects also occur with the spatial properties of objects such as their size, shape, orientation and direction. These latter phenomena are referred to as figural or spatial aftereffects and occur in vision, kinesthesis, the tactile sense, hearing and other senses. Visual spatial aftereffects have been attributed to an afterimage of one object occurring simultaneously with the presentation of another, thus resulting in an illusory effect. This explanation is unacceptable since spatial aftereffects and illusions are often opposite.

In addition to aftereffects within a single sensory modality, they occur also between modalities. Prolonged tilt of the head involving kinesthetic and labyrinthine stimulation results in a visual orientation aftereffect when the head is returned to the upright.

Among the earliest aftereffects to have been noted are those associated with movement. After fixating a moving object, a stationary object appears to move in the opposite direction. Motion aftereffects of objects have also been observed following body movement; an oculogyral effect.

The occurrence of neurons which are specifically sensitive to a particular object property (*e.g.,* left motion direction) suggests a basis for a general theory of adaptation and aftereffect.

# 8.  Perception and Learning

WHETHER perception is among the innate characteristics of the organism or is an outcome of the individual's interactions with his environment is among the fundamental questions with which experimental psychology began. During the eighteenth and nineteenth centuries the issue of innate origins of perception (nativism) versus perception as learned during contact with the environment (empiricism) was often posed in extreme terms. The question today is more often a matter of which aspects of perception occur without prior experience, which are an outcome of learning, and of the manner in which innate and learned perceptual activities interact. Defined as the organism's maintenance of contact with the environment, perception is essential for its adaptation and survival. It would be expected, therefore, that certain features of perception would be manifest at birth and, since the higher animals especially are characterized by a capacity to learn, that other features of perception would emerge and improve with practice. Thus the question with which this chapter will be concerned is: Which features of perception are present at birth or in early infancy and under what conditions do systematic changes in perception occur with practice?

## Perception Without Learning

Aspects of perception which occur without prior practice can be arbitrarily divided into two classes: discrimination, and complex perception. The distinction between these two groups is by no means clearly defined but is roughly the same as that between basic perceptual capacities (Chapter 2) and perceptual stability (Chapters 3–5). The latter group includes the perceptual constancies.

### Unlearned Distance Discrimination

In an experiment reported in 1934, Lashley and Russell raised thirteen rats in complete darkness from birth for a hundred days. Visual stimulation was restricted to a few seconds of very dim illumination each day when the cages were opened for feeding. On the first day in full light each rat was placed on a jumping stand (Fig. 8.1) and encouraged to jump to a platform on which food was available. The distance between stand and platform was varied between 24 and 40 inches. The accuracy of the rat's discrimination of the intervening distance was measured by the force exerted by its leap. To leap 40 inches required a greater force than to leap 24 inches. Even though there were variations in the success achieved in landing on the platform the results were clear in showing that after being reared without visual stimulation the rats did discriminate between different distances between jumping stand and platform. That is, distance discrimination in this situation does not depend on visual experience.

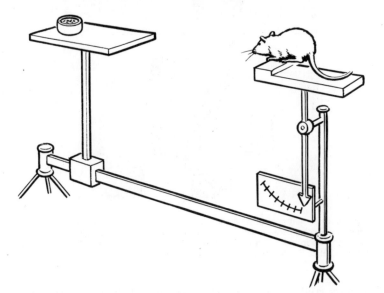

**Figure 8.1** Lashley and Russell experiment; rats reared in darkness discriminate distance between jumping stand and platform as accurately as normally-reared rats. (From D. Krech and R.S. Crutchfield, *Elements of Psychology*, N.Y., Alfred A. Knopf, 1958. By courtesy of D. Krech.)

Lashley and Russell's evidence that distance discrimination occurs without prior visual exposure to space has been confirmed more recently in a series of experiments by Gibson and Walk using a quite different experimental arrangement. The "visual cliff" (Fig. 8.2) consists of a runway across the edge of a steep drop such that on one side is a "deep" and on the other a "shallow". To prevent the animal from actually falling, a sheet of glass is placed under the runway extending across both the steep and shallow sides of the box. Patterned material is placed flush against the underside of the glass on the shallow side and on the floor of the apparatus on the deep side. After showing that a variety of young animals (human infants, cats, lambs, chicks, kids) exhibited a marked tendency to avoid the cliff, Gibson and Walk used the same procedure as Lashley and Russell. Rats were reared for 90 days without pattern vision and then placed on the runway. These experimental animals exhibited the same tendency as light-reared rats to prefer the shallow side and to avoid the deep side of the runway.

**Figure 8.2**  Gibson and Walk's visual cliff; a young animal avoids the "deep" side of a runway across a cliff. Rats reared without pattern vision also avoid the deep side. (From N. Tinbergen, *Animal Behaviour*, N.Y., Time-Life Books, 1965. By courtesy of W. Vandivert.)

The early study by Lashley and Russell and the recent experiments of Gibson and Walk and other investigators show convincingly that depth or distance discrimination occurs without prior practice in the light. This finding is not surprising when, as Gibson and Walk point out: "The survival of a species requires that its members develop discrimination of depth by the time they take up independent locomotion, whether at one day (the chick and goat), 3 to 4 weeks (the rat and the cat) or 6 to 10 months (the human infant). That such a vital capacity does not depend on possibly fatal accidents of learning in the lives of individuals is consistent with evolutionary theory."*

### Unlearned Perceptual Constancy

Size constancy, the capacity to resolve the equivocal size of an object's retinal projection is, as noted in Chapter 3, dependent on information for the distance between observer and object. If, as so convincingly demonstrated

*From E.J. Gibson and R.D. Walk, The visual cliff. In *Sci. Amer.*, 1960, 202, 64-71.

by Lashley and Russell and by Gibson and Walk, distance discrimination is not learned visually, it could be expected that resolution of size to an approximation to object size would also occur without prior exposure to visual stimulation. A series of experiments by Bower in the last few years (Bower, 1966) suggest strongly that both size and shape constancy occur at early stages of infant development.

The essential feature of Bower's investigations was the conditioning of a head-turning response to indicate perception of an object of a certain size. Bower presented a white cube 30 centimetres on a side at a distance of 1 metre to infants aged between 6 and 8 weeks. When the child turned its head even slightly, as little as half an inch, a switch was closed and a recorder operated by it. When this response was made with the cube present it was reinforced by the experimenter appearing and saying "peekaboo". When the head-turning response to the 30 centimetre cube was firmly established, three new conditions were introduced. The 30 centimetre cube at 3 metres, a 90 centimetre cube at 1 metre, and the 90 centimetre cube at 3 metres. The first of these three conditions resulted in a smaller retinal image and the third in the same retinal image size as for the 30 centimetre object (but with a larger object). The second condition gave a different retinal projection for a different object but at the same distance. Although the first and second conditions elicited fewer responses than the training condition, the third condition elicited substantially fewer than all other conditions. The general conclusion is that objects at the same distance elicit responses suggestive of constancy. An object at a much greater distance but giving rise to the same size retinal image as the training object does not elicit responses with similar frequency. There is evidence, therefore, for size constancy soon after birth. Bower has also demonstrated the occurrence of shape constancy with similar methods.

## Motion Parallax and Distance Discrimination

Gibson and Walk, and Bower, have obtained further evidence that the stimulus basis of unlearned distance discrimination is motion parallax, the difference in the extent and velocity of movement of the retinal projections of objects at different distances as the eyes or head move. Bower adduced evidence for the role of motion parallax by covering one eye of his infant subjects, a procedure which eliminated retinal disparity. The monocular group performed as well as binocular subjects in terms of frequency of head-turning. Likewise, Gibson and Walk eliminated as far as possible all distance information except that provided by monocular parallax and showed that animals continued to avoid the steep side of the visual cliff (Fig. 8.2).

The general conclusion that can be drawn from these various studies is that there are aspects of space perception which are present at a very early stage of development. It is clear that capacity to discriminate distance and to respond to objects in terms of their objective size is of biological significance. The range and extent of these unlearned or quickly-learned discriminations and complex perceptual processes such as are involved in constancy are far from fully explored; it is conceivable that other classes of perceptual constancy and illusion (Chapters 3, 4 and 5) can be observed early in development.

# Classes of Learned Perception

There has been a tendency, often implicit, to treat the processes involved in learning to perceive as different in certain ways from those involved in learning to make overt responses. Whether the individual learns to discriminate visually between two shapes or colours or learns to make an intricate motor response sequence such as tying a shoe-lace, sensory information is involved. An individual depends on visual stimulus information in learning to discriminate patterns and on proprioceptive (kinesthetic and muscular) information in making an appropriate response. Information for discrimination derives in the first instance from the external environment and for appropriate responding from the individual's movements and postures. Without appropriate sensory information neither task could be learned. An individual with deficiencies of the visual system would have difficulty in learning to discriminate visually, as would an individual with deficiencies of the kinesthetic-muscular sensory systems in learning a complex motor skill. In other words, individuals learn to discriminate between stimuli generated by their own responses as they do between external stimuli. From this viewpoint, a distinction between "perceptual" and "motor" learning is unwarranted, for both are dependent on sensory information.

If it is recognized that the processes underlying all learning are probably similar, it is convenient to distinguish three classes of situation in which changes in perception occur with practice; discrimination learning, relationship learning, and learning to resolve stimulus equivocalities. The first class refers to progressive refinement or improvement in discriminating between, for example, wavelengths, spatial separations, chemical concentrations and tonal frequencies. The second class refers to progressive changes in behaviour when the relationships between input from two sensory modalities (*e.g.,* vision and kinesthesis) are modified, as would occur if a prism or lens were placed in front of the eyes. The third class refers to changes in the resolution of equivocal stimuli through prior exposure to certain resolving information. These three classes of perceptual situation seem to encompass most cases in which changes in perception (contact with the environment) occur with practice.

## DISCRIMINATION LEARNING

There are numerous everyday examples and anecdotal accounts of the extraordinary refinement achieved in making certain classes of perceptual judgment. The wine-taster and tea-taster can classify the beverages on the basis of their taste into many more categories than the untrained individual. William James, nearly eighty years ago, referred to a farmer who could reach into a barrel of flour and judge whether the flour at the bottom or top was from wheat grown in Iowa or Tennessee. The Australian black-tracker can follow the course taken by another person on the basis of stimulus information which an untrained person cannot use. E. J. Gibson refers to the remarkable case of Julia Brace, said to be employed in an asylum to sort linen, after it came from laundering, by her sense of smell. Extensive practice in numerous industrial tasks leads to great refinement in discriminating such properties as colour, size, smell deficiencies in products and variations in sounds. The blind learn to discriminate symbols using the tactile sense and to read on the basis of tactile information.

Systematic studies of "discrimination training" fall into two major categories: those concerned with progressive changes in acuity and sensitivity thresholds, and with absolute and relative judgments of spatial and other properties.

### Changes in Acuity and Sensitivity

Acuity refers generally to the individual's ability to discriminate spatial detail such as separation, misalignment and shape, and sensitivity to his ability to detect either the occurrence of or changes in energy (Chapter 2). Both abilities improve progressively with practice.

As early as 1858 Volkman showed that tactile acuity, the smallest distance between two points on the skin judged as double, could be halved with practice, an improvement which transferred to hitherto untested areas of the skin. Another early investigation is that of Dressler, in 1894, who found that the two-point threshold decreased from 21 to 4·1 millimetres after between 1000 and 2000 trials. Using the inner side of the arm as a test area and extending the practice over four weeks, Dressler also showed transfer from one arm to the same area of the other arm. The effect of practice on one area was to reduce the threshold from as much as 21 millimetres (pre-training threshold) to about 5 mm on the other arm. Since these early experiments similar findings have been reported by numerous investigators in connection with tactile spatial acuity.

Experiments essentially similar in aim and outcome are those of McFadden in the 1940s, who demonstrated improvements in visual acuity with practice. The acuity task in one experiment was the judgment of separation ("oneness" or "twoness") of a pair of black lines. With repeated trials the observers were able to judge "twoness' at increasing distances from the pattern, *i.e.,* at increasingly smaller visual angles subtended by the white interspace between the two lines. In general terms, increases in visual spatial acuity occurs with numerous patterns and occurs under conditions of both central (foveal) and peripheral vision.

The evidence concerning changes in sensitivity as a function of repeated judgments is less clear-cut than that relating to spatial acuity. Titchener, in his 1905 text book *Experimental Psychology*, noted that such changes seemed to occur, and experimental enquiries since have led from time to time to reports of change in the absolute threshold. Changes have been noted in the absolute threshold for pressure stimulation on the skin but not for taste sensitivity. Experiments on aircraft pilots with deficient colour vision show that this ability improves with practice.

### Changes in Absolute and Relative Judgments

In her detailed review of changes in perceptual judgments with practice, Eleanor J. Gibson pointed out that the distinction between "absolute" and "relative" judgments is somewhat artificial. In judging the absolute length, distance or height of an object, reference must be made to a learned scale of sizes, whereas in relative judgments the property is compared with a standard value of that property. The difference between the two situations is in the use of a scale or standard which has been learned (absolute judgment) or a scale or standard which is available at the time the judgment is made, or at least immediately prior to the judgment (relative judgment). One example of each will be sufficient to indicate the general trends in judgments with practice.

In an early but nonetheless relevant experiment Thorndike and Woodworth (1901) set their observers the task of judging the areas of various geometrical shapes such as rectangles, triangles and circles. All six observers showed progressive improvement (*i.e.,* more accurate estimations) of the shape on which they were practiced, and for some this improvement transferred to different shapes. That is, with continued practice and correction ("knowledge of results"), accuracy in the absolute estimation of area progressively improved. The results of practice are much the same in the case of relative judgments, where the observer is required to compare values of an object property with that of a standard. For example, relative pitch discrimination improves with practice provided that the observer's errors are corrected.

### Nature of Discrimination Learning

As pointed out in the introduction to this chapter a distinction between "perceptual" or "discrimination" learning and "motor" or "response" learning is difficult to justify because learning must depend on sensory information whether the information derives from visual, auditory, tactile, kinesthetic or proprioceptive sources. The laws and principles which apply to the learning of a motor skill probably also apply to discrimination learning. Although it is sometimes stated or implied that reinforcement does not occur in many of the perceptual learning situations, such a view is, to say the least, without firm foundation. The mere fact that the experimental situation in a discrimination learning study is directed towards improvement in discriminatory behaviour may itself be the basis of reward. The observer is reinforced by knowledge of results.

The important point to recognize in considering discrimination learning is that the individual is *capable* of achieving a high degree of refinement in discriminating between and responding to object properties. Whether or not he achieves a degree of refinement to the limit of his capacity is dependent upon the conditions of training; number of trials, reinforcement, and other factors which influence the learning process.

Gibson and Gibson, in discussing perceptual learning in 1955, concluded that the process is essentially one of differentiation; during the course of repeated stimulation the observer comes to "discover higher order variables of stimulation...". The outcome of this ability to respond in terms of more complex variables is increasing refinement in differentiating features of stimulation.

## LEARNING NEW RELATIONSHIPS BETWEEN INFORMATION FROM DIFFERENT SYSTEMS

Consider a situation in which an observer reaches out and runs his hand across the horizontal surface of a table while visually observing both his hand and the table. Presumably he would judge the table top to be flat and horizontal both visually and kinesthetically. The sensory information from both the visual and kinesthetic-tactile senses indicates horizontality. The visual information for horizontality is in agreement with that provided by the kinesthetic and tactile senses.

A question of long standing concerns the perceptual outcome of changing, by artificial means, the spatial relationship between two sensory channels. One means of introducing such a state of affairs is to interpose an optical system between the object and the eye so that object's apparent visual orientation is different from its kinesthetic-tactile orientation. One such arrangement is shown in Fig. 8.3. The effect of the two Dove prisms is to project a slanted image of a horizontal object. Thus, visually the object may be judged as tilted at 20 degrees when in fact it is horizontal. If the observer closes his eyes he can set the pivoted bar to a close approximation to the true horizontal by moving one hand to and fro across its edge and operating a control which rotates the bar with his other hand. Now, if the observer

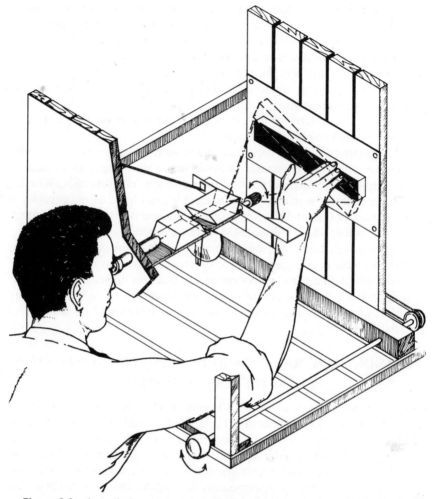

**Figure 8.3**  An optical arrangement consisting of two Dove prisms which tilts the retinal image of a horizontal bar. (From R.H. Day and G. Singer, The effect of spatial judgments on the perceptual aftereffects resulting from prismatically-transformed vision. In *Austral. J. Psychol.*, 1966, 18, 63–70.)

opens his eyes and adjusts the bar to apparent horizontality while both viewing it through the prisms and moving his hand to and fro, a dramatic change takes place. Instead of setting it to a close approximation to the true horizontal he sets it at an angle of about 15–20 degrees in the direction opposite to the optically induced tilt of the bar. That is, if the orientation of the bar is optically transformed through 20 degrees, with the left side higher, the observer adjusts it to apparent horizontality, with the left side 15–20 degrees lower to compensate for the optical distortion at the eye, an effect which can be called behavioural compensation (Day & Singer, 1967).

With head and body upright and normal conditions of illumination a certain pattern of stimulation at the retina signals horizontality. Likewise, if the hand is moved from side to side across a horizontal surface certain patterns of stimulation in the finger, wrist, elbow and shoulder joints signal horizontality. Under almost all conditions, visual and kinesthetic information for horizontality (or any other direction) are in accord. But if visual information is suddenly transformed by refracting light through an optical device as in Fig. 8.3, a new relationship between visual and kinesthetic information for spatial direction must be learned. A quite different pattern of kinesthetic stimulation arising in joints and tendons is now associated with horizontality. This can be demonstrated by an extension of the procedure outlined above in connection with the conditions depicted in Fig. 8.3. If, after setting the bar to the horizontal on a number of occasions as described, the observer now closes his eyes and adjusts the bar to the horizontal using only the kinesthetic sense, the new direction (the left side of the bar lower) persists, an effect which can be called persistence of response. That is, because of visual transformation of direction a new pattern of kinesthetic stimulation is associated with horizontality, a pattern which persists after vision is occluded.

### Dominance of Visual Information

In the example of behavioural compensation (the development of a new pattern of kinesthetic stimulation associated with spatial direction) given above, information from the kinesthetic system for horizontality underwent change. Since the hand was moved across the physically horizontal (but visually transformed bar), why did not vision change? After all, the kinesthetic sense was being stimulated by the true horizontal while the individual viewed through the optical system. Why should not kinesthetic information for horizontality remain constant and stable and the optically transformed visual information eventually come to signal horizontality? The answer is simply that in spatial judgments, visual information is dominant over tactile and kinesthetic information. There is considerable support for the often quoted but somewhat glib statement that man is a visual animal. If visual space is transformed by arranging optical systems such as lenses, prisms or mirrors before the eye, information for kinesthetic and tactile space undergoes change to conform with the visual.

Visual dominance in judgments of size, and the manner in which kinesthetic-tactile information for size undergoes change with the optical transformation of size, has recently been demonstrated in a simple but elegant fashion by Rock and Harris. These investigators placed a small plastic square on a piece of cloth (Fig. 8.4). The subject viewed the square through a minifying lens so that it was visually smaller than its true size and at the same time grasped the square with his fingers from beneath the cloth. The observer was then asked to give his impression of the size of the square either by drawing it or by picking out a square of the same size under normal viewing conditions. The results were clear cut. Subjects either drew or chose a square *smaller* than the one they saw reduced but felt unreduced. The visual dominated the kinesthetic-tactile information. Much the same occurs as under conditions shown in Fig. 8.3. When the subject views a horizontal bar which is optically slanted he judges it kinesthetically to be slanted. Similarly, when he views a 1-inch square which is optically reduced he judges it kinesthetically to be smaller.

In summary, if the relationship between visual and kinesthetic information for spatial properties (size, shape, direction) is altered by interposing

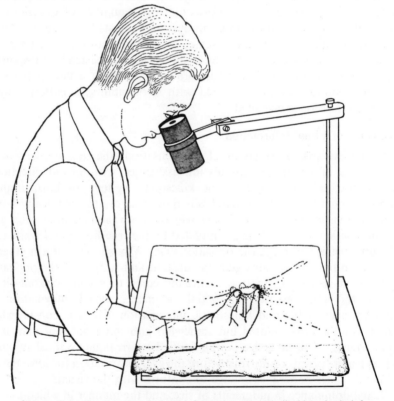

**Figure 8.4** Dominance of visual information over tactile-kinesthetic information for size. When viewing an object through a lens which reduces the size of the retinal image and "feeling" it simultaneously through a cloth, a subject judges size in terms of the transformed visual information. (From I. Rock and C.S. Harris, Vision and touch. In *Scientific American*, 1967, 216, 96–107. Copyright ©, 1967, by Scientific American Inc. All rights reserved.)

an optical system between object and eye, visual information is dominant. An object which is physically horizontal but visually slanted by an optical system is set into a slanted position to appear visually horizontal. If the hand is moved to and fro across the bar it is judged kinesthetically to be horizontal even though it is slanted. This change in kinesthetic information for horizontality (behavioural compensation) tends to persist (persistence of response) so that a later judgment of horizontality made kinesthetically without vision continues to exhibit the change. A new relationship between visual and kinesthetic information for horizontality has been learned. New kinesthetic sensations are associated with horizontality. The learning is rapid and may occur in a single trial. In the next section it will be seen that behavioural compensation, a change in the kinesthetic, tactile and muscular information with optically transformed visual input, occurs in a variety of more complex situations.

## Behavioural Compensation

For the purpose of discussing behavioural compensation, subjective space can be specified in terms of three planes, the frontal, median and horizontal, intersecting at right angles at the centre of the head as shown in Fig. 8.5. In the situation depicted in Fig. 8.3 both the apparent horizontal

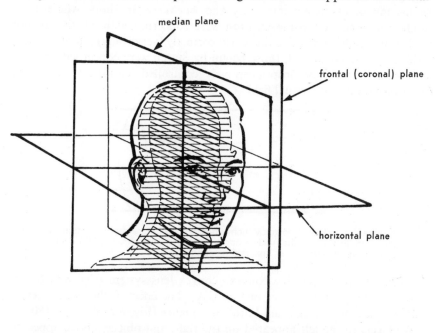

**Figure 8.5** Representation of the median, horizontal and frontal (coronal) planes of a human observer. Each plane can be transformed, *i.e.*, tilted, rotated, reversed or inverted, by an appropriate arrangement of lenses, mirrors and prisms.

and the medial planes are transformed so that a vertical or horizontal object lying in a plane parallel to the frontal plane (a fronto-parallel plane) is judged as tilted. Using mirrors, prisms and lenses either singly or in combination it is possible to transform the apparent frontal, median and horizontal planes about their longitudinal or transverse axes (Fig. 8.5) to any desired angle.

Behavioural compensation, learning new responses to transformed sensory input from the environment, has been studied from two independent points of view. The first series of studies, which began with experiments by George Stratton late in the last century, were designed to answer the question: "If visual space is distorted does the observer in the course of his contact with the environment eventually learn to perceive his environment as it actually is?" The experiments of George Stratton resulted in a long series of enquiries which continue still. The second problem concerned the manner in which individuals learn to make appropriate responses to a changed relationship between visual and proprioceptive information. The standard apparatus developed by Starch in 1910 consisted of a mirror in which the hand was viewed, and a screen to occlude direct view of the hand. The observer was usually required to trace a pattern, observing both pattern and hand in the mirror, so that movements of the hand towards the observer were seen in the mirror as movements away and *vice versa*. In short, whereas the studies initiated by George Stratton were concerned with whether or not we learn visually to perceive the world correctly (veridically) after the visual field is optically distorted, those begun by Starch were concerned with the nature and course of proprioceptively controlled learning with optical transformation of the visual field.

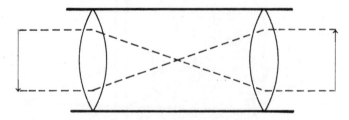

**Figure 8.6** Optical device which when placed before the eye rotates the retinal projections of the median and horizontal planes through 180 degrees so that objects are seen as upside down and reversed.

Stratton wore a double convexo-convex lens system (Fig. 8.6) before one eye for a period of three or four days. The effect of the optical device was to rotate the medial and horizontal planes (Fig. 8.5) through 180° so that objects to the left appeared on the right and objects above appeared below (and *vice versa* in each case). Although Stratton's descriptions of the visual perceptual outcomes of long-term optical transformation are ambiguous, careful reading of his account suggests that changes in visual appearances were, at the most, slight. His behaviour, walking, sitting down, bending etc., at first clumsy and difficult, became progressively refined so that at the end of the transformation period Stratton was "at home" in his reversed and inverted visual environment. In other words, even though the relationship between visual and proprioceptive information was grossly altered, Stratton learned to make appropriate responses. Since Stratton's early studies similar experiments have been conducted using similar but improved optical systems which gave a greater field of view (Stratton's was quite small) and were binocular rather than monocular. The experiments of Ewert in the early 1930s and the more recent studies of Snyder and Pronko in 1952 in which observers wore the 180° transforming device for about a month (only removing it in the dark to sleep), by and large confirm Stratton's findings. In Snyder and Pronko's experiment one observer reported after a month of transformation that the visual scene was reversed and inverted *compared with pre-transformation appearances* but that it was no longer strange or disturbing. Of course, after this protracted period he had learned to make appropriate responses to his reversed perceptual world. In Fig. 8.7 is shown the typical course of learning for a complex task following the onset of 180° visual spatial transformation of the visual field.

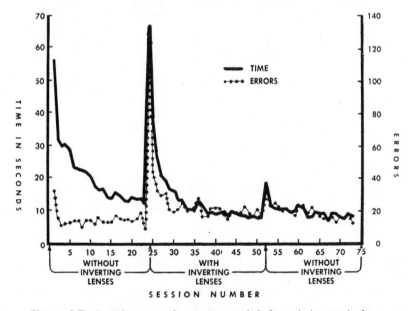

**Figure 8.7** Learning curve for a motor task before, during, and after a period of 180 degrees transformation of the median and horizontal planes. (From F.W. Snyder and N.H. Pronko, *Vision with Spatial Inversion*, Wichita, University of Wichita Press, 1952. By courtesy of F.W. Snyder and N.H. Pronko.)

In addition to the numerous investigations of the outcome of gross changes in visual space occasioned by devices such as that shown in Fig. 8.3 there have been many experiments in which smaller transformations have been used. For example, a wedge prism interposed between object and eye transforms the apparent median plane through an angle determined by prism angle. An object which is actually straight ahead (*i.e.,* in the observer's median plane) viewed through a prism may appear 10 degrees to the left (or right). In reaching for the object the observer at first misses it but after a few responses he reaches accurately. With these smaller transformations the rate of learning the new relationship between visual and proprioceptive information is generally greater than with the large ones.

**Figure 8.8** Mirror-tracing apparatus; the mirror transforms the frontal plane through 180 degrees so that when the hand moves towards the body it is seen as receding and *vice versa.* (From F.W. Geldard, *Fundamentals of Psychology*, N.Y., John Wiley & Sons Inc., 1962. By courtesy of John Wiley & Sons Inc.)

The apparatus shown in Fig. 8.8 serves to transform the frontal plane through 180° so that objects in front appear behind but objects behind are obscured by the observer's body. As the observer moves his hand towards the mirror, *i.e.,* away from himself, it seems to move away from the plane of the mirror and *vice versa.* The effect is *essentially* similar to that achieved by the arrangement shown in Fig. 8.3 in that one of the main planes is apparently rotated through 180°, thus reversing the apparent location of objects, including the limbs when they are in view. In much the same manner as shown by Stratton for median and horizontal plane transformations, 180° rotation of the frontal plane disrupts behaviour initially, but after a series of practice trials the individual performs fast and accurately in tracing around a pattern.

### Persistence of Response

The progressive improvement in behaviour following spatial transformation of the visual field (*i.e.,* modification of the spatial relationship between vision and proprioception) is referred to as behavioural compensation. This class of learning is merely a special instance of motor learning, the progressive development of adaptive responses with practice. Like all learning, behavioural compensation generalizes or transfers to alternative situations. If after learning to make appropriate responses with reversals of the frontal (Fig. 8.8) or median and horizontal (Fig. 8.3) planes the optical system is removed, thus restoring the normal situation, the responses previously learned tend to persist for a time. Such persistence of response patterns appropriate to one situation is often referred to as an aftereffect and unfortunately confused with perceptual aftereffects (Chapter 7). Response persistence is essentially the typical transfer or response generalization observable in many learning tasks. Consider a prism placed between object and eye so that an object straight ahead is apparently 15° to the right. If the observer is instructed to reach out quickly and touch the object without observing his hand, he will reach 15° to the right and miss it. After a series of trials he will learn to reach in the appropriate direction and touch the object (behavioural compensation). The kinesthetic information which previously signalled "straight ahead" now signals "15 degrees right". The prism is now removed and after dissipation of any visual perceptual aftereffect which may have developed (see next section), the observer again reaches out quickly to touch the object without viewing his hand. The object now appears straight ahead. Since kinesthetic information for the true straight ahead now signals "15 degrees right", an association learned during the transformation period, the observer will reach about 15° to the left. Reaching in this latter direction is persistence of response. Kinesthetic information for direction has been modified while viewing through the prism, and the new association between kinesthetic and visual information carries over to the restored normal viewing conditions. This is essentially what happens in the situations studied by Stratton, Ewert, and Synder and Pronko. It would probably occur also in the mirror-drawing situation were responses studied following behavioural compensation.

### Persistence of Response and Perceptual Aftereffects

If an observer regards a pattern of straight vertical lines after a period during which he inspects a pattern of slanted or curved lines the straight vertical lines are judged to be slanted or curved in the opposite direction to the original pattern. This is a typical instance of the perceptual aftereffect described in Chapter 7. Persistence of response refers to the transfer or generalization of proprioceptively mediated responses learned during transformed sensory stimulation to a non-transformed or normal situation. Prisms and lenses also have the effect of slanting and curving the retinal projections of objectively straight and vertical or horizontal lines. A period of viewing through optical systems followed by their removal allows both perceptual aftereffects *and* persistence of response to occur. The two effects may be demonstrated to occur independently of each other, but since they are both frequently generated together there has been a tendency to confuse them. One is a sensory adaptive change and the other a learned effect of considerably greater duration. Unfortunately many experiments, both early and recent, have been so designed as to confound the two phenomena.

### Summary of Relationship Learning

The spatially-extended environment can be specified in terms of the median, frontal and horizontal planes (Fig. 8.5) intersecting at right angles at the centre of the head. Under normal conditions the observer's proprioceptively mediated responses (reaching, walking, throwing) are appropriate to the true spatial position and location of objects in the environment. What is visually horizontal is, for the most part, kinesthetically horizontal. What is visually to the left or right is kinesthetically left or right, and so on. By means of optical systems involving prisms, lenses and mirrors the median, frontal and horizontal planes can be apparently transformed so that there is a discrepancy or discord between the visual and proprioceptive information for position, direction and orientation of objects. If the observer's visual field is so transformed over a sufficiently extended period and he is given the opportunity to practice, the proprioceptive responses become progressively more appropriate to the transformed conditions. Instead of reaching to the right for an object actually to the left the observer learns eventually to reach to the left. Visual appearances do not alter unless the optical device results in perceptual adaptation. The proprioceptive information comes to agree with the transformed visual information. When normal visual conditions are restored, the learned responses developed during the period of transformation (behavioural compensation) tend to persist, an effect called here persistence of response. Behavioural compensation is a special case of motor learning and persistence of response a special instance of response generalization or transfer of training. Since conditions which result in behavioural compensation and consequent persistence of response may also induce perceptual adaptation (with consequent aftereffect) perceptual aftereffects and response persistence frequently occur together and are confused.

## PERCEPTUAL RESOLUTION AND LEARNING

The basis of the perceptual resolution of equivocal sensory projections of object properties such as orientation, size, shape and reflectance has been discussed in detail in Chapters 3, 4, 5 and 6. The projection of these properties at the receptors is so ambiguous that their perception in terms of approximations to the true value of the property is dependent on additional information from proprioceptive or exteroceptive systems. Depending on the nature of this information, the equivocal projection is resolved to a close approximation to the objective value of the property (perceptual constancy) or to a poor approximation (perceptual illusion), If there is no source of resolving information then perceptual instability occurs (Chapter 6).

The information on which perceptual resolution depends may under certain conditions be learned, so that resolution in the direction of either constancy or illusion can occur in the absence of the information itself. This aspect of the relation between learning and perception has been recognized for a considerable time as "the role of past experience in perception". Some aspects of this form of perceptual learning were discussed in Chapter 6.

### Visual Orientation Resolution

In Chapter 3 it was noted that the orientation of the visual image of an object is ambiguous as a source of information for object orientation, since it is an outcome of both observer and object tilt. The visual framework or background is the determinant of judged orientation under normal visual conditions. Both orientation constancy and illusion (Zöllner's illusion) are points on a continuum of orientation judgments, a particular judgment representing one point on the continuum.

Consider a situation similar to that used originally by Asch and Witkin (Chapter 3) but modified so that a *luminous* rod in a tilted room can be adjusted by the observer to apparent verticality. If an observer is required to adjust the rod to apparent verticality against the background of a room tilted at about 20° right, the rod is set at about 14–15° to the right, an instance of underconstancy or illusion in visual judgments of orientation. Now, if the rod is luminous and the seated observer is required to set it to the vertical in the dark, he normally does so with only a degree or so of error. If, however, just prior to the adjustment the lights are switched on and off quickly so that the observer is given a fleeting glimpse of the tilted room his subsequent adjustment to the vertical tends in the direction of room tilt. That is, *prior exposure to a tilted framework or surround gives rise to resolution of object tilt in the direction of surround tilt* (Austin, 1967; see also Day, 1968).

At first sight this effect might be interpreted as a visual spatial aftereffect, prior stimulation by a slanted field resulting in a vertical object appearing slanted in the opposite direction and adjustment to the apparent vertical in the opposite direction. That the effect is not a perceptual aftereffect has been shown in a series of intriguing experiments by Austin. Austin used very brief exposures of the tilted room and allowed sufficient time to elapse between exposure of the tilted room and presentation of the luminous rod such that any *perceptual* aftereffect would have dissipated. Even after prolonged periods in the dark the effect of the tilted environment could be detected. Prior familiarization with visual resolving information for object orientation determines judgments of orientation. The observer learns in a few trials the information necessary to resolve equivocal projections of object properties.

## Controlled and Uncontrolled Learning of Resolving Information

In the last example perceptual resolution of object orientation derived from controlled exposure to field or background orientation. The information necessary for object orientation was learned from a situation presented before the object was presented alone. Even though the information was not present at the time the object (the luminous rod) was presented it had been learned and served to resolve the equivocal visual projection of the rod. Previously acquired information relevant to the perceptual resolution of equivocal projections of object properties does not often derive from such carefully-controlled conditions. On the contrary, such learned or "stored" information accrues during the course of normal contacts with the environment. There are many perceptual phenomena which result from the resolution of equivocalities through information learned in the haphazard process of environmental contact. Such effects are often referred to as deriving from "past experience". This phrase simply implies that the information on which perceptual resolution depends has been learned as a result of prior exposure to the relevant information. Some instances of this haphazard acquisition of resolving information for equivocal retinal projections were discussed in Chapter 6 in connection with unstable figures and objects.

## Resolution of Object Movement

Visual autokinetic movement occurs when there is a lack of resolving information provided by a stationary or moving background. In the absence of such information the visual image of a visible object in an otherwise dark or featureless environment is equivocal. Perceptual instability is the outcome. The role of learned resolving information in determining the *direction* of movement was demonstrated by Comalli, Werner and Wapner in 1957. These investigators presented lighted silhouettes of a running horse, a running boy and an arrow in a dark room in two orientations, facing right and facing left. The judged direction of motion during a 30-second period for each object tended significantly in the direction in which the objects faced.

Later experiments have confirmed the role of learned information on direction of autokinetic motion.

If prior exposure to a tilted room affects subsequent judgments of object orientation, an effect which is not attributable to perceptual adaptation and aftereffect, it is provocative to consider the effect of prior exposure to a moving field on subsequent judgments of object movement, Since the motion, including the stationariness, of the retinal image of an object is equivocal, it is likely that prior exposure of a leftward-moving field would result in a stationary object viewed later in the dark being judged as moving leftward. No such study has so far been conducted. In investigating the hypothesis, however, it would be essential to leave sufficient time between exposure of the moving field and presentation of the object, for perceptual adaptation (Chapter 7) to dissipate completely.

### Resolution of Object Colour

The spectral composition of light falling on the retina is determined jointly by the composition of the illuminant and the selective absorption of the surface from which it is reflected. For this reason the retinal stimulus is ambiguous from the viewpoint of object colour.

As early as 1907 Hering argued that the judged colour of an object was determined in part by "memory" for the colour of certain familiar objects. He stated: "The colour in which we have oftenest seen an external thing impresses itself indelibly on our memory and becomes a fixed characteristic of the memory image. What the layman calls the real colour of a thing is a colour which has become firmly attached to the thing in his memory; I might call it the memory colour of the thing."*

The prototype of many more recent studies concerned with the role of prior exposure to objects with certain colours is that of Duncker in 1939. Duncker cut out the shape of a leaf and a donkey from the same green material and presented to the observer in red light. His hypothesis was that a leaf being a familiar green object would be matched to a greener variable than the donkey shape. The hypothesis was confirmed, for the green sector of a colour-wheel was adjusted to 60° to match the colour of the leaf and to 29° to match that of the donkey.

There have been many criticisms of Duncker's experiment and many subsequent attempts to refine the procedures in the interest of more adequate experimental control of such factors as prior exposure, instructions to the observer and methods of responding. It cannot be said as yet that the phenomenon of memory colour, the tendency to judge the colour of an object in terms of its characteristic colour, is fully confirmed. Perhaps one of the deficiencies in the methods used to study memory colour is the use of a

*Hering, E. *Outlines of a Theory of the Light Sense*. (Translation by L.M. Hurvich and D. Jameson.) Cambridge, Mass.: Harvard University Press 1964.

variable, usually an adjustable colour-wheel, to match the colour of a simultaneously presented familiar object. The variable itself may well destroy the slight memory colour effect. An improved method would seem to be that of simply asking the observer to vary the colour of the object itself until it is, say, *red* in the same way as the observer in Austin's experiment was required to adjust the luminous rod to the *vertical* after exposure to a tilted background. If the subject were presented with "nonsense" shapes of different colours, say, red, yellow and green, and later asked to adjust the colour of each of these shapes to the same red, there would probably be differences between them determined by their colours during prior presentation. The matching procedure in such experiments would probably operate to minimize memory colour effects by providing cues for colour. If the observer in the autokinetic situation described earlier in this chapter was presented with a moving object to *match* the apparent movement of the stationary object, the mere presence of the matching object would probably either severely reduce autokinetic movement or eliminate it completely.

# Perception, Learning and Behaviour

The three perceptual conditions outlined under which learning occurs are probably not exhaustive, It is enough to note, however, that "perceptual learning" is by no means confined to progressive refinement or improvement in the individual's ability to differentiate or discriminate between features of the impinging stimulus. In so far as learning or, for that matter, almost all aspects of behaviour, are dependent in some degree on sensory input, all classes of learning can be thought of as perceptual. The distinction often made between "perceptual" or "discrimination" learning, on the one hand, and "response" or "motor" learning on the other is, to say the least, artificial. The major point of difference is to be found in the sensory information on the basis of which learning occurs. Discrimination learning is dependent among other things on sensory stimulation at the exteroceptors, the receptors of the eye, ear, skin etc. Motor learning rests upon stimulation of the receptors associated with joints, tendons, muscles etc., the proprioceptive systems. In this sense a distinction between perception and overt behaviour is difficult to justify. Behaviour and its modification with practice are largely dependent on sensory input whether the sources of stimulation are removed from the organism or derived from its own activities.

# Summary

Certain aspects of visual perception occur without previous visual experience. Perception of depth and distance by rats occurs without exposure to the visual environment and visual size and shape constancy can be observed in very young human infants.

Although some features of perception are innate, much perception is dependent upon experience with the environment. It is convenient to consider three classes of learning in perception; discrimination learning, learning new relationships between information from different systems, and learning resolving information for ambiguous stimuli.

Discrimination learning includes the extraordinary refinements which can be achieved in such tasks as wine and tea-tasting and in the discrimination of colours, shapes, smells and sounds. Perceptual acuity and sensitivity can be improved by practice.

If the stimulus input into one system is modified the individual learns a new relationship between that system and another. The perceptual learning of a new relationship between sensory systems can be observed when visual input is changed by placing an optical system such as a prism or lens before the eyes. Behaviour is initially disrupted but new co-ordination is established after a period of practice.

The perceptual resolution of equivocal sensory projections of object properties such as size, shape and orientation may also depend on learned information. If a subject is exposed to a tilted room for a period and is then shown a vertical bar of light in the dark, the latter apparently is tilted in a direction opposite to the room. It is possible to show that this effect is not a spatial aftereffect but is an outcome of learned or stored resolving information for the ambiguous retinal orientation of the bar.

# References

Addams, R.A. An account of a peculiar optical phaenomenon seen after having looked at a moving body. *Phil. Mag.*, 1834, 5, 373.

Akita, M., Graham, C.H., and Hsia, Y. Maintaining an absolute hue in the presence of different background colours. *Vision Res.*, 1964, 4, 539–556.

Amoore, J.E., Johnston, W., and Rubin, M. The stereochemical theory of odor. *Sci. Amer.*, 1964, 211. (Sci. Amer. Reprint No. 297.)

Amoore, J.E., Rubin, M., and Johnston, J.W. The stereochemical theory of olfaction. *Proceedings of the Scientific Section of the Toilet Goods Association*, Special Supplement, No. 37, 1962.

Ansbacher, H.C. Distortion in the perception of real movement. *J. exp. Psychol.*, 1944, 34, 1–23.

Asch, S.E., and Witkin, H.A. Studies in space orientation: I. Perception of the upright with displaced visual fields. *J. exp. Psychol.*, 1948, 38, 325–337.

Aubert, H. Eine Scheinbare Beteunde Drehung von Objekten bei Neigung des Kopfes Mach Rechts Oder Links. *Arch. path. Anat. Physiol.*, 1861, 20, 381–393.

Aubert H. Die Bewegungsempfindung. *Arch. ges. Physiol.*, 1886, 39, 347–370.

Austin, M. Studies in perceptual spatial adaptation and its aftereffect. Unpublished PhD thesis, University of Sydney, 1968.

Barlow, H.B., and Hill, R.M. Evidence for a physiological explanation of the waterfall phenomenon and figural after-effects. *Nature*, 1963, 200, 1345-1347.

Beck, J., and Gibson, J.J. The relation of apparent shape to apparent slant in the preparation of objects. *J. exp. Psychol.*, 1955, 50, 125-133.

Beidler, L.M. Mechanisms of gustatory and olfactory receptor stimulation. In Rosenblith, W.A.(Ed.), *Sensory Communication*, Cambridge, Mass.: The M.I.T. Press, 1961.

Bower, T.G.R. The visual world of infants. *Sci. Amer.*, 1966, 215, 80–97.

Boynton, R.M. Recognition of critical targets among irrelevant forms. In Wulfeck, J.W., and Taylor, J.H. (Eds), *Form Discrimination as Related to Military Problems*. Washington, D.C.: National Research Council, 1957.

Braunstein, M.L. The perception of depth through motion. *Psychol. Bull.*, 1962, 59, 422–433.

Brett, J.R. The eye. In Brown, M. (Ed.), *The Physiology of Fishes*, Vol. 2. New York: Academic Press, Inc., 1957.

Brosgole, L. *An analysis of induced motion*. Technical Report. Navtradeveen IH-48, 1966, U.S. Naval Training Device Center.

Brown, J.F. On time perception in visual movement fields. *Psychol. Forsch.*, 1931, 14, 233–248.

Brown, J.F. The visual perception of velocity. *Psychol. Forsch.*, 1931, 14, 199–232.

Brunswik, E. Zur Entwicklung der Albedowahrnehmung. *Z. Psychol.*, 1929, 109, 40–115.

Bugelski, B.R., and Alampay, D.A. The role of frequency in developing perceptual sets. *Canad. J. Psychol.*, 1961, 15, 206–212.

185

Bullock, J.H., and Diecke, F.P.J. Properties of an infra-red receptor. *J. Physiol.*, 1956, 134, 47–87.

Collins, J.K. A study of the aftereffect of seen movement. Unpublished MA thesis, University of Sydney, 1965.

Comalli, P.E., Werner, H., and Wapner, S. Studies in physiognomic perception: III. Effect of directional dynamics and meaning induced sets on autokinetic motion. *J. Psychol.*, 1957, 43, 289–299.

Curthoys, I.S. The effect of binaural adaptation and masking on auditory localisation. Unpublished PhD thesis, Monash University, 1968.

Day, R.H. Studies in perception. *Aust. Psychol.*, 1968, 2, 109-126.

Day, R.H. Perceptual constancy of auditory direction with head rotation. *Nature,* 1968, 219, 501-502.

Day, R.H., and Power, R.P. Frequency of apparent reversal of rotary motion in depth as a function of shape and pattern. *Aust. J. Psychol.*, 1963, 15, 162-174.

Day, R.H., and Power, R.P. Apparent reversal (oscillation) of rotary motion in depth: An investigation and a general theory. *Psychol. Rev.*, 1965, 72, 117–127.

Day, R.H., and Singer, G. The effects of spatial judgments on the perceptual aftereffects resulting from prismatically transformed vision. *Aust. J. Psychol.*, 1966, 18, 63-70.

Day, R.H., and Singer, G. Sensory adaptation and behavioural compensation with spatially transformed vision and hearing. *Psychol. Bull.*, 1967, 67, 307–322.

DeValois, R.L. Color vision mechanisms in monkey. *J. gen. Psychiol.*, 1960, 43, 115-128 (special supplement).

Dresslar, F.B. Studies in the psychology of touch. *Amer. J. Psychol.*, 1894, 6, 313–368.

Duncker, K. The influence of past experience upon perceptual properties. *Amer. J. Psychol.*, 1939, 52, 225–265.

Emmert, E. Grössenverhältnisse der Nachbilder. *Klin. Monatsbl. d. Augenheilk*, 1881, 19, 443–450.

Ewert, P.H. A study of the effect of inverted retinal stimulation upon spatially co-ordinated behavior. *Genetic Psychol. Monographs*, 1930, 7, Nos 3–4.

Forgus, R.H. *Perception: The Basic Process in Cognitive Development*. New York: McGraw-Hill, 1966.

Galanter, E. Contemporary psychophysics. In Newcomb, T.M. (Ed.), *New Directions in Psychology*. New York: Holt, Rinehart and Winston, 1962.

Ganz, L., and Day, R.H. An analysis of the satiation fatigue mechanism of figural after-effects. *Amer. J. Psychol.,* 1965, 78, 345-361.

Gelb, A., Farbenkonstanz der Sehdinge. *Handbuch der Normalen und Pathologischen Physiologie*, 1929, 12, 594–678.

Gibson, E.J. Improvement in perceptual judgments as a function of controlled practice or training. *Psychol. Bull.*, 1953, 50, 401–431.

Gibson, E.J., and Walk, R.D. The "visual cliff". *Sci. Amer.*, 1960, 202, 64–71.

Gibson, J.J. Adaptation, after-effect and contrast in the perception of curved lines. *J. exp. Psychol.*, 1933, 16, 1–31.

Gibson, J.J. Adaptation with negative after-effect. *Psychol. Rev.*, 1937, 44, 222–244.

Gibson, J.J. *Perception of the Visual World*, Boston: Houghton Mifflin Co., 1950.

Gibson, J.J., and Gibson, E.J. Perceptual learning: Differentiation or enrichment. *Psychol. Rev.*, 1955, 62, 32–41.

Gibson, J.J., and Radner, M. Adaptation, after-effect, and contrast in the perception of tilted lines: I. Quantitative studies. *J. exp. Psychol.*, 1937, 20, 453–467.

Gogel, W.C., Wist, E.R., and Harker, G.S. A test of the invariance of the ratio of perceived size to perceived distance. *Amer. J. Psychol.*, 1963, 66, 537–553.

Graham, C.H., *et al. Vision and Visual Perception*. New York: John Wiley & Sons, Inc., 1965.

Graham, C.H., Brown, R.H., and Mote, F.A. The relation of size of stimulus and intensity in the human eye: I. Intensity thresholds for white light. *J. exp. Psychol.*, 1939, 24, 555–573.

Granit, R. On inhibition in the after-effect of seen movement. *Brit. J. Psychol.*, 1928, 19, 147-157.

Graybiel, A., and Clark, B. Validity of the oculogravic illusion as a specific indicator of otolith function. *Aerospace Med.*, 1965, 36, 1173–1181.

Graybiel, A., and Niven, J.I. *Persistence of the autokinetic illusion in persons with bilateral injury or destruction of the labyrinth of the inner ear.* Project NM001 110100, Report No. 41, 1956. Pensacola, School of Aviation Medicine.

Gregory, R.L. Distortion of visual space as inappropriate constancy scaling. *Nature*, 1963, 119, 678.

Gregory, R.L. Visual illusions. In Foss, B.M. (Ed.), *New Horizons in Psychology.* Harmondsworth: Penguin Books, 1966.

Gregory, R.L. *Eye and Brain.* London: Weidenfeld & Nicolson, 1966.

Grether, W.F. Instrument reading: I. The design of long-scale indicators for speed and accuracy of quantitative readings. *J. Appl. Psychol.*, 1949, 33, 363–372.

Hardy, A.C. *Handbook of Colorimetry.* Cambridge, Mass.: Technology Press, 1936.

Hartline, H.K. The discharge of nerve impulses from the single visual sense cell. *Cold Spring Harbor Symposia on Quantitative Biology*, 1935, 3, 245–250.

Hartline, H.K. The response of single optic nerve fibers of the vertebrate eye to illumination of the retina. *Amer. J. Physiol.*, 1938, 121, 400–415.

Helson, H. Fundamental problems in color vision: I. The principle governing changes in hue, saturation and lightness of non-selective samples in chromatic illumination. *J. exp. Psychol.*, 1938, 23, 439–476.

Helson, H. Some factors and implications of color constancy. *J. opt. Soc. Amer.*, 1943, 33, 555–567.

Henning, H. *Der Geruch* (2nd edn) Leipzig: Barth, 1924.

Hering, E. *Outlines of a Theory of the Light Sense.* (English translation, L.M. Hurvich and D. Jameson) Cambridge, Mass.: Harvard University Press, 1964.

Hess, C., and Pretori, H. Messende Untersuchungen über die Gesetzmässigkeit des simultanen Helligkeitscontrastes. *Arch. Ophthal.*, 1894, 40, 1–24.

Holway, A.H., and Boring, E.G. Determinants of apparent visual size with distance variant. *Amer. J. Psychol.*, 1941, 54, 21–37.

Howard, I.P. An investigation of a satiation process in the reversible perspective of revolving skeletal shapes. *Quart. J. exp. Psychol.*, 1961, 13, 19–33.

James, W. *Principle of Psychology.* New York: Henry Holt, 1890.

Jameson, D., and Hurvich, L.M. Complexities of perceived brightness. *Science,* 1961, 133, 174–179.

Jenkins, W.O. The tactual discrimination of shapes for coding aircraft-type controls. In Fitts, P.M. (Ed.), *Psychological Research on Equipment Design.* U.S. Army Airforce Research Report, 1947.

Kaufman, L., and Rock, I. The moon illusion. *Sci. Amer.*, 1962, 207, 120–132.

Kenyon, F.C. A curious optical illusion with an electric fan. *Science*, 1898, 8, 371-372.

Kilpatrick, F.P. (Ed.). *Human Behavior from the Transactional Point of View.* Washington: Office of Naval Research, 1953.

Kilpatrick, F.P., and Ittleson, W.H. Three demonstrations involving the visual perception of movement. *J. exp. Psychol.*, 1951, 42, 394–402.

Kleint, H. Versuche über die Wahrnehmung. *Z. Psychol.*, 1937, 140, 109.

Köhler, W., and Wallach, H. Figural after-effects: An investigation of visual processes. *Proc. Amer. Phil. Soc.*, 1944, 88, 269–357.

Krech, D., and Crutchfield, R.S. *Elements of Psychology*. New York: Alfred A. Knopf, 1958.

Kreig, W.J.S. *Functional Neuroanatomy*. Evanston, Illinois: Brain Books, 1953.

Lashley, K.S., and Russell, J.T. The mechanism of vision: XI. A preliminary test of innate organization. *J. genet. Psychol.*, 1934, 45, 136–144.

Leibowitz, H., and Moore, D. Role of accommodation and convergence in the perception of size. *J. Opt. Soc. Amer.*, 1966, 56, 1120–1123.

Lissman, H.W. Electric location in fishes. *Sci. Amer.*, 1963, 208, 50–59.

Lissman, H.W., and Machin, K.E. The mechanism of object location in *Gymnarchus niloticus* and similar fish. *J. exp. Biol.*, 1958, 35, 451–486.

Lowenstein, E. *The Senses*. Harmondsworth: Penguin Books, 1966.

McAdam, D.L. Specification of small chromaticity differences. *J. Opt. Soc. Amer.*, 1943, 33, 18–26.

McCormick, E.J. *Human Factors Engineering*, New York: McGraw-Hill Book Company, 1957.

McFadden, H.B. *Three Studies in Psychological Optics: I. The Permanence of the Effects of Training on Visual Acuity*. Duncan, Oklahoma: Optometric Extension Program, 1941, 1–10.

Mach, E. Uber die Wirkung der raumlichen Vertheilung des Lichtreizes auf die Netzhaut. *Classe der kaiserlichen Akad. der Wissen*, 1865, 52, 303–322.

Mach, E. Uber den Physiologischen Effect raumlich vertheilter Lichtreize (Zweite Abhandlung) *Classe der kaiserlichen Akad. der Wissen*, 1866, 52, 131–144.

MacNichol, E.F. Three-pigment color vision. *Sci. Amer.*, 1964, 211, 48–56.

Marshall, A.J., and Stanley, G. The apparent length of light and dark arcs seen peripherally in rotary motion. *Aust. J. Psychol.*, 1964, 16, 120-128.

Matin, L., and MacKinnon, G.E. Autokinetic movement: Selective manipulation of directional components by image stabilization. *Science*, 1964, 143, 147–148.

Metzger, W. *Gesetze des Schens*. Frankfurt: Kramer, 1936.

Miller, E.F., and Graybiel, A. Comparison of autokinetic movement perceived by normal persons and deaf subjects with bilateral labyrinthine defects. *Aerospace Med.*, 1962, 33, 1077–1080.

Müller, G.E. Ueber das Aubertsche Phänomen. *Z. Sinnensphysiol.*, 1916, 49, 109–244.

Munson, W.A., and Gardner, M.B. Loudness patterns: A new approach. *J. Acoust. Soc. Amer.*, 1950, 22, 177–190.

Necker, L.A. Observations on some remarkable phaenomenon seen in Switzerland; and an optical phaenomenon which occurs on viewing of a crystal or geometrical solid. *Phil. Mag.*, 1832, 1, 329–337.

Over, R. Context and movement as factors influencing haptic illusions. *Aust. J. Psychol.*, 1966, 18, 262-265.

Pheiffer, C.H., Eure, S.B., and Hamilton, C.B. Reversing figures and eye movements. *Amer. J. Psychol.*, 1956, 69, 452–455.

Pollack, R.H. Figural after-effects: Quantitative studies of displacement. *Aust. J. Psychol.*, 1958, 10, 269–277.

Power, R.P. The apparent reversal of rotary motion in depth. Unpublished MA thesis, University of Sydney, 1964.

Power, R.P. Studies in the apparent reversal of rotary motion in depth. Unpublished doctoral dissertation, University of Sydney, 1966.

Pritchard, R.M. Visual illusions viewed as stabilized retinal images. *Quart. J. exp. Psychol.*, 1958, 10, 77–81.

Pritchard, R.M., Heron, W., and Hebb, D.O. Visual perception approached by the method of stabilized images. *Canad. J. Psychol.*, 1960, 14, 67–77.

Purdy, D. Spectral hue as a function of intensity. *Amer. J. Psychol.*, 1931, 43, 541–559.

Purkinje, J.A. Beiträge zur Nähren Kenntniss des Schwindels aus Heutognostischen Daten. In Chotak, K.J. (Ed.), *Purkyne's sebrane spisy (operaomnia)* 2, 1937, 23-24. (Purkinje's paper appeared originally in 1820.)

Ratliff, F., and Hartline, H.K. The responses of *Limulus* optic nerve fibers to patterns of illumination on the receptor mosaic. *J. gen. Physiol.*, 1959, 42, 1241–1255.

Ratliffe, F. *Mach Bands: Quantitative Studies on Neural Networks in the Retina.* San Francisco: Holden-Day, 1965.

Révész, G. Lassen sich die bekannten geometrisch—optischen Täuschungen auch in haptischen Gebiet nachweisen. *J. f. Psychol. Psychotherapie*, 1953, 1, 464–478.

Rice, C.E. Human echo perception. *Science*, 1967, 155, 656–664.

Riggs, L.A., Ratliff, F., Cornsweet, J.C., and Cornsweet, T.N. The disappearance of steadily fixated visual test objects. *J. Optical Soc. Amer.*, 1953, 43, 495–501.

Rock, I., and Harris, C.S. Vision and touch. *Sci. Amer.*, 1967, 216, 96–107.

Rock, I., and Kaufman, L. The moon illusion: II. *Science*, 1962, 136, 1023-1031.

Roeder, K.D., and Treat, A.E. The detection and evasion of bats by moths. *American Scientist*, 1961, 49, 135–148.

Rubin, E. *Visuelle Wahrgenommene Figuren.* Copenhagen: Gyldendalske, 1921.

Rudel, R.G., and Teuber, H.A.L. Decrement of visual and haptic Müller-Lyer illusion on repeated trials: a study of crossmodal transfer. *Quart. J. exp. Psychol.*, 1963, 15, 125–131.

Sanford, E.C. *A Course in Experimental Psychology.* London: D.C. Heath & Company, 1897.

Schroeder, H. Ueber eine optische Inversion bei Betrachtung verkehrter, durch optische Vorrichtung entworfener, physischer Bilder. *Ann. Phys. Chem.*, 1858, 181, 298–311.

Schwartz, E. Bau und Funktzion der Seitenlinie des Stresfenhechtlings (*Aplocheilus lineatus* Cuv. u. Val.). *Z. vergl. Physiol.*, 1965, 50, 55–87.

Sherif, M. A study of some social factors in perception. *Arch. Psychol. N.Y.*, 1935, 187, 60.

Snyder, F.W., and Pronko, N.H. *Vision with Spatial Inversion.* Wichita: University of Wichita Press, 1952.

Starch, D.A. A demonstration of the trial and error method of learning. *Psychol. Bull.*, 1910, 7, 20–23.

Stevens, S.S., and Davis, H. *Hearing: Its Physiology and Psychology.* New York: John Wiley & Sons, Inc., 1938.

Stewart, E.C. The Gelb effect. *J. exp. Psychol.*, 1959, 57, 235–242.

Stratton, G.M. Some preliminary experiments on vision without inversion of the retinal image. *Psychol. Rev.*, 1896, 3, 611–617.

Tausch, R. Optische Tauschungen als artifizielle Effekte der Gestaltungs prozesse von Grössen und Formenkontanz in der naturlichen Raumwahrnehmung. *Psychol. Forsch.*, 1954, 24, 299–348.

Théiry, A. Weber geometrisch—optische Täuschungen. *Phil. Stud.*, 1896, 12, 67–126.

Thompson, S.P. Some new optical illusions. *J. Science*, 1879, 16, 234–240.

Thompson, S.P. Optical illusions of motion. *Brain*, 1880, 3, 289–298.

Thorndike, R.L., and Woodworth, R.S. The influence of improvement in one mental function upon the efficiency of other functions. *Psychol. Rev.*, 1901, 8, 247–261, 384–395, 553–564.

Thouless, R.H. Phenomenal regression to the real object: I. *Brit. J. Psychol.*, 1931, 21, 339–359.

Thouless, R.H. Phenomenal regression to the real object: II. *Brit. J. Psychol.*, 1931, 22, 1–30.

Tinbergen, N. *Animal Behavior*, New York: Time—Life Books, 1965.

Titchener, E.B. *Experimental Psychology Student's Manual.* New York: Macmillan & Co., 1901.

Titchener, E.B. *A Textbook of Psychology.* New York: Macmillan & Co., 1919.

Verhoeff, F.W. A theory of binocular perspective. *Amer. J. Physiol. Opt.*, 1925, 6, 416–448 (an English translation of Verhoeff's paper which was originally published in 1902).

Volkmann, A.W. Weber den Einfluss der Webung. *Leipzig Berichte, Math. phys. Classe*, 1858, 10, 38–69.

van Bergeijk, W.A., Pierce, J.R., and David, E.E. *Waves and the Ear.* London: Heinemann Educational Books Ltd., 1958.

von Holst, E. Relations between the central nervous system and the peripheral. *Brit. J. Anim. Behav.*, 1954, 2, 89–94.

von Holst, E. Aktive Leistungen der wenschlichen Gesichswahrnehmung. *Studium Generate.*, 1957, 10, 231–243.

Wade, N.J. The effect of body posture on visual orientation. Unpublished PhD thesis, Monash University, 1968.

Wallach, H. Brightness constancy and the nature of achromatic colors. *J. exp. Psychol.*, 1948, 38, 310–324.

Wallach, H. The perception of motion. *Sci. Amer.*, 1959, 208, 56–60. (Sci. Amer. Reprint No. 409.)

Wallach, H., and Kravitz, J. The measurement of the constancy of visual direction and of its adaptation. *Psychonomic Sci.*, 1965, 2, 217–218.

Webster, F.A. Active energy radiating systems: The bat and ultrasonic principles II; acoustical control of airborne interceptions by bats. In *Proc. Internat. Cong. Technology and Blindness*, Vol. I, 1963, 49–135.

Wertheimer, M. Experimentelle Studien über das Sehen von Bewegung. *Z. Psychol.*, 1912, 61, 161f.

Wheatstone, C. On some remarkable and hitherto unobserved, phenomena of binocular vision: I. *Phil. Trans.*, Pt I, 1838, 371–394 and II, *Phil Mag.*, 1852, 3, 504–523.

Witkin, H.A., and Asch, S.E. Studies in space orientation: IV. Further experiments on perception of the upright with displaced visual fields. *J. exp. Psychol.*, 1948, 38, 762–782.

Zotterman, Y. Studies in the neural mechanism of taste. In Rosenblith, W.A. (Ed.), *Sensory Communication*, Cambridge, Mass.: The M.I.T. Press, 1961.

Zwaademaker, H. *L'odorat.* Paris: Doin, 1925.

Zwaademaker, H. An intellectual history of a physiologist with psychological aspirations. In Murchison, C. (Ed.), *A History of Psychology in Autobiography*. Worcester: Clark University Press, 1930, 491–576.

# Index